Economic Sophisms

FRÉDÉRIC BASTIAT

Economic Sophisms, F. Bastiat
Jazzybee Verlag Jürgen Beck
86450 Altenmünster, Loschberg 9
Deutschland

ISBN: 9783988687067

Translated by Patrick James Stirling (1809 – 1891)

www.jazzybee-verlag.de
admin@jazzybee-verlag.de

Printed by Libri Plureos GmbH, Friedensallee 273, 22763 Hamburg

CONTENTS:

FRÉDÉRIC BASTIAT (1801–1850): FRENCH ECONOMIST AND CHAMPION OF FREE TRADE

Early Life and Education

Frédéric Bastiat was born on June 29, 1801, in Bayonne, France, to a merchant family. His father was a successful businessman in the bustling port city, which exposed young Bastiat early to the world of commerce and trade. He received his education at the prestigious colleges of Saint-Sever and Sorèze, institutions that provided him with a solid foundation in classical learning and critical thinking.

Early Career and Personal Development

In 1818, at age 17, Bastiat entered his uncle's counting house in Bayonne, beginning what was expected to be a traditional mercantile career. However, the mundane routines of commercial bookkeeping and trade administration proved deeply unsatisfying to his intellectual nature. After seven years of this work, he made a pivotal decision in 1825 to leave the business world behind.

When his grandfather died, Bastiat inherited a property in Mugron, a small town in the Landes region of southwestern France. This inheritance provided him with the financial independence to pursue his true interests. He became a gentleman farmer, managing his estate while dedicating his considerable leisure time to intensive study, reading, and philosophical reflection. This period of intellectual development would prove crucial to his later contributions to economic thought.

Political Awakening and Local Involvement

The Revolution of 1830, which brought Louis-Philippe to power and established the July Monarchy, filled Bastiat with enthusiasm for liberal reform. This political awakening led him to become more involved in local affairs. In 1831, he was appointed as a justice of the peace (juge de paix) for his canton, a position that gave him insight into local disputes and social issues. The following year, in 1832, he was elected to the General Council of the Landes (conseil général), where he gained valuable experience in regional governance and policy-making.

First Publications and Local Advocacy

Bastiat's writing career began in 1834 with his first pamphlet, which addressed local concerns. Between 1841 and 1844, he published three additional pamphlets, all focusing on taxation issues that directly affected his region. These early works demonstrated his ability to analyze complex economic problems and present clear, compelling arguments for reform.

Discovery of the Free Trade Movement

A chance subscription to an English newspaper, the Globe and Traveller, proved to be a turning point in Bastiat's intellectual development. Through this publication, he learned about the Anti-Corn-Law League, a powerful British movement led by Richard Cobden and John Bright that campaigned against protective tariffs on grain imports. The League's arguments for free trade resonated deeply with Bastiat's own economic thinking.

For two years, Bastiat carefully studied the British free trade movement, analyzing its strategies, arguments, and successes. This research convinced him that France needed a similar campaign to combat its own protectionist policies.

Rise to National Prominence

In 1844, Bastiat published his breakthrough article "Sur l'influence des tarifs anglais et français" (On the Influence of English and French Tariffs) in the influential Journal des Économistes. This piece attracted widespread attention in French intellectual circles and established his reputation as a formidable economic thinker. He followed this success with additional articles, including the first installment of his brilliant "Sophismes Économiques" (Economic Sophisms), a series that would become one of his most celebrated works.

The Paris Years and International Connections

In 1845, Bastiat moved to Paris to oversee the publication of "Cobden et la Ligue, ou l'agitation anglaise pour la liberté des échanges" (Cobden and the League, or the English Agitation for Free Trade). The French capital's economists welcomed him warmly, recognizing his talent and dedication to liberal economic principles.

From Paris, Bastiat traveled to London and Manchester, where he met personally with Cobden, Bright, and other prominent leaders of the Anti-Corn-Law League. These meetings strengthened his resolve and provided him with practical insights into organizing an effective free trade campaign.

Founding the French Free Trade Movement

Upon returning to France, Bastiat discovered that his writings had already begun to influence public opinion. In 1846, he played a crucial role in establishing France's first Free Trade Association (Association pour la Liberté des Échanges) in Bordeaux. The movement's rapid growth across the country soon required his full-time attention, prompting him to permanently relocate from his peaceful estate in Mugron to the bustling political center of Paris.

Exhausting Campaign for Economic Reform

The eighteen months following his move to Paris were marked by extraordinary productivity and exhausting labor. Bastiat took on multiple demanding roles simultaneously: he served as secretary of the association's central committee, organized and maintained correspondence with branch societies throughout France, lobbied government ministers, raised funds through subscriptions, and edited the weekly newspaper "Libre-Échange."

His intellectual output during this period was remarkable. He continued contributing to the Journal des Économistes while also writing for three other periodicals. He addressed public meetings in Paris and provincial cities, and delivered a comprehensive lecture series on political economy principles to students at the law and medical schools. This relentless pace of work came at a severe cost to his health, as he pushed himself beyond his physical limits in service of his cause.

Initially, the free trade movement appeared to be gaining momentum and seemed poised for success. However, the political forces supporting protectionism proved much stronger in France than they had been in England, and the opposition was better organized and more entrenched. The movement's progress was abruptly halted by the Revolution of February 1848, which overthrew the July Monarchy and established the Second Republic.

Confronting the Socialist Challenge

The 1848 Revolution brought socialist and communist ideas, which had been developing over the previous three decades, into temporary prominence. The establishment of National Workshops and other socialist experiments posed a direct challenge to the liberal economic principles Bastiat championed.

Despite his deteriorating health and the loss of his voice due to the throat condition that was slowly killing him, Bastiat courageously defended his principles during this critical period. Although he could barely speak in the Constituent Assembly, where he had been elected as a representative, he continued to offer wise counsel as vice-president of the finance committee and wielded his pen with remarkable skill and energy.

Prolific Anti-Socialist Writings

Between 1848 and 1850, Bastiat produced an extraordinary series of pamphlets and essays that systematically dismantled socialist arguments and exposed the connections between socialism and protectionism. His major works from this period included "Propriété et Loi" (Property and Law), "Justice et Fraternité" (Justice and Fraternity), "Propriété et Spoliation" (Property and Plunder), "L'État" (The State), "Baccalauréat et Socialisme" (The Baccalaureate and Socialism), "Protectionisme et Communisme" (Protectionism and Communism), "Capital et Rente" (Capital and Interest), "Maudit Argent" (Cursed Money), "Spoliation et Loi" (Plunder and Law), "Gratuité du Credit" (Free Credit), and "Ce qu'on voit et ce qu'on ne voit pas" (What Is Seen and What Is Not Seen).

These works demonstrated Bastiat's unique approach to combating socialism. Rather than creating straw-man arguments or engaging in abstract theoretical criticism, he carefully studied the actual proposals and arguments of socialism's most popular advocates, patiently analyzed their reasoning, and demonstrated conclusively that their policies, however well-intentioned, were based on false premises and would lead to harmful consequences.

The Harmonies Project and Final Years

While engaged in this intense polemical work, Bastiat was simultaneously developing his grand theoretical project: a comprehensive reconstruction of economic science based on the principle that "interests, left to themselves, tend to harmonious combinations, and to the progressive preponderance of the general good."

The first volume of this ambitious work, "Les Harmonies économiques" (Economic Harmonies), was published in early 1850. This book represented his attempt to provide a positive, systematic exposition of economic principles that would complement his earlier critical works.

Death and Legacy

In the autumn of 1850, while working on the second volume of Economic Harmonies, Bastiat's declining health forced him to seek relief in Italy's warmer climate. He traveled to Pisa and Florence before reaching Rome, but the change of scenery could not halt the progression of his illness. On December 24, 1850, Frédéric Bastiat died in Rome at the age of 49, his great work left unfinished.

Assessment of Bastiat's Contributions

Bastiat's life work can be evaluated across three distinct but interconnected dimensions:

Champion of Free Trade

While the general principles of free trade had been established by earlier economists like Adam Smith and David Ricardo, Bastiat made unique contributions to the cause. He demonstrated with unprecedented clarity how free trade principles could be practically applied to French agriculture, commerce, and manufacturing. His "Economic Sophisms" remains the most complete, effective, and witty critique of protectionism ever written, systematically demolishing protectionist arguments through rigorous logic and brilliant satire.

Opponent of Socialism

Among French economists of his era, Bastiat had no equal as a critic of socialism. He distinguished himself by engaging directly with socialist ideas as they were actually presented by their most prominent advocates, rather than attacking simplified or distorted versions. He carefully examined their proposals and arguments, treating them with intellectual honesty while demonstrating their fundamental flaws. His anti-socialist writings from 1848-1850 provide an unmatched arsenal of rational arguments against collectivist economic theories.

Economic Theorist

Bastiat's most ambitious but incomplete contribution was his attempt to reconstruct economic science on new foundations. Through his battles with both protectionists and socialists, he developed a unifying vision: the fundamental harmony of human interests when left free from artificial interference. He identified what he saw as the crucial error in both protectionist and socialist thinking—the assumption that human interests are naturally antagonistic, with capital inevitably exploiting labor, manufacturing destroying agriculture, foreign trade harming domestic producers, and consumers opposing producers.

Bastiat believed that previous schools of economic thought had failed to fully grasp the truth that human interests, when not subject to arbitrary government intervention, naturally tend toward harmonious cooperation and mutual benefit. This insight, he argued, provided the key to understanding both individual prosperity and social progress.

His vision of economic harmony represented a sophisticated attempt to demonstrate that a free market economy, far from being a realm of conflict and exploitation, naturally promotes cooperation, mutual benefit, and social progress. Though his early death prevented him from fully developing this theory, his insights continue to influence economic thought and policy debates to this day.

TRANSLATOR'S PREFACE.

Bastiat's two great works on Political Economy—the Sophismes Économiques, and the Harmonies Économiques—may be regarded as counterparts of each other. He himself so regarded them: "the one," he says, "pulls down, the other builds up." His object in the Sophismes was to refute the fallacies of the Protectionist school, then predominant in France, and so to clear the way for the establishment of what he maintained to be the true system of economic science, which he desired to found on a new and peculiar theory of value, afterwards fully developed by him in the *Harmonies.* Whatever difference of opinion may exist among economists as to the soundness of this theory, all must admire the irresistible logic of the *Sophismes*, and "the sallies of wit and humour," which, as Mr Cobden has said, make that work as "amusing as a novel."

The system of Bastiat having thus a *destructive* as well as a *constructive* object, a *negative* as well as a *positive* design, it is perhaps only doing justice to his great reputation as an economist to put the English reader in a position to judge of that system as a whole. Hence the present translation of the *Sophismes* is intended as a companion volume to the translation of the *Harmonies.*

It is unnecessary for me to say more here by way of preface, the gifted author having himself explained the design of the work in a short but lucid introduction.

P.J.S.

ECONOMIC SOPHISMS. FIRST SERIES.

INTRODUCTION.

My design in this little volume is to refute some of the arguments which are urged against the Freedom of Trade.

I do not propose to engage in a contest with the protectionists; but rather to instil a principle into the minds of those who hesitate because they sincerely doubt.

I am not one of those who say that Protection is founded on men's interests. I am of opinion rather that it is founded on errors, or, if you will, upon *incomplete truths*. Too many people fear liberty, to permit us to conclude that their apprehensions are not sincerely felt.

It is perhaps aiming too high, but my wish is, I confess, that this little work should become, as it were, the *Manual* of those whose business it is to pronounce between the two principles. Where men have not been long accustomed and familiarized to the doctrine of liberty, the sophisms of protection, in one shape or another, are constantly coming back upon them. In order to disabuse them of such errors when they recur, a long process of analysis becomes necessary; and every one has not the time required for such a process—legislators less than others. This is my reason for endeavouring to present the analysis and its results cut and dry.

But it may be asked, Are the benefits of liberty so hidden as to be discovered only by Economists by profession?

* *The first series of the Sophismes Économiques appeared in the end of 1845; the second series in 1848.—Editor.*

We must confess that our adversaries have a marked advantage over us in the discussion. In very few words they can announce a half-truth; and in order to demonstrate that it is *incomplete*, we are obliged to have recourse to long and dry dissertations.

This arises from the nature of things. Protection concentrates on one point the good which it produces, while the evils which it inflicts are spread over the masses. The one is visible to the naked eye; the other only to the eye of the mind. In the case of liberty, it is just the reverse.

In the treatment of almost all economic questions, we find it to be so.

You say, Here is a machine which has turned thirty workmen into the street.

Or, Here is a spendthrift who encourages every branch of industry.

Or, The conquest of Algeria has doubled the trade of Marseilles.

Or, The budget secures subsistence for a hundred thousand families.

You are understood at once and by all. Your propositions are in themselves clear, simple, and true. What are your deductions from them?

Machinery is an evil.

Luxury, conquests, and heavy taxation, are productive of good.

And your theory has all the more success that you are in a situation to support it by a reference to undoubted facts.

On our side, we must decline to confine our attention to the cause, and its direct and immediate effect. We know that this very effect in its turn becomes a cause. To judge correctly of a measure, then, we must trace it through the whole chain of results to its definitive effect. In other words, we are forced to *reason* upon it.

But then clamour gets up: You are theorists, metaphysicians, idealists, utopian dreamers, *doctrinaires*; and all the prejudices of the popular mind are roused against us.

What, under such circumstances, are we to do? We can only invoke the patience and good sense of the reader, and set our deductions, if we can, in a light so clear, that truth and error must show themselves plainly, openly, and without disguise,—and that the victory, once gained, may remain on the side of restriction, or on that of freedom.

And here I must set down an essential observation.

Some extracts from this little volume have already appeared in the *Journal des Economistes*.

In a critique, in other respects very favourable, from the pen of M. le Vicomte de Romanet, he supposes that I demand the suppression of customs. He is mistaken. I demand the suppression of the protectionist *regime*. We don't refuse taxes to the Government, but we desire, if possible, to dissuade the governed from taxing one another. Napoleon said that "the customhouse should not be made an instrument of revenue, but a means of protecting industry." We maintain the contrary, and we contend that the customhouse ought not to become in the hands of the working classes an instrument of reciprocal rapine, but that it may be used as an instrument of revenue as legitimately as any other. So far are we—or, to speak only for myself, so far am I—from demanding the suppression of customs, that I see in that branch of revenue our future anchor of safety. I believe our resources are capable of yielding to the Treasury immense returns; and to speak plainly, I must add, that, seeing how slow is the spread of sound economic doctrines, and so rapid the increase of our budgets, I am disposed to count more upon the necessities of the Treasury than on the force of enlightened opinion for furthering the cause of commercial reform.

You ask me, then, What is your conclusion? and I reply, that here there is no need to arrive at a conclusion. I combat sophisms; that is all.

But you rejoin, that it is not enough to pull down—it is also necessary to build up. True; but to destroy an error, is to build up the truth which stands opposed to it.

After all, I have no repugnance to declare what my wishes are. I desire to see public opinion led to sanction a law of customs conceived nearly in these terms:—

Articles of primary necessity to pay a duty, ad valorem, of 5 per cent.

Articles of convenience, 10 per cent.

Articles of luxury, 15 to 20 per cent.

These distinctions, I am aware, belong to an order of ideas which are quite foreign to Political Economy strictly so called, and I am far from thinking them as just and useful as they are commonly supposed to be. But this subject does not fall within the compass of my present design.

I. ABUNDANCE, SCARCITY.

Which is best for man, and for society, abundance or scarcity?

What! you exclaim, can that be a question? Has any one ever asserted, or is it possible to maintain, that scarcity is at the foundation of human wellbeing?

Yes, this has been asserted, and is maintained every day; and I hesitate not to affirm that the *theory of scarcity* is much the most popular. It is the life of conversation, of the journals, of books, and of the tribune; and strange as it may seem, it is certain that Political Economy will have fulfilled its practical mission when it has established beyond question, and widely disseminated, this very simple proposition: "The wealth of men consists in the abundance of commodities."

Do we not hear it said every day, "The foreigner is about to inundate us with his products?" Then we fear abundance.

Did not M. Saint Cricq exclaim, "Production is excessive?" Then he feared abundance.

Do workmen break machines? Then they fear excess of production, or abundance.

Has not M. Bugeaud pronounced these words, "Let bread be dear, and agriculturists will get rich?" Now, bread cannot be dear but because it is scarce. Therefore M. Bugeaud extols scarcity.

Does not M. d'Argout urge as an argument against sugar-growing the very productiveness of that industry? Does he not say, "Beetroot has no future, and its culture cannot be extended, because a few acres devoted to its culture in each department would supply the whole consumption of France?" Then, in his eyes, good lies in sterility, in dearth, and evil in fertility and abundance.

The *Presse*, the *Commerce*, and the greater part of the daily papers, have one or more articles every morning to demonstrate to the Chambers and the Government, that it is sound policy to raise legislatively the price of all things by means of tariffs. And do the Chambers and the Government not obey the injunction? Now tariffs can raise prices only by diminishing the *supply* of commodities in the market! Then the journals, the Chambers, and the Minister, put in practice the theory of scarcity, and I am justified in saying that this theory is by far the most popular.

How does it happen that in the eyes of workmen, of publicists, and statesmen, abundance should appear a thing to be dreaded, and scarcity advantageous? I propose to trace this illusion to its source.

We remark that a man grows richer in proportion to the return yielded by his exertions, that is to say, in proportion as he sells his commodity at a *higher price*. He sells at a higher price in proportion to the rarity, to the scarcity, of the article he produces. We conclude from this, that, as far as he is concerned at least, scarcity enriches him. Applying successively the same reasoning to all other producers, we construct the *theory of scarcity*. We next proceed to apply this theory, and, in order to favour producers generally, we raise prices artificially, and cause a scarcity of all commodities, by prohibition, by restriction, by the suppression of machinery, and other analogous means.

The same thing holds of abundance. We observe that when a product is plentiful, it sells at a lower price, and the producer gains less. If all producers are in the same situation, they are all poor. Therefore it is abundance that ruins society And as theories are soon reduced to practice, we see the law struggling against the abundance of commodities.

This sophism in its more general form may make little impression, but applied to a particular order of facts, to a certain branch of industry, to a given class, of producers, it is extremely specious; and this is easily explained. It forms a syllogism which is not *false*, but *incomplete*. Now, what is *true* in a syllogism is always and necessarily present to the mind. But *incompleteness* is a negative quality, an absent *datum*, which it is very possible, and indeed very easy, to leave out of account.

Man produces in order to consume. He is at once producer and consumer. The reasoning which I have just explained considers him only in the first of these points of view. Had the second been taken into account, it would have led to an opposite conclusion. In effect, may it not be said:—

The consumer is richer in proportion as he *purchases* all things cheaper; and he purchases things cheaper in proportion to their abundance; therefore it is abundance which enriches him. This reasoning, extended to all consumers, leads to the *theory of plenty*.

It is the notion of *exchange* imperfectly understood which leads to these illusions. If we consider our personal interest, we recognise distinctly that it is double. As *sellers* we have an interest in dearness, and consequently in scarcity; as *buyers*, in cheapness, or what amounts to the same thing, in the abundance of commodities. We cannot, then, found our reasoning on one or other of these interests before inquiring which of the two coincides and is identified with the general and permanent interest of mankind at large.

If man were a solitary animal, if he laboured exclusively for himself, if he consumed directly the fruit of his labour—in a word, *if he did not exchange*—the theory of scarcity would never have appeared in the world. It is too evident that, in that case, abundance would be advantageous, from whatever quarter it came, whether from the result of his industry, from ingenious tools, from powerful machinery of his invention, or whether due to the fertility of the soil, the liberality of nature, or even to a mysterious *invasion* of products brought by the waves and left by them upon the shore. No solitary man would ever have thought that in order to encourage his labour and render it more productive, it was necessary to break in pieces the instruments which saved it, to neutralize the fertility of the soil, or give back to the sea the good things it had brought to his door. He would perceive at once that labour is not an end, but a means; and that it would be absurd to reject the result for fear of doing injury to the means by which that result was accomplished. He would perceive that if he devotes two hours a day to providing for his wants, any circumstance (machinery, fertility, gratuitous gift, no matter what) which saves him an hour of that labour, the result remaining the same, puts that hour at his disposal, and that he can devote it to increasing his enjoyments; in short, he would see that *to save labour* is nothing else than *progress*.

But *exchange* disturbs our view of a truth so simple. In the social state, and with the separation of employments to which it leads, the production and consumption of a commodity are not mixed up and confounded in the same individual. Each man comes to see in his labour no longer a means but an end. In relation to each commodity, exchange creates two interests, that of the producer and that of the consumer; and these two interests are always directly opposed to each other.

It is essential to analyze them, and examine their nature.

Take the case of any producer whatever, what is his immediate interest? It consists of two things: 1st, that the fewest possible number of persons should devote themselves to his branch of industry; 2dly, that the greatest possible number of persons should be in quest of the article he produces. Political economy explains it more succinctly in these terms, Supply very limited, demand very extended; or in other words still, Competition limited, demand unlimited.

What is the immediate interest of the consumer? That the supply of the product in question should be extended, and the demand restrained.

Seeing, then, that these two interests are in opposition to each other, one of them must necessarily coincide with social interests in general, and the other be antagonistic to them.

But which of them should legislation favour, as identical with the public good—if, indeed, it should favour either?

To discover this, we must inquire what would happen if the secret wishes of men were granted.

In as far as we are producers, it must be allowed that the desire of every one of us is anti-social. Are we vine-dressers? It would give us no great regret if hail should shower down on all the vines in the world except our own: *this is the theory of scarcity.* Are we iron-masters? Our wish is, that there should be no other iron in the market but our own, however much the public may be in want of it; and for no other reason than that this want, keenly felt and imperfectly satisfied, shall ensure us a higher price: this *is still the theory of scarcity.* Are we farmers? We say with M. Bugeaud, Let bread be dear, that is to say, scarce, and agriculturists will thrive: always the same theory, *the theory of scarcity.*

Are we physicians? We cannot avoid seeing that certain physical ameliorations, improving the sanitary state of the country, the development of certain moral virtues, such as moderation and temperance, the progress of knowledge tending to enable each man to take better care of his own health, the discovery of certain simple remedies of easy application, would be so many blows to our professional success. In as far as we are physicians, then, our secret wishes would be anti-social. I do not say that physicians form these secret wishes. On the contrary, I believe they would hail with joy the discovery of a universal panacea; but they would not do this as physicians, but as men, and as Christians. By a noble abnegation of self', the physician places himself in the consumer's point of view. But as exercising a profession, from which he derives his own and his family's subsistence, his desires, or, if you will, his interests, are anti-social.

Are we manufacturers of cotton stuffs? We desire to sell them at the price most profitable to ourselves. We should consent willingly to an interdict being laid on all rival manufactures; and if we could venture to give this wish public expression, or hope to realize it with some chance of success, we should attain our end, to some extent, by indirect means; for example, by excluding foreign fabrics, in order to diminish the *supply,* and thus produce, forcibly and to our profit, a *scarcity* of clothing.

In the same way, we might pass in review all other branches of industry, and we should always find that the producers, as such, have anti-social views. "The shopkeeper," says Montaigne, "thrives only by the irregularities of youth; the farmer by the high price of corn, the architect by the destruction of houses, the officers of justice by lawsuits and quarrels. Ministers of religion derive their distinction and employment from our vices and our death. No physician rejoices in the health of his friends, nor soldiers in the peace of their country; and so of the rest."

Hence it follows that if the secret wishes of each producer were realized, the world would retrograde rapidly towards barbarism. The sail would supersede steam, the oar would supersede the sail, and general traffic would be carried on by the carrier's waggon; the latter would be superseded by the mule, and the mule by the pedlar. Wool would exclude cotton, cotton in its turn would exclude wool, and so on until the dearth of all things had caused man himself to disappear from the face of the earth.

Suppose for a moment that the legislative power and the public force were placed at the disposal of Mimeral's committee, and that each member of that association had the privilege of bringing in and sanctioning a favourite law, is it difficult to divine to what sort of industrial code the public would be subjected?

If we now proceed to consider the immediate interest of the consumer, we shall find that it is in perfect harmony with the general interest, with all that the welfare of society calls for. When the purchaser goes to market, he desires to find it well stocked. Let the seasons be propitious for all harvests; let inventions more and more marvellous bring within reach a greater and greater number of products and enjoyments; let time and labour be saved; let distances be effaced by the perfection and rapidity of transit; let the spirit of justice and of peace allow of a diminished weight of taxation; let barriers of every kind be removed;—in all this the interest of the consumer runs parallel with the public interest. The consumer may push his secret wishes to a chimerical and absurd length, without these wishes becoming antagonistic to the public welfare. He may desire that food and shelter, the hearth and the roof, instruction and morality, security and peace, power and health, should be obtained without exertion, and without measure, like the dust of the highways, the water of the brook, the air which we breathe; and yet the realization of his desires would not be at variance with the good of society.

It may be said that if these wishes were granted, the work of the producer would become more and more limited, and would end with being stopped for want of aliment. But why? Because, on this extreme supposition, all imaginable wants and desires would be fully satisfied. Man, like Omnipotence, would create all things by a simple act of volition. Well, on this hypotheses, what reason should we have to regret the stoppage of industrial production?

I made the supposition, not long ago, of the existence of an assembly composed of workmen, each member of which, in his capacity of producer, should have the power of passing a law embodying his *secret wish*, and I said that the code which would emanate from that assembly would be monopoly systematized, the theory of scarcity reduced to practice.

In the same way, a chamber in which each should consult exclusively his own immediate interest as a consumer, would tend to systematize liberty, to suppress all restrictive measures, to overthrow all artificial barriers—in a word, to realize the *theory of plenty*.

Hence it follows:

That to consult exclusively the immediate interest of the producer, is to consult an interest which is anti-social.

That to take for basis exclusively the immediate interest of the consumer, would be to take for basis the general interest.

Let me enlarge on this view of the subject a little, at the risk of being prolix.

A radical antagonism exists between seller and buyer.*

The former desires that the subject of the bargain should be scarce, its supply limited, and its price high.

The latter desires that it should be *abundant*, its supply large, and its price low.

The laws, which should be at least neutral, take the part of the seller against the buyer, of the producer against the consumer, of dearness against cheapness,** of scarcity against abundance.

** The author has modified somewhat the terms of this proposition in a posterior work.—See Harmonies Économiques, chapter xi.—Editor.*

*** We have not in French a substantive to express the idea opposed to that of dearness (cheapness). It is somewhat remarkable that the popular instinct expresses the idea by this periphrase, marche avantageux, bon marche'. The protectionists would do well to reform this locution, for it implies an economic system opposed to theirs.*

They proceed, if not intentionally, at least logically, on this datum: *a nation is rich when it is in want of everything.*

For they say, it is the producer that we must favour by securing him a good market for his product. For this purpose it is necessary to raise the price, and in order to raise the price we must restrict the supply; and to restrict the supply is to create scarcity.

Just let us suppose that at the present moment, when all these laws are in full force, we make a complete inventory, not in value, but in weight, measure, volume, quantity, of all the commodities existing in the country, which are fitted to satisfy the wants and tastes of its inhabitants—corn, meat, cloth, fuel, colonial products, etc.

Suppose, again, that next day all the barriers which oppose the introduction of foreign products are removed.

Lastly, suppose that in order to test the result of this reform, they proceed three months afterwards to make a new inventory.

Is it not true that there will be found in France more corn, cattle, cloth, linen, iron, coal, sugar, etc., at the date of the second, than at the date of the first inventory?

So true is this, that our protective tariffs have no other purpose than to hinder all these things from reaching us, to restrict the supply, and prevent depreciation and abundance.

Now I would ask, Are the people who live under our laws better fed because there is *less* bread, meat, and sugar in the country? Are they better clothed, because there is *less* cloth and linen? Better warmed, because there is *less* coal? Better assisted in their labour, because there are *fewer* tools and *less* iron, copper, and machinery?

But it may be said, If the foreigner *inundates* us with his products, he will carry away our money.

And what does it matter? Men are not fed on money. They do not clothe themselves with gold, or warm themselves with silver. What matters it whether there is more or less money in the country, if there is more bread on our sideboards, more meat in our larders, more linen in our wardrobes, more firewood in our cellars.

Restrictive laws always land us in this dilemma:—

Either you admit that they produce scarcity, or you do not. If you admit it, you avow by the admission that you inflict on the people all the injury in your power. If you do not admit it, you deny having restricted the supply and raised prices, and consequently you deny having favoured the producer.

What you do is either hurtful or profitless, injurious or ineffectual. It never can be attended with any useful result.

II. OBSTACLE, CAUSE.

The obstacle mistaken for the cause,—scarcity mistaken for abundance,—this is the same sophism under another aspect; and it is well to study it in all its phases.

Man is originally destitute of everything.

Between this destitution and the satisfaction of his wants, there exist a multitude of *obstacles* which labour enables us to surmount. It is curious to inquire how and why these very obstacles to his material prosperity have come to be mistaken for the cause of that prosperity.

I want to travel a hundred miles. But between the starting-point and the place of my destination, mountains, rivers, marshes, impenetrable forests, brigands—in a word, *obstacles*—interpose themselves; and to overcome these obstacles, it is necessary for me to employ many efforts, or, what comes to the same thing, that others should employ many efforts for me, the price of which I must pay them. It is clear that I should have been in a better situation if these obstacles had not existed.

On his long journey through life, from the cradle to the grave, man has need to assimilate to himself a prodigious quantity of alimentary substances, to protect himself against the inclemency of the weather, to preserve himself from a number of ailments, or cure himself of them. Hunger, thirst, disease, heat, cold, are so many obstacles strewn along his path. In a state of isolation he must overcome them all, by hunting, fishing, tillage, spinning, weaving, building; and it is clear that it would be better for him that these obstacles were less numerous and formidable, or, better still, that they did not exist at all. In society, he does not combat these obstacles personally, but others do it for him; and in return he employs himself in removing one of those obstacles which are encountered by his fellow-men.

It is clear also, considering things in the gross, that it would be better for men in the aggregate, or for society, that these obstacles should be as few and feeble as possible.

But when we come to scrutinize the social phenomena in detail, and men's sentiments as modified by the introduction of exchange, we soon perceive how they have come to confound wants with wealth, the obstacle with the cause.

The separation of employments, the division of labour, which results from the faculty of exchanging, causes each man, instead of struggling on his own account to overcome all the obstacles which surround him, to combat only *one* of them; he overcomes that one not for himself but for his fellow-men, who in turn render him the same service.

The consequence is that this man, in combating this obstacle which it is his special business to overcome for the sake of others, sees in it the immediate source of his own wealth. The greater, the more formidable, the more keenly felt this obstacle is, the greater will be the remuneration which his fellow-men will be disposed to accord him; that is to say, the more ready will they be to remove the obstacles which stand in his way.

The physician, for example, does not bake his own bread, or manufacture his own instruments, or weave or make his own coat. Others do these things for him, and in return he treats the diseases with which his patients are afflicted. The more numerous, severe, and frequent these diseases are, the more others consent, and are obliged, to do for his personal comfort. Regarding it from this point of view, disease, that general obstacle to human happiness, becomes a cause of material prosperity to the individual physician. The same argument applies to all producers in their several departments. The shipowner derives his profits from the obstacle called *distance*; the agriculturist from that called *hunger*; the manufacturer of cloth from that called *cold*; the schoolmaster lives upon *ignorance*; the lapidary upon *vanity*; the attorney on *cupidity*; the notary upon possible *bad faith*,—just as the physician lives upon the diseases of men. It is quite true, therefore, that each profession has an immediate interest in the continuation, nay in the extension, of the special obstacle which it is its business to combat.

Observing this, theorists make their appearance, and, founding a system on their individual sentiments, tell us: Want is wealth, labour is wealth, obstacles to material prosperity are prosperity. To multiply obstacles is to support industry.

Then statesmen intervene. They have the disposal of the public force; and what more natural than to make it available for developing and multiplying obstacles, since this is developing and multiplying wealth? They say, for example: If we prevent the importation of iron from places where it is abundant, we place an obstacle in the way of its being procured. This obstacle, keenly felt at home, will induce men to pay in order to be set free from it. A certain number of our fellow-citizens will devote themselves to combating it, and this obstacle will make their fortune. The greater the obstacle is—that is, the scarcer, the more inaccessible, the more difficult to transport, the more distant from the place where it is to be used, the mineral sought for becomes—the more hands will be engaged in the various ramifications of this branch of industry. Exclude, then, foreign iron, create an obstacle, for you thereby create the labour which is to overcome it.

The same reasoning leads to the proscription of machinery.

Here, for instance, are men who are in want of casks for the storage of their wine. This is an obstacle; and here are other men whose business it is to remove that obstacle by making the casks that are wanted. It is fortunate, then, that this obstacle should exist, since it gives employment to a branch of national industry, and enriches a certain number of our fellow-citizens. But then we have ingenious machinery invented for felling the oak, cutting it up into staves, and forming them into the wine-casks that are wanted. By this means the obstacle is lessened, and so are the gains of the cooper. Let us maintain both at their former elevation by a law, and put down the machinery.

To get at the root of this sophism, it is necessary only to reflect that human labour is not the *end*, but the *means. It never remains unemployed.* If one obstacle is removed, it does battle with another; and society is freed from two obstacles by the same amount of labour which was formerly, required for the removal of one. If the labour of the cooper is rendered unnecessary in one department, it will soon take another direction. But how and from what source will it be remunerated? From the same source exactly from which it is remunerated at present; for when a certain amount of labour becomes disposable by the removal of an obstacle, a corresponding amount of remuneration becomes disposable also. To maintain that human labour will ever come to want employment, would be to maintain that the human race will cease to encounter obstacles. In that case labour would not only be impossible; it would be superfluous.

We should no longer have anything to do, because we should be omnipotent; and we should only have to pronounce our *fiat* in order to ensure the satisfaction of all our desires and the supply of all our wants.*

** See post, ch. xiv. of second series of Sophismes Economiques, and ch. iii. and xi. of the Harmonies Économiques.*

III. EFFORT, RESULT.

We have just seen that between our wants and the satisfaction of these wants, obstacles are interposed. We succeed in overcoming these obstacles, or in diminishing their force by the employment of our faculties. We may say in a general way, that industry is an effort followed by a result.

But what constitutes the measure of our prosperity, or of our wealth? Is it the result of the effort? or is it the effort itself? A relation always subsists between the effort employed and the result obtained. Progress consists in the relative enhancement of the second or of the first term of this relation.

Both theses have been maintained; and in political economy they have divided the region of opinion and of thought.

According to the first system, wealth is the result of labour, increasing as the relative *proportion of result to effort increases.* Absolute perfection, of which God is the type, consists in the infinite distance interposed between the two terms—in this sense, effort is *nil*, result infinite.

The second system teaches that it is the effort itself which constitutes the measure of wealth. To make progress is to increase the relative proportion *which effort bears to result.* The ideal of this system may be found in the sterile and eternal efforts of Sisyphus.*

The first system naturally welcomes everything which tends to diminish *pains* and augment *products*; powerful machinery which increases the forces of man, exchange which allows him to derive greater advantage from natural agents distributed in various proportions over the face of the earth, intelligence which discovers, experience which proves, competition which stimulates, etc.

Logically, the second invokes everything which has the effect of increasing pains and diminishing products; privileges, monopolies, restrictions, prohibitions, suppression of machinery, sterility, etc.

It is well to remark that the *universal practice* of mankind always points to the principle of the first system. We have never seen, we shall never see, a man who labours in any department, be he agriculturist, manufacturer, merchant, artificer, soldier, author, or philosopher, who does not devote all the powers of his mind to work better, to work with more rapidity, to work more economically—in a word, to effect *more with less.*

The opposite doctrine is in favour only with theorists, deputies, journalists, statesmen, ministers—men, in short, born to make experiments on the social body.

** For this reason, and for the sake of conciseness, the reader will pardon us for designating this system in the sequel by the name of sisyphism.*

At the same time, we may observe, that in what concerns themselves personally, they act as every one else does, on the principle of obtaining from labour the greatest possible amount of useful results.

Perhaps I may be thought to exaggerate, and that there are no true *sisyphists.*

If it be argued that in practice they do not press their principle to its most extreme consequences, I willingly grant it. This is always the case when one sets out with a false principle. Such a principle soon leads to results so absurd and so mischievous that we are obliged to stop short. This is the reason why practical industry never admits *sisyphism*; punishment would follow error too closely not to expose it. But in matters of speculation, such as theorists and statesmen deal in, one may pursue a false principle a long time before discovering its falsity by the complicated consequences to which men were formerly strangers; and when at last its falsity is found out, the authors take refuge in the opposite principle, turn round, contradict themselves, and seek their justification in a modern maxim of incomparable absurdity: in political economy, there is no inflexible rule, no absolute principle.

Let us see, then, if these two opposite principles which I have just described do not predominate by turns, the one in practical industry, the other in industrial legislation.

I have already noticed the saying of M. Bugeaud (that "when bread is dear, agriculturists become rich"); but in M. Bugeaud are embodied two separate characters, the agriculturist and the legislator.

As an agriculturist, M. Bugeaud directs all his efforts to two ends,—to save labour, and obtain cheap bread. When he prefers a good plough to a bad one; when he improves his pastures; when, in order to pulverize the soil, he substitutes as much as possible the action of the atmosphere for that of the harrow and the hoe; when he calls to his aid all the processes of which science and experiment have proved the efficacy,—he has but one object in view, viz., to diminish *the proportion of effort to result.* We have indeed no other test of the ability of a cultivator, and the perfection of his processes, than to measure to what extent they have lessened the one and added to the other. And as all the farmers in the world act upon this principle, we may assert that the effort of mankind at large is to obtain, for their own benefit undoubtedly, bread and all other products cheaper, to lessen the labour needed to procure a given quantity of what they want.

This incontestable tendency of mankind once established, should, it would seem, reveal to the legislator the true principle, and point out to him in what way he should aid industry (in as far as it falls within his province to aid it); for it would be absurd to assert that human laws should run counter to the laws of Providence.

And yet we have heard M. Bugeaud, as a deputy, exclaim: "I understand nothing of this theory of cheapness; I should like better to see bread dearer and labour more abundant." And following out this doctrine, the deputy of the Dordogne votes legislative measures, the effect of which is to hamper exchanges, for the very reason that they procure us indirectly what direct production could not procure us but at greater expense.

Now, it is very evident that M. Bugeaud's principle as a deputy is directly opposed to the principle on which he acts as an agriculturist. To act consistently, he should vote against all legislative restriction, or else import into his farming operations the principle which he proclaims from the tribune. We should then see him sow his corn in his most sterile fields, for in this way he would succeed in *working much to obtain little.* We should see him throwing aside the plough, since hand-culture would satisfy his double wish for dearer bread and more abundant labour.

Restriction has for its avowed object, and its acknowledged effect, to increase labour.

It has also for its avowed object, and its acknowledged effect, to cause dearness, which means simply scarcity of products; so that, carried out to its extreme limits, it is pure *sisyphism*, such as we have defined it,—*labour infinite, product nil.*

Baron Charles Dupin, the light of the peerage, it is said, on economic science, accuses railways of *injuring navigation*; and it is certain that it is of the nature of a more perfect, to restrict the use of a less perfect means of conveyance. But railways cannot hurt navigation except by attracting traffic; and they cannot attract traffic but by conveying goods and passengers more cheaply; and they cannot convey them more cheaply but by *diminishing the proportion which the effort employed bears to the result obtained*, seeing that that is the very thing which constitutes cheapness. When, then, Baron Dupin deplores this diminution of the labour employed to effect a given result, it is the doctrine of *sisyphism* which he preaches. Logically, since he prefers the ship to the rail, he should prefer the cart to the ship, the pack-saddle to the cart, and the pannier to all other known means of conveyance, for it is the latter which exacts the most labour with the least result.

"Labour constitutes the wealth of a people," said M. de Saint-Cricq, that Minister of Commerce who has imposed so many restrictions upon trade. We must not suppose that this was an elliptical expression, meaning, "The results of labour constitute the wealth of a people." No, this economist distinctly intended to affirm that it is the *intensity* of labour which is the measure of wealth, and the proof of it is, that from consequence to consequence, from one restriction to another, he induced France (and in this he thought he was doing her good) to expend double the amount of labour, in order, for example, to provide herself with an equal quantity of iron. In England, iron was then at eight francs, while in France it cost sixteen francs. Taking a day's labour at one franc, it is clear that France could, by means of exchange, procure a quintal of iron by subtracting eight days' work from the aggregate national labour. In consequence of the restrictive measures of M. de Saint-Cricq, France was obliged to expend sixteen days' labour in order to provide herself with a quintal of iron by direct production. Double the labour for the same satisfaction, hence double the wealth. Then it follows that wealth is not measured by the result, but by the intensity of the labour. Is not this *sisyphism* in all its purity?

And in order that there may be no mistake as to his meaning, the Minister takes care afterwards to explain more fully his ideas; and as he had just before called the intensity of labour *wealthy* he goes on to call the more abundant results of that labour, or the more abundant supply of things proper to satisfy our wants, *poverty.* "Everywhere," he says, "machinery has taken the place of manual labour; everywhere production superabounds; everywhere the equilibrium between the faculty of producing, and the means of consuming, is destroyed." We see, then, to what, in M. de Saint-Cricq's estimation, the critical situation of the country was owing—it was to having produced too much, and her labour being too intelligent, and too fruitful. We were too well fed, too well clothed, too well provided with everything; a too rapid production surpassed all our desires. It was necessary, then, to put a stop to the evil, and for that purpose, to force us, by restrictions, to labour more in order to produce less.

I have referred likewise to the opinions of another Minister of Commerce, M. d'Argout. They deserve to be dwelt upon for an instant. Desiring to strike a formidable blow at beet-root culture, he says, "Undoubtedly, the cultivation of beet-root is useful, *but this utility is limited.* The developments attributed to it are exaggerated. To be convinced of this, it is sufficient to observe that this culture will be necessarily confined within the limits of consumption. Double, triple, if you will, the present consumption of France, *you will always find that a very trifling portion of the soil will satisfy the requirements of that consumption.*" (This is surely rather a singular subject of complaint!) "Do you desire proof of this? How many *hectares* had we under beet-root in 1828? 3130, which is equivalent to 1-10, 540th of our arable land. At the present time, when indigenous sugar supplies one-third of our consumption, how much land is devoted to that culture? 16,700 *hectares*, or 1-1978th of the arable land, or 45 *centiares* in each commune. Suppose indigenous sugar already supplied our whole consumption, we should have only 48,000 hectares under beet-root, or 1-689th of the arable land."*

There are two things to be remarked upon in this citation—the facts and the doctrine. The facts tend to prove that little land, little capital, and little labour are required to produce a large quantity of sugar, and that each commune of France would be abundantly provided by devoting to beet-root cultivation one hectare of its soil. The doctrine consists in regarding this circumstance as adverse, and in seeing in the very power and fertility of the new industry, *a limit to its utility.*

* It is fair to M. d'Argout to say that he put this language in the mouth of the adversaries of beet-root culture. But he adopts it formally, and sanctions it besides, by the law which it was employed to justify.

I do not mean to constitute myself here the defender of beet-root culture, or a judge of the strange facts advanced by M. d'Argout; * but it is worth while to scrutinize the doctrine of a statesman, to whom France for a long time entrusted the care of her agriculture and of her commerce.

I remarked in the outset that a variable relation exists between an industrial effort and its result; that absolute imperfection consists in an infinite effort without any result; absolute perfection in an unlimited result without any effort; and perfectibility in the progressive diminution of effort compared with the result.

But M. d'Argout tells us there is death where we think we perceive life, and that the importance of any branch of industry is in direct proportion to its powerlessness. What are we to expect, for instance, from the cultivation of beet-root? Do you not see that 48,000 *hectares* of land, with capital and manual labour in proportion, are sufficient to supply all France with sugar? Then, this is a branch of industry of limited utility; limited, of course, with reference to the amount of labour which it demands, the only way in which, according to the ex-Minister, any branch of industry can be useful. This utility would be still more limited, if, owing to the fertility of the soil, and the richness of the beet-root, we could reap from 24,000 hectares, what at present we only obtain from 48,000. Oh! were only twenty times, a hundred times, more land, capital, and labour necessary to *yield us the same result*, so much the better. We might build some hopes on this new branch of industry, and it would be worthy of state protection, for it would offer a vast field to our national industry. But to produce much with little! that is a bad example, and it is time for the law to interfere.

** Supposing that 48,000 or 50,000 hectares were sufficient to supply the present consumption, it would require 150,000 for triple that consumption, which M. d'Argout admits as possible. Moreover, if beet-root entered into a six years' rotation of crops, it would occupy successively 900,000 hectares, or 1-38th of the arable land.*

But what is true with regard to sugar, cannot be otherwise with regard to bread. If, then, the *utility* of any branch of industry is to be estimated not by the amount of satisfactions it is fitted to procure us with a determinate amount of labour, but, on the contrary, by the amount of labour which it exacts in order to yield us a determinate amount of satisfactions, what we ought evidently to desire is, that each acre of land should yield less corn, and each grain of com less nourishment; in other words, that our land should be comparatively barren; for then the quantity of land, capital, and manual labour that would be required for the maintenance of our population would be much more considerable; we could then say that the demand for human labour would be in direct proportion to this barrenness. The aspirations of MM. Bugeaud, Saint-Cricq, Dupin, and d'Argout, would then be satisfied; bread would be dear, labour abundant, and France rich—rich at least in the sense in which these gentlemen understand the word.

What we should desire also is, that human intelligence should be enfeebled or extinguished; for, as long as it survives, it will be continually endeavouring to augment *the proportion which the end bears to the means, and which the product bears to the labour.* It is in that precisely that intelligence consists.

Thus, it appears that *sisyphism* has been the doctrine of all the men who have been intrusted with our industrial destinies. It would be unfair to reproach them with it. This principle guides Ministers only because it is predominant in the Chambers; and it predominates in the Chambers only because it is sent there by the electoral body, and the electoral body is imbued with it only because public opinion is saturated with it.

I think it right to repeat here that I do not accuse men such as MM. Bugeaud, Dupin, Saint-Cricq, and d'Argout of being absolutely and under all circumstances *sisyphists.* They are certainly not so in their private transactions; for in these they always desire to obtain *by way of exchange* what would cost them dearer to procure *by direct production*; but I affirm they are *sisyphists* when they hinder the country from doing the same thing.*

* See on the same subject, *Sophismes Économiques*, second
series, ch. xvi., post, and *Harmonies Économiques*, ch. vi.

IV. TO EQUALIZE THE CONDITIONS OF PRODUCTION.

It has been said.....but in case I should be accused of putting sophisms into the mouths of the protectionists, I shall allow one of their most vigorous athletes to speak for them.

"It has been thought that protection in our case should simply represent the difference which exists between the cost price of a commodity which we produce and the cost price of the same commodity produced by our neighbours.... A protective duty calculated on this basis would only ensure free competition....; free competition exists only when there is equality in the conditions and in the charges. In the case of a horse race, we ascertain the weight which each horse has to carry, and so equalize the conditions; without that there could be no fair competition. In the case of trade, if one of the sellers can bring his commodity to market at less cost, he ceases to be a competitor, and becomes a monopolist.... Do away with this protection which represents the difference of cost price, and the foreigner invades our markets and acquires a monopoly."*

"Every one must wish, for his own sake, as well as for the sake of others, that the production of the country should be protected against foreign competition, *whenever the latter can furnish products at a lower price.*"**

* *M. le Vicomte de Romanet.*

** *Matthieu le Dombasle.*

This argument recurs continually in works of the protectionist school. I propose to examine it carefully, and I solicit earnestly the reader's patience and attention. I shall consider, first of all, the inequalities which are attributable to nature, and afterwards those which are attributable to diversity of taxation.

In this, as in other cases, we shall find protectionist theorists viewing their subject from the producer's stand-point, whilst we advocate the cause of the unfortunate consumers, whose interests they studiously keep out of sight. They institute a comparison between the field of industry and the *turf*. But as regards the latter, the race is at once the *means* and the *end*. The public feels no interest in the competition beyond the competition itself. When you start your horses, your *end*, your object, is to find out which is the swiftest runner, and I see your reason for equalizing the weights. But if your *end*, your object, were to secure the arrival of some important and urgent news at the winning-post, could you, without inconsistency, throw obstacles in the way of any one who should offer you the best means of expediting your message? This is what you do in commercial affairs. You forget the end, the object sought to be attained, which is material prosperity; you disregard it, you sacrifice it to a veritable *petitio principii*; in plain language, you are begging the question.

But since we cannot bring our opponents to our point of view, let us place ourselves in theirs, and examine the question in its relations with production.

I shall endeavour to prove,

1st, That to level and equalize the conditions of labour, is to attack exchange in its essence and principle.

2d, That it is not true that the labour of a country is neutralized by the competition of more favoured countries.

3d, That if that were true, protective duties would not equalize the conditions of production.

4th, That liberty, freedom of trade, levels these conditions as much as they can be levelled.

5th, That the least favoured countries gain most by exchange.

I. To level and equalize the conditions of labour is not simply to cramp exchanges in certain branches of trade, it is to attack exchange in its principle, for its principle rests upon that very diversity, upon those very inequalities of fertility, aptitude, climate, and temperature, which you desire to efface. If Guienne sends wine to Brittany, and if Brittany sends corn to Guienne, it arises from their being placed under different conditions of production. Is there a different law for international exchanges? To urge against international exchanges that inequality of conditions which gives rise to them, and explains them, is to argue against their very existence.

If protectionists had on their side sufficient logic and power, they would reduce men, like snails, to a state of absolute isolation. Moreover, there is not one of their sophisms which, when submitted to the test of rigorous deductions, does not obviously tend to destruction and annihilation.

II. It is not true, in point of *fact*, that inequality of conditions existing between two similar branches of industry entails necessarily the ruin of that which is least favourably situated. On the turf, if one horse gains the prize, the other loses it; but when two horses are employed in useful labour, each produces a beneficial result in proportion to its powers; and if the more vigorous renders the greater service, it does not follow that the other renders no service at all. We cultivate wheat in all the departments of France, although there are between them enormous differences of fertility; and if there be any one department which does not cultivate wheat, it is because it is not profitable to engage in that species of culture in that locality. In the same way, analogy shows us that under the *regime* of liberty, in spite of similar differences, they produce wheat in all the countries of Europe; and if there be one which abandons the cultivation of that grain, it is because it is found *more for its interest* to give another direction to the employment of its land, labour, and capital And why should the fertility of one department not paralyze the agriculturist of a neighbouring department which is less favourably situated? Because the economic phenomena have a flexibility, an elasticity, *levelling powers*, so to speak, which appear to have altogether escaped the notice of the protectionist school. That school accuses us of being given up to system; but it is the protectionists who are systematic in the last degree, if the spirit of system consists in bolstering up arguments which rest upon one fact instead of upon an aggregation of facts. In the example which we have given, it is the difference in the value of lands which compensates the difference in their fertility. Your field produces three times more than mine. Yes, but it has cost you ten times more, and I can still compete with you. This is the whole mystery. And observe, that superiority in some respects leads to inferiority in others. It is just because your land is more fertile that it is dearer; so that it is not *accidentally*, but *necessarily*, that the equilibrium is established, or tends to be established; and it cannot be denied that liberty is the *regime* which is most favourable to this tendency.

I have referred to a branch of agricultural industry; I might as well have referred to industry in a different department. There are tailors at Quimper, and that does not hinder there being tailors also in Paris, though the latter pay a higher rent, and live at much greater expense. But then they have a different set of customers, and that serves not only to redress the balance, but to make it incline to their side.

When we speak, then, of equalizing the conditions of labour, we must not omit to examine whether liberty does not give us what we seek from an arbitrary system.

This natural levelling power of the economic phenomena is so important to the question we are considering, and at the same time so fitted to inspire us with admiration of the providential wisdom which presides over the equitable government of society, that I must ask permission to dwell upon it for a little.

The protectionist gentlemen tell us: Such or such a people have over us an advantage in the cheapness of coal, of iron, of machinery, of capital—we cannot compete with them.

We shall examine the proposition afterwards under all its aspects. At present, I confine myself to the inquiry whether, when a superiority and an inferiority are both present, they do not possess in themselves, the one an ascending, the other a descending force, which must ultimately bring them back to a just equilibrium.

Suppose two countries, A and B. A possesses over B all kinds of advantages. You infer from this, that every sort of industry will concentrate itself in A, and that B is powerless. A, you say, sells much more than it buys; B buys much more than it sells. I might dispute this, but I respect your hypothesis.

On this hypothesis, labour is much in demand in A, and will soon rise in price there.

Iron, coal, land, food, capital, are much in demand in A, and they will soon rise in price there.

Contemporaneously with this, labour, iron, coal, land, food, capital, are in little request in B, and will soon fall in price there.

Nor is this all. While A is always selling, and B is always buying, money passes from B to A. It becomes abundant in A, and scarce in B.

But abundance of money means that we must have plenty of it to buy everything else. Then in A, to the *real dearness* which arises from a very active demand, there is added a *nominal dearness*, which is due to a redundancy of the precious metals.

Scarcity of money means that little is required for each purchase. Then in B a *nominal cheapness* comes to be combined with *real cheapness*.

In these circumstances, industry will have all sorts of motives—motives, if I may say so, carried to the highest degree of intensity—to desert A and establish itself in B.

Or, to come nearer what would actually take place under such circumstances, we may affirm that sudden displacements being so repugnant to the nature of industry, such a transfer would not have been so long delayed, but that from the beginning, under the free *regime*, it would have gradually and progressively shared and distributed itself between A and B, according to the laws of supply and demand—that is to say, according to the laws of justice and utility.

And when I assert that if it were possible for industry to concentrate itself upon one point, that very circumstance would set in motion an irresistible decentralizing force, I indulge in no idle hypothesis.

Let us listen to what was said by a manufacturer in addressing the Manchester Chamber of Commerce (I omit the figures by which he supported his demonstration):—

"Formerly we exported stuffs; then that exportation gave place to that of yams, which are the raw material of stuffs; then to that of machines, which are the instruments for producing yarn; afterwards to the exportation of the capital with which we construct our machines; finally, to that of our workmen and our industrial skill, which are the source of our capital. All these elements of labour, one after the other, are set to work wherever they find the most advantageous opening, wherever the expense of living is cheaper and the necessaries of life are moat easily procured; and at the present day, in Prussia, in Austria, in Saxony, in Switzerland, in Italy, we see manufactures on an immense scale founded and supported by English capital, worked by English operatives, and directed by English engineers."

You see very clearly, then, that nature, or rather that Providence, more wise, more far-seeing than your narrow and rigid theory supposes, has not ordered this concentration of industry, this monopoly of all advantages upon which you found your reasoning as upon a fact which is unalterable and without remedy. Nature has provided, by means as simple as they are infallible, that there should be dispersion, diffusion, solidarity, simultaneous progress; all constituting a state of things which your restrictive laws paralyze as much as they can; for the tendency of such laws is, by isolating communities, to render the diversity of condition much more marked, to prevent equalization, hinder fusion, neutralize countervailing circumstances, and segregate nations, whether in their superiority or in their inferiority of condition.

III. In the third place, to contend that by a protective duty you equalize the conditions of production, is to give currency to an error by a deceptive form of speech. It is not true that an import duty equalizes the conditions of production. These remain, after the imposition of the duty, the same as they were before. At most, all that such a duty equalizes are *the conditions of sale.* It may be said, perhaps, that I am playing upon words, but I throw back the accusation. It is for my opponents to show that *production and sale* are synonymous terms; and if they cannot do this, I am warranted in fastening upon them the reproach, if not of playing on words, at least of mixing them up and confusing them.

To illustrate what I mean by an example: I suppose some Parisian speculators to devote themselves to the production of oranges. They know that the oranges of Portugal can be sold in Paris for a penny apiece, whilst they, on account of the frames and hot-houses which the colder climate would render necessary, could not sell them for less than a shilling as a remunerative price. They demand that Portuguese oranges should have a duty of elevenpence imposed upon them. By means of this duty, they say, the *conditions af production* will be equalized; and the Chamber, giving effect, as it always does, to such reasoning, inserts in the tariff a duty of elevenpence upon every foreign orange.

Now, I maintain that the *conditions of production* are in nowise changed. The law has made no change on the heat of the sun of Lisbon, or on the frequency and intensity of the frosts of Paris. The ripening of oranges will continue to go on naturally on the banks of the Tagus, and artificially on the banks of the Seine—that is to say, much more human labour will be required in the one country than in the other. The conditions of sale are what have been equalized. The Portuguese must now sell us their oranges at a shilling, elevenpence of which goes to pay the tax. That tax will be paid, it is evident, by the French consumer. And look at the whimsical result. Upon each Portuguese orange consumed, the country will lose nothing, for the extra elevenpence charged to the consumer will be paid into the treasury. This will cause displacement, but not loss. But upon each French orange consumed there will be a loss of elevenpence, or nearly so, for the purchaser will certainly lose that sum, and the seller as certainly will not gain it, seeing that by the hypothesis he will only have received the cost price. I leave it to the protectionists to draw the inference.

IV. If I have dwelt upon this distinction between the conditions of production and the conditions of sale, a distinction which the protectionists will no doubt pronounce paradoxical, it is because it leads me to inflict on them another, and a much stranger, paradox, which is this: Would you equalize effectually the conditions of production, leave exchange free.

Now, really, it will be said, this is too much; you must be making game of us. Well, then, were it only for curiosity, I entreat the gentlemen protectionists to follow me on to the conclusion of my argument. It will not be long. I revert to my former illustration.

Let us suppose for a moment that the average daily wage which a Frenchman earns is equal to a shilling, and it follows incontestably that to produce directly an orange in France, a day's work, or its equivalent, is required; while to produce the value of a Portuguese orange, only a twelfth part of that day's labour would be necessary; which means exactly this, that the sun does at Lisbon what human labour does at Paris. Now, is it not very evident that if I can produce an orange, or, what comes to the same thing, the means of purchasing one, with a twelfth part of a day's labour, I am placed, with respect to this production, under exactly the same conditions as the Portuguese producer himself, excepting the carriage, which must be at my expense. It is certain, then, that liberty equalizes the conditions of production direct or indirect, as far as they can be equalized, since it leaves no other difference, but the inevitable one arising from the expense of transport.

I add, that liberty equalizes also the conditions of enjoyment, of satisfaction, of consumption, with which the protectionists never concern themselves, and which are yet the essential consideration, consumption being the end and object of all our industrial efforts. In virtue of free trade, we enjoy the sun of Portugal like the Portuguese themselves. The inhabitants of Havre and the citizens of London are put in possession, and on the same conditions, of all the mineral resources which nature has bestowed on Newcastle.

V. Gentlemen protectionists, you find me in a paradoxical humour; and I am disposed to go further still. I say, and I sincerely think, that if two countries are placed under unequal conditions of production, *it is that one of the two which is least favoured by nature which has most to gain by free trade.* To prove this, I must depart a little from the usual form of such a work as this. I shall do so nevertheless, first of all, because the entire question lies there, and also because it will afford me an opportunity of explaining an economic law of the highest importance, and which, if rightly understood, appears to me to be fitted to bring back to the science all those sects who, in our day, seek in the land of chimeras that social harmony which they fail to discover in nature. I refer to the law of consumption, which it is perhaps to be regretted that the majority of economists have neglected.

Consumption is the *end* and final cause of all the economic phenomena, and it is in consumption consequently that we must expect to find their ultimate and definitive solution.

Nothing, whether favourable or unfavourable, can abide permanently with the producer. The advantages which nature and society bestow upon him, the inconveniences he may experience, glide past him, so to speak, and are absorbed and mixed up with the community in as far as the community represents consumers. This is an admirable law both in its cause and in its effects, and he who shall succeed in clearly describing it is entitled, in my opinion, to say, "I have not passed through life without paying my tribute to society." Everything which favours the work of production is welcomed with joy by the producer, for the *immediate effect* of it is to put him in a situation to render greater service to the community, and to exact from it a greater remuneration. Every circumstance which retards or interrupts production gives pain to the producer, for the *immediate effect* of it is to circumscribe his services, and consequently his remuneration. *Immediate* good or ill circumstances—fortunate or unfortunate—necessarily fall upon the producer, and leave him no choice but to accept the one and eschew the other.

In the same way, when a workman succeeds in discovering an improved process in manufactures, the *immediate* profit from the improvement results to him. This was necessary, in order to give his labour an intelligent direction; and it is just, because it is fair that an effort crowned with success should carry its recompense along with it.

But I maintain that these good or bad effects, though in their own nature permanent, are not permanent as regards the producer. If it had been so, a principle of progressive, and, therefore, of indefinite, inequality would have been introduced among men, and this is the reason why these good or evil effects become very soon absorbed in the general destinies of the human race.

How is this brought about? I shall show how it takes place by some examples.

Let us go back to the thirteenth century. The men who then devoted themselves to the art of copying received for the service which they rendered *a remuneration regulated by the general rate of earnings.** Among them there arose one who discovered the means of multiplying copies of the same work rapidly. He invented printing.

In the first instance, one man was enriched, and many others were impoverished. At first sight, marvellous as the invention proves itself to be, we hesitate to decide whether it is hurtful or useful. It seems to introduce into the world, as I have said, an indefinite element of inequality. Guttemberg profits by his invention, and extends his invention with its profits indefinitely, until he has ruined all the copyists. As regards the public, in the capacity of consumer, it gains little; for Guttemberg takes care not to lower the price of his books, but just enough to undersell his rivals.

But the intelligence which has introduced harmony into the movements of the heavenly bodies, has implanted it also in the internal mechanism of society. We shall see the economic advantages of the invention when it has ceased to be individual property, and has become for ever the common patrimony of the masses.

At length the invention comes to be known. Guttemberg is no longer the only printer; others imitate him. Their profits' at first are large. They are thus rewarded for having been the first to imitate the invention; and it is right that it should be so, for this higher remuneration was necessary to induce them to concur in the grand definite result which is approaching. They gain a great deal, but they gain less than the inventor, for *competition* now begins its work. The price of books goes on falling. The profit of imitators goes on diminishing in proportion as the invention becomes of older date; that is to say, in proportion as the imitation becomes less meritorious.....

* *The author, here and elsewhere, uses the French word profits; but it is clear from the context that he does not refer to the returns from capital, in which sense alone the English economists employ the term profits. We have therefore substituted the words earnings or wages.— Translator,*

The new branch of industry at length reaches its normal state; in other words, the remuneration of printers ceases to be exceptionally high, and comes, like that of the copyist, to be *regulated by the ordinary rate of earnings.* Here we have production, as such, brought back to the point from which it started. And yet the invention is not the less an acquisition; the saving of time, of labour, of effort to produce a given result, that is, to produce a determinate number of copies, is not the less realized. But how does it show itself? In the cheapness of books. And to whose profit? To the profit of the consumer, of society, of the human race. The printers, who have thenceforth no exceptional merit, no longer receive exceptional remuneration. As men, as consumers, they undoubtedly participate in the advantages which the invention has conferred upon the community. But that is all. As printers, as producers, they have returned to the ordinary condition of the other producers of the country. Society pays them for their labour, and not for the utility of the invention. The latter has become the common and gratuitous heritage of mankind at large.

I confess that the wisdom and the beauty of these laws call forth my admiration and respect. I see in them Saint-Simonianism:

To each according to his capacity; to each capacity according to its works. I see in them, communism; that is, the tendency of products to become the *common* heritage of men; but a Saint-Simonianism, a communism, regulated by infinite prescience, and not abandoned to the frailties, the passions, and the arbitrary will of men.

What I have said of the art of printing, may be affirmed of all the instruments of labour, from the nail and the hammer to the locomotive and the electric telegraph. Society becomes possessed of all through its more abundant consumption, and *it enjoys all gratuitously*, for the effect of inventions and discoveries is to reduce the price of commodities; and all that part of the price which has been annihilated, and which represents the share invention has in production, evidently renders the product gratuitous to that extent. All that remains to be paid for is the human labour, the immediate labour, /and it is paid for without reference to the result of the invention, at least when that invention has passed through the cycle I have just described—the cycle which it is designed to pass through. I send for a tradesman to my house; he comes and brings his saw with him; I pay him two shillings for his day's work, and he saws me twenty-five boards. Had the saw not been invented, he would probably not have made out to furnish me with one, and I should have had to pay him the same wages for his day's work. The *utility* produced by the saw is then, as far as I am concerned, a gratuitous gift of nature, or rather it is a part of that inheritance which, *in common* with all my brethren, I have received from my ancestors. I have two workmen in my field. The one handles the plough, the other the spade. The result of their labour is very different, but the day's wages are the same, because the remuneration is not proportioned to the utility produced, but to the effort, the labour, which is exacted.

I entreat the reader's patience, and beg him to believe that I have not lost sight of free trade. Let him only have the goodness to remember the conclusion at which I have arrived: *Remuneration is not in proportion to the utilities which the producer brings to market, but to his labour.**

* *It is true that labour does not receive a uniform remuneration. It may be more or less intense, dangerous, skilled, etc. Competition settles the usual or current price in each department—and this is the fluctuating price of which I speak.*

I have drawn my illustrations as yet from human inventions. Let us now turn our attention to natural advantages.

In every branch of production, nature and man concur. But the portion of utility which nature contributes is always gratuitous. It is only the portion of utility which human labour contributes which forms the subject of exchange, and, consequently, of remuneration. The latter varies, no doubt, very much in proportion to the intensity of the labour, its skill, its promptitude, its suitableness, the need there is of it, the temporary absence of rivalry, etc. But it is not the less true, in principle, that the concurrence of natural laws, which are common to all, counts for nothing in the price of the product.

We do not pay for the air we breathe, although it is so *useful* to us, that, without it, we could not live two minutes. We do not pay for it, nevertheless; because nature furnishes it to us without the aid of human labour. But if, for example, we should desire to separate one of the gases of which it is composed, to make an experiment, we must make an exertion; or if we wish another to make that exertion for us, we must sacrifice for that other an equivalent amount of exertion, although we may have embodied it in another product. Whence we see that pains, efforts, and exertions are the real subjects of exchange. It is not, indeed, the oxygen gas that I pay for, since it is at my disposal everywhere, but the labour necessary to disengage it, labour which has been saved me, and which must be recompensed. Will it be said that there is something else to be paid for, materials, apparatus, etc.? Still, in paying for these, I pay for labour. The price of the coal employed, for example, represents the labour necessary to extract it from the mine and to transport it to the place where it is to be used.

We do not pay for the light of the sim, because it is a gift of nature. But we pay for gas, tallow, oil, wax, because there is here human labour to be remunerated; and it will be remarked that, in this case, the remuneration is proportioned, not to the utility produced, but to the labour employed, so much so that it may happen that one of these kinds of artificial light, though more intense, costs us less, and for this reason, that the same amount of human labour affords us more of it.

Were the porter who carries water to my house to be paid in proportion to the *absolute utility* of water, my whole fortune would be insufficient to remunerate him. But I pay him in proportion to the exertion he makes. If he charges more, others will do the work, or, if necessary, I will do it myself. Water, in truth, is not the subject of our bargain, but the labour of carrying it. This view of the matter is so important, and the conclusions which I am about to deduce from it throw so much light on the question of the freedom of international exchanges, that I deem it necessary to elucidate it by other examples.

The alimentary substance contained in potatoes is not very costly, because we can obtain a large amount of it with comparatively little labour. We pay more for wheat, because the production of it costs a greater amount of human labour. It is evident that if nature did for the one what it does for the other, the price of both would tend to equality. It is impossible that the producer of wheat should permanently gain much more than the producer of potatoes. The law of competition would prevent it.

If by a happy miracle the fertility of all arable lands should come to be augmented, it would not be the agriculturist, but the consumer, who would reap advantage from that phenomenon for it would resolve itself into abundance and cheapness. There would be less labour incorporated in each quarter of corn, and the cultivator could exchange it only for a smaller amount of labour worked up in some other product. If, on the other hand, the fertility of the soil came all at once to be diminished, nature's part in the process of production would be less, that of human labour would be greater, and the product dearer. I am, then, warranted in saying that it is in consumption, in the human element, that all the economic phenomena come ultimately to resolve themselves. The man who has failed to regard them in this light, to follow them out to their ultimate effects, without stopping short at *immediate* results, and viewing them from the *producer's* standpoint, can no more be regarded as an economist than the man who should prescribe a draught, and, instead of watching its effect on the entire system of the patient, should inquire only how it affected the mouth and throat, could be regarded as a physician.

Tropical regions are very favourably situated for the production of sugar and of coffee. This means that nature does a great part of the work, and leaves little for human labour to do. But who reaps the advantage of this liberality of nature? Not the producing countries, for competition causes the price barely to remunerate the labour. It is the human race that reaps the benefit, for the result of nature's liberality is cheapness, and cheapness benefits everybody.

Suppose a temperate region where coal and iron-ore are found on the surface of the ground, where one has only to stoop down to get them. That, in the first instance, the inhabitants would profit by this happy circumstance, I allow. But competition would soon intervene, and the price of coal and iron-ore would go on falling, till the gift of nature became free to all, and then the human labour employed would be alone remunerated according to the general rate of earnings.

Thus the liberality of nature, like improvements in the processes of production, is, or continually tends to become, under the law of competition, the common and gratuitous patrimony of consumers, of the masses, of mankind in general. Then, the countries which do not possess these advantages have everything to gain by exchanging their products with those countries which possess them, because the subject of exchange is *labour*, apart from the consideration of the natural utilities worked up with that labour; and the countries which have incorporated in a given amount of their labour the greatest amount of these *natural utilities*, are evidently the most favoured countries. Their products which represent the least amount of human labour are the least profitable; in other words, they *are cheaper*, and if the whole liberality of nature resolves itself into *cheapness*, it is evidently not the producing, but the consuming, country which reaps the benefit.

Hence we see the enormous absurdity of consuming countries which reject products for the very reason that they are cheap. It is as if they said, "We want nothing that nature gives us. You ask me for an effort equal to two, in exchange for a product which I cannot create without an effort equal to four; you can make that effort, because in your case nature does half the work. Be it so; I reject your offer, and I shall wait until your climate, having become more inclement, will force you to demand from me an effort equal to four, in order that I may treat with you *on a footing of equality.*"

A is a favoured country. B is a country to which nature has been less bountiful. I maintain that exchange benefits both, but benefits B especially; because exchange is not an exchange of *utilities for utilities*, but *of value for value.* Now A includes *a greater amount of utility in the same value*, seeing that the utility of a product includes what nature has put there, as well as what labour has put there; whilst value includes only what labour has put there. Then B makes quite an advantageous bargain. In recompensing the producer of A for his labour only, it receives into the bargain a greater amount of natural utility than it has given.

This enables us to lay down the general rule: Exchange is a barter of *values*; value under the action of competition being made to represent labour, exchange becomes a barter of equal labour. What nature has imparted to the products exchanged is on both sides given *gratuitously and into the bargain*; whence it follows necessarily that exchanges effected with countries the most favoured by nature are the most advantageous.

The theory of which in this chapter I have endeavoured to trace the outlines would require great developments. I have glanced at it only in as far as it bears upon my subject of free trade. But perhaps the attentive reader may have perceived in it the fertile germ which in the rankness of its maturity will not only smother protection, but, along with it, *Fourierisrme, Saint-Simonianisme, communisme*, and all those schools whose object it is to exclude from the government of the world the law of *competition.* Regarded from the producer's point of view, competition no doubt frequently clashes with our *immediate* and individual interests; but if we change our point of view and extend our regards to industry in general, to universal prosperity—in a word, to *consumption*—we shall find that competition in the moral world plays the same part which equilibrium does in the material world. It lies at the root of true communism, of true socialism, of that equality of conditions and of happiness so much desired in our day; and if so many sincere publicists, and well-meaning reformers seek after the *arbitrary*, it is for this reason—that they do not understand liberty.*

* *The theory sketched in this chapter, is the same which, four years afterwards, was developed in the* Harmonies Économiques. *Remuneration reserved exclusively for human labour; the gratuitous nature of natural agents; progressive conquest of these agents, to the profit of mankind, whose common property they thus become; elevation of general wellbeing and tendency to relative equalization of conditions; we recognise here the essential elements of the most important of all the works of Bastiat.—Editor.*

V. OUR PRODUCTS ARE BURDENED WITH TAXES.

We have here again the same sophism. We demand that foreign products should be taxed to neutralize the effect of the taxes which weigh upon our national products. The object, then, still is to equalize the conditions of production. We have only a word to say, and it is this: that the tax is an artificial obstacle which produces exactly the same result as a natural obstacle, its effect is to enhance prices. If this enhancement reach a point which makes it a greater loss to create the product for ourselves than to procure it from abroad by producing a counter value, *laissez faire*, let well alone. Of two evils, private interest will do well to choose the least. I might, then, simply refer the reader to the preceding demonstration; but the sophism which we have here to combat recurs so frequently in the lamentations and demands, I might say in the challenges, of the protectionist school, as to merit a special discussion.

If the question relate to one of those exceptional taxes which are imposed on certain products, I grant readily that it is reasonable to impose the same duty on the foreign product. For example, it would be absurd to exempt foreign salt from duty; not that, in an economical point of view, France would lose anything by doing so, but the reverse. Let them say what they will, principles are always the same; and France would gain by the exemption as she must always gain by removing a natural or artificial obstacle. But in this instance the obstacle has been interposed for purposes of revenue. These purposes must be attained; and were foreign salt sold in our market duty free, the Treasury would lose its hundred millions of francs (four millions sterling); and must raise that sum from some other source. There would be an obvious inconsistency in creating an obstacle, and failing in the object. It might have been better to have had recourse at first to another tax than that upon French salt. But I admit that there are certain circumstances in which a tax may be laid on foreign commodities, provided it is not *protective*, but fiscal.

But to pretend that a nation, because she is subjected to heavier taxes than her neighbours, should protect herself by tariffs against the competition of her rivals, in this is a sophism, and it is this sophism which I intend to attack.

I have said more than once that I propose only to explain the theory, and lay open, as far as possible, the sources of protectionist errors. Had I intended to raise a controversy, I should have asked the protectionists why they direct their tariffs chiefly against England and Belgium, the most heavily taxed countries in the world? Am I not warranted in regarding their argument only as a pretext? But I am not one of those who believe that men are prohibitionists from self-interest, and not from conviction. The doctrine of protection is too popular not to be sincere. If the majority had faith in liberty, we should be free. Undoubtedly it is self-interest which makes our tariffs so heavy; but conviction is at the root of it. "The will," says Pascal, "is one of the principal organs of belief." But the belief exists nevertheless, although it has its root in the will, and in the insidious suggestions of egotism.

Let us revert to the sophism founded on taxation.

The State may make a good or a bad use of the taxes which it levies. When it renders to the public services which are equivalent to the value it receives, it makes a good use of them. And when it dissipates its revenues without giving any service in return, it makes a bad use of them.

In the first case, to affirm that the taxes place the country which pays them under conditions of production more unfavourable than those of a country which is exempt from them, is a sophism. We pay twenty millions of francs for justice and police; but then we have them, with the security they afford us, and the time which they save us; and it is very probable that production is neither more easy nor more active in those countries, if there are any such, where the people take the business of justice and police into their own hands. We pay many hundreds of millions (of francs) for roads, bridges, harbours, and railways. Granted; but then we have the benefit of these roads, bridges, harbours, and railways; and whether we make a good or a bad bargain in constructing them, it cannot be said that they render us inferior to other nations, who do not indeed support a budget of public works, but who have no public works. And this explains why, whilst accusing taxation of being a cause of industrial inferiority, we direct our tariffs especially against those countries which are the most heavily taxed. Their taxes, well employed, far from deteriorating, have ameliorated, *the conditions of production* in these countries. Thus we are continually arriving at the conclusion that protectionist sophisms are not only not true, but are the very reverse of true.*

* *See Harmonies Économiques, ch. xvii.*

If taxes are improductive, suppress them, if you can; but assuredly the strangest mode of neutralizing their effect is to add individual to public taxes. Fine compensation truly! You tell us that the State taxes are too much; and you give that as a reason why we should tax one another!

A protective duty is a tax directed against a foreign product; but we must never forget that it falls back on the home consumer. Now the consumer is the tax-payer. The agreeable language you address to him is this: "Because your taxes are heavy, we raise the price of everything you buy; because the State lays hold of one part of your income, we hand over another to the monopolist."

But let us penetrate a little deeper into this sophism, which is in such repute with our legislators, although the extraordinary thing is that it is just the very people who maintain unproductive taxes who attribute to them our industrial inferiority, and in that inferiority find an excuse for imposing other taxes and restrictions.

It appears evident to me that the nature and effects of protection would not be changed, were the State to levy a direct tax and distribute the money afterwards in premiums and indemnities to the privileged branches of industry.

Suppose that while foreign iron cannot be sold in our market below eight francs, French iron cannot be sold for less than twelve francs.

On this hypothesis, there are two modes in which the State can secure the home market to the producer.

The first mode is to lay a duty of five francs on foreign iron. It is evident that that duty would exclude it, since it could no longer be sold under thirteen francs, namely, eight francs for the cost price, and five francs for the tax, and at that price it would be driven out of the market by French iron, the price of which we suppose to be only twelve francs. In this case, the purchaser, the consumer, would be at the whole cost of the protection.

Or again, the State might levy a tax of five francs from the public, and give the proceeds as a premium to the ironmaster. The protective effect would be the same. Foreign iron would in this case be equally excluded; for our ironmaster can now sell his iron at seven francs, which, with the five francs premium, would make up to him the remunerative price of twelve francs. But with home iron at seven francs the foreigner could not sell his for eight, which by the supposition is his lowest remunerative price.

Between these two modes of going to work, I can see only one difference. The principle is the same; the effect is the same; but in the one, certain individuals pay the price of protection; in the other, it is paid for by the nation at large.

I frankly avow my predilection for the second mode. It appears to me more just, more economical, and more honourable; more just, because if society desires to give largesses to some of its members, all should contribute; more economical, because it would save much expense in collecting, and get us rid of many restrictions; more honourable, because the public would then see clearly the nature of the operation, and act accordingly.

But if the protectionist system had taken this form, it would have been laughable to hear men say, "We pay heavy taxes for the army, for the navy, for the administration of justice, for public works, for the university, the public debt, etc.—in all exceeding a milliard [£40,000,000 sterling]. For this reason, the State should take another milliard from us, to relieve these poor ironmasters, these poor shareholders in the coal-mines of Anzin, these unfortunate proprietors of forests, these useful men who supply us with cod-fish."

Look at the subject closely, and you will be satisfied that this is the true meaning and effect of the sophism we are combating. It is all in vain; you cannot *give money* to some members of the community but by taking it from others. If you desire to ruin the tax-payer, you may do so. But at least do not banter him by saying, "In order to compensate your losses, I take from you again as much as I have taken from you already." To expose fully all that is false in this sophism would be an endless work. I shall confine myself to three observations. You assert that the country is overburdened with taxes, and on this fact you found an argument for the protection of certain branches of industry. But we have to pay these taxes in spite of protection. If, then, a particular branch of industry presents itself, and says, "I share in the payment of taxes; that raises the cost price of my products, and I demand that a protecting duty should also raise their selling price," what does such a demand amount to? It amounts simply to this, that the tax should be thrown over on the rest of the community. The object sought for is to be reimbursed the amount of the tax by a rise of prices. But as the Treasury requires to have the full amount of all the taxes, and as the masses have to pay the higher price, it follows that they have to bear not only their own share of taxation but that of the particular branch of industry which is protected. But we mean to protect everybody, you will say. I answer, in the first place, that that is impossible; and, in the next place, that if it were possible, there would be no relief. I would pay for you, and you would pay for me; but the tax must be paid all the same.

You are thus the dupes of an illusion. You wish in the first instance to pay taxes in order that you may have an army, a navy, a church, a university, judges, highways, etc., and then you wish to free from taxation first one branch of industry, then a second, then a third, always throwing back the burden upon the masses. You do nothing more than create interminable complications, without any other result than these complications themselves. Show me that a rise of price caused by protection falls upon the foreigner, and I could discover in your argument something specious. But if it be true that the public pays the tax before your law, and that after the law is passed it pays for protection and the tax into the bargain, truly I cannot see what is gained by it.

But I go further, and maintain that the heavier our taxes are, the more we should hasten to throw open our ports and our frontiers to foreigners less heavily taxed than ourselves. And why? In order to throw back upon them a greater share of our burden. Is it not an incontestable axiom in political economy that taxes ultimately fall on the consumer? The more, then, our exchanges are multiplied, the more will foreign consumers reimburse us for the taxes incorporated and worked up in the products we sell them; whilst we in this respect will have to make them a smaller restitution, seeing that their products, according to our hypothesis, are less heavily burdened than ours.

In fine, have you never asked yourselves whether these heavy burdens on which you found your argument for a prohibitory regime are not caused by that very regime? If commerce were free, what use would you have for your great standing armies and powerful navies?.... But this belongs to the domain of politics.

Et ne confondons pas, pour trop approfondir,
Leurs affaires avec les nôtres.

VI. BALANCE OF TRADE.

Our adversaries have adopted tactics which are rather embarrassing. Do we establish our doctrine? They admit it with the greatest possible respect. Do we attack their principle? They abandon it with the best grace in the world. They demand only one thing—that our doctrine, which they hold to be true, should remain relegated in books, and that their principle, which they acknowledge to be vicious, should reign paramount in practical legislation. Resign to them the management of tariffs, and they will give up all dispute with you in the domain of theory.

"Assuredly," said M. Gauthier de Rumilly, on a recent occasion, "no one wishes to resuscitate the antiquated theories of the balance of trade." Very right, Monsieur Gauthier, but please to remember that it is not enough to give a passing slap to error, and immediately afterwards, and for two hours together, reason as if that error were truth.

Let me speak of M. Lestiboudois. Here we have a consistent reasoner, a logical disputant. There is nothing in his conclusions which is not to be found in his premises. He asks nothing in practice, but what he justifies in theory. His principle may be false; that is open to question. But, at any rate, he has a principle. He believes, and he proclaims it aloud, that if France gives ten, in order to receive fifteen, she loses five; and it follows, of course, that he supports laws which are in keeping with this view of the subject "The important thing to attend to," he says, "is that the amount of our importations goes on augmenting, and exceeds the amount of our exportations—that is to say, France every year purchases more foreign products, and sells less of her own. Figures prove this. What do we see? In 1842, imports exceeded exports by 200 millions. These facts appear to prove in the clearest manner that national industry is not sufficiently protected, that we depend upon foreign labour for our supplies, that the competition of our rivals oppresses our industry. The present law appears to me to recognise the fact, which is not true according to the economists, that when we purchase we necessarily sell a corresponding amount of commodities. It is evident that we can purchase, not with our usual products, not with our revenue, not with the results of permanent labour, but with our capital, with products which have been accumulated and stored up, those intended for reproduction—that is to say, that we may expend, that we may dissipate, the proceeds of anterior economies, that we may impoverish ourselves, that we may proceed on the road to ruin, and consume entirely the national capital. This is exactly what we are doing. Every year we give away 200 millions of francs to the foreigner."

Well, here is a man with whom we can come to an understanding. There is no hypocrisy in this language. The doctrine of the balance of trade is openly avowed. France imports 200 millions more than she exports. Then we lose 200 millions a year. And what is the remedy? To place restrictions on importation. The conclusion is unexceptionable.

It is with M. Lestiboudois, then, that we must deal, for how can we argue with M. Gauthier? If you tell him that the balance of trade is an error, he replies that that was what he laid down at the beginning. If you say that the balance of trade is a truth, he will reply that that is what he proves in his conclusions.

The economist school will blame me, no doubt, for arguing with M. Lestiboudois. To attack the balance of trade, it will be said, is to fight with a windmill.

But take care. The doctrine of the balance of trade is neither so antiquated, nor so sick, nor so dead as M. Gauthier would represent it, for the entire Chamber—M.

Gauthier himself included—has recognised by its votes the theory of M. Lestiboudois.

I shall not fatigue the reader by proceeding to probe that theory, but content myself with subjecting it to the test of facts.

We are constantly told that our principles do not hold good, except in theory. But tell me, gentlemen, if you regard the books of merchants as holding good in practice? It appears to me that if there is anything in the world which should have practical authority, when the question regards profit and loss, it is commercial accounts. Have all the merchants in the world come to an understanding for centuries to keep their books in such a way as to represent profits as losses, and losses as profits? It may be so, but I would much rather come to the conclusion that M. Lestiboudois is a bad economist.

Now, a merchant of my acquaintance having had two transactions, the results of which were very different, I felt curious to compare the books of the counting-house with the books of the Customhouse, as interpreted by M. Lestiboudois to the satisfaction of our six hundred legislators.

M. T. despatched a ship from Havre to the United States, with a cargo of French goods, chiefly those known as *articles de Paris*, amounting to 200,000 francs. This was the figure declared at the Customhouse. When the cargo arrived at New Orleans it was charged with 10 per cent, freight and 30 per cent, duty, making a total of 280,000 francs. It was sold with 20 per cent, profit, or 40,000 francs, and produced a total of 320,000 francs, which the consignee invested in cottons. These cottons had still for freight, insurance, commission, etc., to bear a cost of 10 per cent. so that when the new cargo arrived at Havre it had cost 352,000 francs, which was the figure entered in the Customhouse books. Finally M. T. realized upon this return cargo 20 per cent, profit, or 70,400 francs; in other words, the cottons were sold for 422,400 francs.

If M. Lestiboudois desires it, I shall send him an extract from the books of M. T. He will there see *at the credit* of the *profit and loss* account—that is to say, as profits—two entries, one of 40,000, another of 70,400 francs, and M. T. is very sure that his accounts are accurate.

And yet, what do the Customhouse books tell M. Lestiboudois regarding this transaction? They tell him simply that France exported 200,000 francs' worth, and imported to the extent of 352,000 francs; whence the honourable deputy concludes "*that she had expended, and dissipated the profits of her anterior economies, that she is impoverishing herself that she is on the high road to ruin, and has given away to the foreigner 152,000 francs of her capital.*"

Some time afterwards, M. T. despatched another vessel with a cargo also of the value of 200,000 francs, composed of the products of our native industry. This unfortunate ship was lost in a gale of wind after leaving the harbour, and all M. T. had to do was to make two short entries in his books, to this effect:—

"*Sundry goods debtors to X*, 200,000 francs, for purchases of different commodities despatched by the ship N.

"*Profit and loss debtors to sundry goods*, 200,000 francs, in consequence of *definitive and total loss* of the cargo."

At the same time, the Customhouse books bore an entry of 200.000 francs in the list of exportations; and as there was no corresponding entry to make in the list of importations, it follows that M. Lestiboudois and the Chamber will see in this shipwreck a clear and net profit for France of 200,000 francs.

There is still another inference to be deduced from this, which is, that according to the theory of the balance of trade, France has a very simple means of doubling her capital at any moment. It is enough to pass them through the Customhouse, and then pitch them into the sea. In this case the exports will represent the amount of her capital, the imports will be *nil*, and even impossible, and we shall gain all that the sea swallows up.

This is a joke, the protectionists will say. It is impossible' we could give utterance to such absurdities. You do give utterance to them, however, and, what is more, you act upon them, and impose them on your fellow-citizens to the utmost of your power.

The truth is, it would be necessary to take the balance of trade *backwards [au rebours]*, and calculate the national profits from foreign trade by the excess of imports over exports. This excess, after deducting costs, constitutes the real profit. But this theory, which is true, leads directly to free trade. I make you a present of it, gentlemen, as I do of all the theories in the preceding chapters. Exaggerate it as much as you please—it has nothing to fear from that test. Suppose, if that amuses you, that the foreigner inundates us with all sorts of useful commodities without asking anything in return, that our imports are *infinite* and exports *nil*, I defy you to prove to me that we should be poorer on that account.

VII. OF THE MANUFACTURERS

OF CANDLES, WAX-LIGHTS, LAMPS, CANDLESTICKS, STREET LAMPS, SNUFFERS, EXTINGUISHERS, AND OF THE PRODUCERS OF OIL, TALLOW, ROSIN, ALCOHOL, AND, GENERALLY, OF EVERYTHING CONNECTED WITH LIGHTING.

To Messieurs the Members of the Chamber of Deputies.

Gentlemen,—You are on the right road. You reject abstract theories, and have little consideration for cheapness and plenty Your chief care is the interest of the producer. You desire to emancipate him from external competition, and reserve the *national market for national industry.*

We are about to offer you an admirable opportunity of applying your—what shall we call it? your theory? No; nothing is more deceptive than theory; your doctrine? your system? your principle? but you dislike doctrines, you abhor systems, and as for principles, you deny that there are any in social economy: we shall say, then, your practice, your practice without theory and without principle.

We are suffering from the intolerable competition of a foreign rival, placed, it would seem, in a condition so far superior to ours for the production of light, that he absolutely *inundates our national market* with it at a price fabulously reduced. The moment he shows himself, our trade leaves us—all consumers apply to him; and a branch of native industry, having countless ramifications, is all at once rendered completely stagnant. This rival, who is no other than the Sun, wages war to the knife against us, and we suspect that he has been raised up by *perfidious Albion* (good policy as times go); inasmuch as he displays towards that haughty island a circumspection with which he dispenses in our case.

What we pray for is, that it may please you to pass a law ordering the shutting up of all windows, sky-lights, dormer-windows, outside and inside shutters, curtains, blinds, bull's-eyes; in a word, of all openings, holes, chinks, clefts, and fissures, by or through which the light of the sun has been in use to enter houses, to the prejudice of the meritorious manufactures with which we flatter ourselves we have accommodated our country,—a country which, in gratitude, ought not to abandon us now to a strife so unequal.

We trust, Gentlemen, that you will not regard this our request as a satire, or refuse it without at least previously hearing the reasons which we have to urge in its support.

And, first, if you shut up as much as possible all access to natural light, and create a demand for artificial light, which of our French manufactures will not be encouraged by it?

If more tallow is consumed, then there must be more oxen and sheep; and, consequently, we shall behold the multiplication of artificial meadows, meat, wool, hides, and, above all, manure, which is the basis and foundation of all agricultural wealth.

If more oil is consumed, then we shall have an extended cultivation of the poppy, of the olive, and of rape. These rich and exhausting plants will come at the right time to enable us to avail ourselves of the increased fertility which the rearing of additional cattle will impart to our lands.

Our heaths will be covered with resinous trees. Numerous swarms of bees will, on the mountains, gather perfumed treasures, now wasting their fragrance on the desert air, like the flowers from which they emanate. No branch of agriculture but will then exhibit a cheering development.

The same remark applies to navigation. Thousands of vessels will proceed to the whale fishery; and, in a short time, we shall possess a navy capable of maintaining the honour of France, and gratifying the patriotic aspirations of your petitioners, the undersigned candlemakers and others.

But what shall we say of the manufacture of *articles de Paris?* Henceforth you will behold gildings, bronzes, crystals, in candlesticks, in lamps, in lustres, in candelabra, shining forth, in spacious warerooms, compared with which those of the present day can be regarded but as mere shops.

No poor *resinier* from his heights on the seacoast, no coalminer from the depth of his sable gallery, but will rejoice in higher wages and increased prosperity.

Only have the goodness to reflect, Gentlemen, and you will be convinced that there is, perhaps, no Frenchman, from the wealthy coalmaster to the humblest vender of lucifer matches, whose lot will not be ameliorated by the success of this our petition.

We foresee your objections, Gentlemen, but we know that you can oppose to us none but such as you have picked up from the effete works of the partisans of free trade. We defy you to utter a single word against us which will not instantly rebound against yourselves and your entire policy.

You will tell us that, if we gain by the protection which we seek, the country will lose by it, because the consumer must bear the loss.

We answer:

You have ceased to have any right to invoke the interest of the consumer; for, whenever his interest is found opposed to that of the producer, you sacrifice the former. You have done so for the purpose of *encouraging labour and increasing employment.* For the same reason you should do so again.

You have yourselves obviated this objection. When you are told that the consumer is interested in the free importation of iron, coal, corn, textile fabrics—yes, you reply, but the producer is interested in their exclusion. Well, be it so;—if consumers are interested in the free admission of natural light, the producers of artificial light are equally interested in its prohibition.

But, again, you may say that the producer and consumer are identical. If the manufacturer gain by protection, he will make the agriculturist also a gainer; and if agriculture prosper, it will open a vent to manufactures. Very well; if you confer upon us the monopoly of furnishing light during the day,—first of all, we shall purchase quantities of tallow, coals, oils, resinous substances, wax, alcohol—besides silver, iron, bronze, crystal—to carry on our manufactures; and then we, and those who furnish us with such commodities, having become rich will consume a great deal, and impart prosperity to all the other branches of our national industry.

If you urge that the light of the sun is a gratuitous gift of nature, and that to reject such gifts is to reject wealth itself under pretence of encouraging the means of acquiring it, we would caution you against giving a death-blow to your own policy. Remember that hitherto you have always repelled foreign products, because they approximate more nearly than home products to the character of gratuitous gifts. To comply with the exactions of other monopolists, you have only *half a motive*; and to repulse us simply because we stand on a stronger vantage-ground than others would be to adopt the equation, + x + = -; in other words, it would be to heap *absurdity upon absurdity.*

Nature and human labour co-operate in various proportions (depending on countries and climates) in the production of commodities. The part which nature executes is always gratuitous; it is the part executed by human labour which constitutes value, and is paid for.

If a Lisbon orange sells for half the price of a Paris orange, it is because natural, and consequently gratuitous, heat does for the one, what artificial, and therefore expensive, heat must do for the other.

When an orange comes to us from Portugal, we may conclude that it is furnished in part gratuitously, in part for an onerous consideration; in other words, it comes to us at *half-price* as compared with those of Paris.

Now, it is precisely the *gratuitous half* (pardon the word) which we contend should be excluded. You say, How can natural labour sustain competition with foreign labour, when the former has all the work to do, and the latter only does one-half, the sun supplying the remainder? But if this half being gratuitous, determines you to exclude competition, how should the whole, being gratuitous, induce you to admit competition? If you were consistent, you would, while excluding as hurtful to native industry what is half gratuitous, exclude *a fortiori* and with double zeal, that which is altogether gratuitous.

Once more, when products such as coal, iron, corn, or textile fabrics, are sent us from abroad, and we can acquire them with less labour than if we made them ourselves, the difference is a free gift conferred upon us. The gift is more or less considerable in proportion as the difference is more or less great. It amounts to a quarter, a half, or three-quarters of the value of the product, when the foreigner only asks us for three-fourths, a half, or a quarter of the price we should otherwise pay. It is as perfect and complete as it can be, when the donor (like the sun in furnishing us with light) asks us for nothing. The question, and we ask it formally, is this, Do you desire for our country the benefit of gratuitous consumption, or the pretended advantages of onerous production? Make your choice, but be logical; for as long as you exclude as you do, coal, iron, com, foreign fabrics, in proportion as their price approximates to zero, what inconsistency would it be to admit the light of the sun, the price of which is already at *zero* during the entire day!

VIII. DIFFERENTIAL DUTIES.

A poor vine-dresser of the Gironde had trained with fond enthusiasm a slip of vine, which, after much fatigue and much labour, yielded him, at length, a tun of wine; and his success made him forget that each drop of this precious nectar had cost his brow a drop of sweat. "I shall sell it," said he to his wife, "and with the price I shall buy stuff sufficient to enable you to furnish a trousseau for our daughter." The honest countryman repaired to the nearest town, and met a Belgian and an Englishman. The Belgian said to him: "Give me your cask of wine, and I will give you in exchange fifteen parcels of stuff." The Englishman said: "Give me your wine, and I will give you twenty parcels of stuff; for we English can manufacture the stuff cheaper than the Belgians." But a Customhouse officer, who was present, interposed, and said: "My good friend, exchange with the Belgian if you think proper, but my orders are to prevent you from making an exchange with the Englishman." "What!" exclaimed the countryman; "you wish me to be content with fifteen parcels of stuff which have come from Brussels, when I can get twenty parcels which have come from Manchester?" "Certainly; don't you see that France would be a loser if you received twenty parcels, instead of fifteen?" "I am at a loss to understand you," said the vine-dresser, "And I am at a loss to explain it," rejoined the Customhouse official; "but the thing is certain, for all our deputies, ministers, and journalists agree in this, that the more a nation receives in exchange for a given quantity of its products, the more it is impoverished." The peasant found it necessary to conclude a bargain with the Belgian. The daughter of the peasant got only three-quarters of her trousseau; and these simple people are still asking themselves how it happens that one is ruined by receiving four instead of three; and why a person is richer with three dozens of towels than with four dozens.

IX. IMMENSE DISCOVERY.

At a time when everybody is bent on bringing about a saving in the expense of transport—and when, in order to effect this saving, we are forming roads and canals, improving our steamers, and connecting Paris with all our frontiers by a network of railways—at a time, too, when I believe we are ardently and sincerely seeking a solution of the problem, *how to bring the prices of commodities, in the place where they are to be consumed, as nearly as possible to the level of their prices in the place where they were produced*,—I should think myself wanting to my country, to my age, and to myself, if I kept longer secret the marvellous discovery which I have just made.

The illusions of inventors are proverbial, but I am positively certain that I have discovered an infallible means of bringing products from every part of the world to France, and *vice versa* at a considerable reduction of cost.

Infallible, did I say? Its being infallible is only one of the advantages of my invention.

It requires neither plans, estimates, preparatory study, engineers, mechanists, contractors, capital, shareholders, or Government aid!

It presents no danger of shipwreck, explosion, fire, or collision!

It may be brought into operation at any time!

Moreover—and this must undoubtedly recommend it to the public—it will not add a penny to the Budget, but the reverse. It will not increase the staff of functionaries, but the reverse. It will interfere with no man's liberty, but the reverse.

It is observation, not chance, which has put me in possession of this discovery, and I will tell you what suggested it.

I had at the time this question to resolve:

"Why does an article manufactured at Brussels, for example, cost dearer when it comes to Paris?"

I soon perceived that it proceeds from this: That between Paris and Brussels *obstacles* of many kinds exist. First of all, there is *distance*, which entails loss of time, and we must either submit to this ourselves, or pay another to submit to it. Then come rivers, marshes, accidents, bad roads, which are so many *difficulties* to be surmounted. We succeed in building bridges, in forming roads, and making them smoother by pavements, iron rails, etc. But all this is costly, and the commodity must be made to bear the cost. Then there are robbers who infest the roads, and a body of police must be kept up, etc.

Now, among these *obstacles* there is one which we have ourselves set up, and at no little cost, too, between Brussels and Paris. There are men who lie in ambuscade along the frontier, armed to the teeth, and whose business it is to throw *difficulties* in the way of transporting merchandise from the one country to the other. They are called Customhouse officers, and they act in precisely the same way as ruts and bad roads. They retard, they trammel commerce, they augment the difference we have remarked between the price paid by the consumer and the price received by the producer—that very difference, the reduction of which, as far as possible, forms the subject of our problem.

That problem is resolved in three words: Reduce your tariff.

You will then have done what is equivalent to constructing the Northern Railway without cost, and will immediately begin to put money in your pocket.

In truth, I often seriously ask myself how anything so whimsical could ever have entered into the human brain, as first of all to lay out many millions for the purpose of removing the *natural obstacles* which lie between France and other countries, and then to lay out many more millions for the purpose of substituting *artificial obstacles*, which have exactly the same effect; so much so, indeed, that the obstacle created and the obstacle removed neutralize each other, and leave things as they were before, the residue of the operation being a double expense.

A Belgian product is worth at Brussels 20 francs, and the cost of carriage would raise the price at Paris to 30 francs. The same article made in Paris costs 40 francs. And how do we proceed?

In the first place, we impose a duty of 10 francs on the Belgian product, in order to raise its cost price at Paris to 40 francs; and we pay numerous officials to see the duty stringently levied, so that, on the road, the commodity is charged 10 francs for the carriage, and 10 francs for the tax.

Having done this, we reason thus: The carriage from Brussels to Paris, which costs 10 francs, is very dear. Let us expend two or three hundred millions [of francs] in railways, and we shall reduce it by one half. Evidently, all that we gain by this is that the Belgian product would sell in Paris for 35 francs, viz.

20 francs, its price at Brussels.

10 " duty.

5 " reduced carriage by railway.

Total, 35 francs, representing cost price at Paris.

Now, I ask, would we not have attained the same result by lowering the tariff by 5 francs? We should then have—

20 francs, the price at Brussels.

5 " reduced duty.

10 " carriage by ordinary roads.

Total, 35 francs, representing cost price at Paris.

And by this process we should have saved the 200 millions which the railway cost, plus the expense of Customhouse surveillance, for this last would be reduced in proportion to the diminished encouragement held out to smuggling.

But it will be said that the duty is necessary to protect Parisian industry. Be it so; but then you destroy the effect of your railway.

For, if you persist in desiring that the Belgian product should cost at Paris 40 francs, you must raise your duty to 15 francs, and then you have—

20 francs, the price at Brussels.

15 " protecting duty.

5 " railway carriage.

Total, 40 francs, being the equalized price.

Then, I venture to ask, what, under such circumstances, is the good of your railway?

In sober earnestness, let me ask, is it not humiliating that the nineteenth century should make itself a laughing-stock to future ages by such puerilities, practised with such imperturbable gravity? To be the dupe of other people is not very pleasant, but to employ a vast representative apparatus in order to dupe, and double dupe, ourselves—and that, too, in an affair of arithmetic—should surely humble the pride of this *age of enlightenment.*

X. RECIPROCITY.

We have just seen that whatever increases the expense of conveying commodities from one country to another—in other words, whatever renders transport more onerous—acts in the same way as a protective duty; or if you prefer to put it in another shape, that a protective duty acts in the same way as more onerous transport.

A tariff, then, may be regarded in the same light as a marsh, a rut, an obstruction, a steep declivity—in a word, it is an *obstacle*, the effect of which is to augment the difference between the price which the producer of a commodity receives, and the price which the consumer pays for it. In the same way, it is undoubtedly true that marshes and quagmires are to be regarded in the same light as protective tariffs.

There are people (few in number, it is true, but there are such people) who begin to understand that obstacles are not less obstacles because they are artificial, and that our mercantile prospects have more to gain from liberty than from protection, and exactly for the same reason which makes a canal more favourable to traffic than a steep, roundabout, and inconvenient road.

But they maintain that this liberty must be reciprocal. If we remove the barriers we have erected against the admission of Spanish goods, for example, Spain must remove the barriers she has erected against the admission of ours. They are, therefore, the advocates of *commercial treaties*, on the basis of exact reciprocity, concession for concession; let us make the *sacrifice* of buying, say they, to obtain the advantage of selling.

People who reason in this way, I am sorry to say, are, whether they know it or not, protectionists in principle; only, they are a little more inconsistent than pure protectionists, as the latter are more inconsistent than absolute prohibitionists.

The following apologue will demonstrate this:—

STULTA AND PUERA. There were, no matter where, two towns called Stulta and Puera. They completed at great cost a highway from the one town to the other. When this was done, Stulta said to herself, "See how Puera inundates us with her products; we must see to it." In consequence, they created and paid a body of *obstructives*, so called because their business was to place *obstacles* in the way of traffic coming from Puera. Soon afterwards, Puera did the same.

At the end of some centuries, knowledge having in the interim made great progress, the common sense of Puera enabled her to see that such reciprocal obstacles could only be reciprocally hurtful. She therefore sent a diplomatist to Stulta, who, laying aside official phraseology, spoke to this effect: "We have made a highway, and now we throw obstacles in the way of using it. This is absurd. It would have been better to have left things as they were. We should not, in that case, have had to pay for making the road in the first place, nor afterwards have incurred the expense of maintaining *obstructives*. In the name of Puera, I come to propose to you, not to give up opposing each other all at once—that would be to act upon a principle, and we despise principles as much as you do—but to lessen somewhat the present obstacles, taking care to estimate equitably the respective *sacrifices* we make for this purpose." So spoke the diplomatist. Stulta asked for time to consider the proposal, and proceeded to consult, in succession, her manufacturers and agriculturists. At length, after the lapse of some years, she declared that the negotiations were broken off.

On receiving this intimation, the inhabitants of Puera held a meeting. An old gentleman (they always suspected he had been secretly bought by Stulta) rose and said: The obstacles created by Stulta injure our sales, which is a misfortune. Those which we have ourselves created injure our purchases, which is another misfortune. With reference to the first, we are powerless; but the second rests with ourselves. Let us, at least, get quit of one, since we cannot rid ourselves of both evils. Let us suppress our *obstructives* without requiring Stulta to do the same. Some day, no doubt, she will come to know her own interests better.

A second counsellor, a practical, matter-of-fact man, guiltless of any acquaintance with principles, and brought up in the ways of his forefathers, replied: "Don't listen to that Utopian dreamer, that theorist, that innovator, that economist, that *Stultomaniac.*"

We shall all be undone if the stoppages of the road are not equalized, weighed, and balanced between Stulta and Puera. There would be greater difficulty in going than in coming, in exporting than in importing. We should find ourselves in the same condition of inferiority relatively to Stulta, as Havre, Nantes, Bordeaux, Lisbon, London, Hamburg, and New Orleans, are with relation to the towns situated at the sources of the Seine, the Loire, the Garonne, the Tagus, the Thames, the Elbe, and the Mississippi, for it is more difficult for a ship to ascend than to descend a river. (*A Voice*: Towns at the *embouchures* of rivers prosper more than towns at their source.) This is impossible. (Same Voice: But it is so.) Well, if it be so, they have prospered *contrary to rules*. Reasoning so conclusive convinced the assembly, and the orator followed up his victory by talking largely of national independence, national honour, national dignity, national labour, inundation of products, tributes, murderous competition. In short, he carried the vote in favour of the maintenance of obstacles; and if you are at all curious on the subject, I can point out to you countries, where you will see with your own eyes Road-makers and Obstructives working together on the most friendly terms possible, under the orders of the same legislative assembly, and at the expense of the same taxpayers, the one set endeavouring to clear the road, and the other set doing their utmost to render it impassible.

XI. NOMINAL PRICES.

Do you desire to be in a situation to decide between liberty and protection? Do you desire to appreciate the bearing of an economic phenomenon? Inquire into its effects *upon the abundance or scarcity of commodities*, and not *upon the rise or fall of prices.* Distrust *nominal prices*;* and they will only land you in an inextricable labyrinth.

** I have translated the expression des prix absolus, nominal prices, or actual money prices, because the English economists do not, so far as I remember, make use of the term absolute price.—See post, chap. v. of second series, where the author employs the expression in this sense.— Translator.*

M. Matthieu de Dombasle, after having shown that protection raises prices, adds—

"The enhancement of price increases the expense of living, and *consequently* the price of labour, and each man receives, in the enhanced price of his products, compensation for the higher prices he has been obliged to pay for the things he has occasion to buy. Thus, if every one pays more as a consumer, every one receives more as a producer."

It is evident that we could reverse this argument, and say—"If every one receives more as a producer, every one pays more as a consumer."

Now, what does this prove? Nothing but this, that protection *displaces* wealth uselessly and unjustly. In so far, it simply perpetrates spoliation.

Again, to conclude that this vast apparatus leads to simple compensations, we must stick to the "consequently" of M. de Dombasle, and make sure that the price of labour will not fail to rise with the price of the protected products. This is a question of fact which I remit to M. Moreau de Jonnes, that he may take the trouble to find out whether the rate of wages advances along with the price of shares in the coal-mines of Anzin. For my own part, I do not believe that it does; because, in my opinion, the price of labour, like the price of everything else, is governed by the relation of supply to demand. Now, I am convinced that *restriction* diminishes the supply of coal, and consequently enhances its price; but I do not see so clearly that it increases the demand for labour, so as to enhance the rate of wages; and that this effect should be produced is all the less likely, because the quantity of labour demanded depends on the disposable capital. Now, protection may indeed displace capital, and cause its transference from one employment to another, but it can never increase it by a single farthing.

But this question, which is one of the greatest interest and importance, will be examined in another place.* I return to the subject of *nominal price*; and I maintain that it is not one of those absurdities which can be rendered specious by such reasonings as those of M. de Dombasle.

Put the case of a nation which is isolated, and possesses a given amount of specie, and which chooses to amuse itself by burning each year one half of all the commodities that it possesses. I undertake to prove that, according to the theory of M. de Dombasle, it will not be less rich.

In fact, in consequence of the fire, all things will be doubled in price, and the inventories of property, made before and after the destruction, will show exactly the same *nominal* value. But then what will the country in question have lost? If John buys his cloth dearer, he also sells his corn at a higher price; and if Peter loses on his purchase of corn, he retrieves his losses by the sale of his cloth. "Each recovers, in the extra price of his products, the extra expense of living he has been put to; and if everybody pays as a consumer, everybody receives a corresponding amount as a producer."

All this is a jingling quibble, and not science. The truth, in plain terms, is this: that men consume cloth and corn by fire or by using them, and that the effect is the same *as regards price*, but not *as regards wealth*, for it is precisely in the use of commodities that wealth or material prosperity consists.

In the same way, restriction, while diminishing the abundance of things, may raise their price to such an extent that each party shall be, *pecuniarily speaking*, as rich as before. But to set down in an inventory three measures of corn at 20s., or four measures at 15s., because the result is still sixty shillings,—would this, I ask, come to the same thing with reference to the satisfaction of men's wants?

It is to this, the consumer's point of view, that I shall never cease to recall the protectionists, for this is the end and design of all our efforts, and the solution of all problems.**

** See post, ch. v., second series.—Translator.*

*** To this view of the subject the author frequently reverts. It was, in his eyes, all important; and, four days before his death, he dictated this recommendation:—"Tell M. de F. to treat economical questions always from the consumer's point of view, for the interest of the consumer is identical with that of the human race."—Editor.*

I shall never cease to say to them: Is it, or is it not, true that restriction, by impeding exchanges, by limiting the division of labour, by forcing labour to connect itself with difficulties of climate and situation, diminishes ultimately the quantity of commodities produced by a determinate amount of efforts? And what does this signify, it will be said, if the smaller quantity produced under the *regime* of protection has the same *nominal value* as that produced under the *regime* of liberty? The answer is obvious. Man does not live upon nominal values, but upon real products, and the more products there are, whatever be their price, the richer he is.

In writing what precedes, I never expected to meet with an anti-economist who was enough of a logician to admit, in so many words, that the wealth of nations depends on the value of things, apart from the consideration of their abundance. But here is what I find in the work of M. de Saint-Chamans (p. 210):—

"If fifteen millions' worth of commodities, sold to foreigners, are taken from the total production, estimated at fifty millions, the thirty-five millions' worth of commodities remaining, not being sufficient to meet the ordinary demand, will increase in price, and rise to the value of fifty millions. In that case the revenue of the country will represent a value of fifteen millions additional.... There would then be an increase of the wealth of the country to the extent of fifteen millions, exactly the amount of specie imported."

This is a pleasant view of the matter! If a nation produces in one year, from its agriculture and commerce, a value of fifty millions, it has only to sell a quarter of it to the foreigner to be a quarter richer! Then if it sells the half, it will be one-half richer! And if it should sell the whole, to its last tuft of wool and its last grain of wheat, it would bring up its revenue to 100 millions. Singular way of getting rich, by producing infinite dearness by absolute scarcity!

Again, would you judge of the two doctrines? Submit them to the test of exaggeration.

According to the doctrine of M. de Saint-Chamans, the French would be quite as rich—that is to say, quite as well supplied with all things—had they only a thousandth part of their annual products, because they would be worth a thousand times more.

According to our doctrine, the French would be infinitely rich if their annual products were infinitely abundant, and, consequently, without any value at all.*

* *See post, ch. v. of second series of Sophismes; and ch. vi. of Harmonies Economiques.*

XII. DOES PROTECTION RAISE THE RATE OF WAGES?

An atheist, declaiming one day against religion and priestcraft, became so outrageous in his abuse, that one of his audience, who was not himself very orthodox, exclaimed, "If you go on much longer in this strain, you will make me a convert."

In the same way, when we see our beardless scribblers, our novel-writers, reformers, fops, amateur contributors to newspapers, redolent of musk, and saturated with champagne, stuffing their portfolios with radical prints, or issuing under gilded covers their own tirades against the egotism and individualism of the age—when we hear such people declaim against the rigour of our institutions, groan over the proletariat and the wages system, raise their eyes to Heaven, and weep over the poverty of the working classes (poverty which they never see but when they are paid to paint it),—we are likewise tempted to exclaim, "If you go on longer in this strain, we shall lose all interest in the working classes."

Affectation is the besetting sin of our times. When a serious writer, in a spirit of philanthropy, refers to the sufferings of the working classes, his words are caught up by these sentimentalists, twisted, distorted, and exaggerated, *usque ad 'nauseam.* The grand, the only remedy, it would seem, lies in the high-sounding phrases, association and organization. The working classes are flattered—fulsomely, servilely flattered;

they are represented as in the condition of slaves, and men of common sense will soon be ashamed publicly to espouse their cause, for how can common sense make itself heard in the midst of all this insipid and empty declamation?

Far from us be this cowardly indifference, which would not be justified even by the sentimental affectation which prompts it.

Workmen! your situation is peculiar! They make merchandise of you, as I shall show you immediately.... But no; I withdraw that expression. Let us steer clear of strong language, which may be misapplied; for spoliation, wrapt up in the sophistry which conceals it, may be in full operation unknown to the spoliator, and with the blind assent of his victim. Still, you are deprived of the just remuneration of your labour, and no one is concerned to do you *justice*. If all that was wanted to console you were ardent appeals to philanthropy, to impotent charity, to degrading almsgiving; or if the grand words, organization, communism, *phalanstère*,* were enough for you, truly they would not be spared. But *justice*, simple justice, no one thinks of offering you. And yet, would it not be *just* that when, after a long day's toil, you have received your modest wages, you should have it in your power to exchange them for the greatest amount of satisfactions and enjoyments which you could possibly obtain for them from any one in any part of the world?

* *Allusion to a socialist work of the day.—Translator.*

Some day I may have occasion also to talk to you of association and organization, and we shall then see what you have to expect from those chimeras which now mislead you.

In the meantime, let us inquire whether *injustice* is not done you by fixing legislatively the people from whom you are to purchase the things you have need of—bread, meat, linens, or cloth; and in dictating, if I may say so, the artificial scale of prices which you are to adopt in your dealings.

Is it true that protection, which admittedly makes you pay dearer for everything, and entails a loss upon you in this respect, raises proportionally your wages?

On what does the rate of wages depend?

One of your own class has put it forcibly, thus: When two workmen run after one master, wages fall; they rise when two masters run after one workman.

For the sake of brevity, allow me to make use of this formula, more scientific, although, perhaps, not quite so clear. The rate of wages depends on the proportion which the supply of labour bears to the demand for it.

Now, on what does the *supply* of labour depend?

On the number of men waiting for employment; and on this first element protection can have no effect.

On what does the *demand* for labour depend?

On the disposable capital of the nation. But does the law which says, We shall no longer receive such or such a product from abroad, we shall make it at home, augment the capital? Not in the least degree. It may force capital from one employment to another, but it does not increase it by a single farthing. It does not then increase the demand for labour.

We point with pride to a certain manufacture. Is it established or maintained with capital which has fallen from the moon? No; that capital has been withdrawn from agriculture, from shipping, from the production of wines. And this is the reason why, under the *regime* of protective tariffs, there are more workmen in our mines and in our manufacturing towns, and fewer sailors in our ports, and fewer labourers in our fields and vineyards.

I could expatiate at length on this subject, but I prefer to explain what I mean by an example.

A countryman was possessed of twenty acres of land, which he worked with a capital of £400. He divided his land into four parts, and established the following rotation of crops:—1st, maize; 2d, wheat; 3d, clover; 4th, rye. He required for his own family only a moderate portion of the grain, meat, and milk which his farm produced, and he sold the surplus to buy oil, flax, wine, etc. His whole capital was expended each year in wages, hires, and small payments to the working classes in his neighbourhood. This capital was returned to him in his sales, and even went on increasing year by year; and our countryman, knowing very well that capital produces nothing when it is unemployed, benefited the working classes by devoting the annual surplus to enclosing and clearing his land, and to improving his agricultural implements and farm buildings. He had even some savings in the neighbouring town with his banker, who, of course, did not let the money lie idle in his till, but lent it to shipowners and contractors for public works, so that these savings were always resolving themselves into wages.

At length the countryman died, and his son, who succeeded him, said to himself, "My father was a dupe all his life. He purchased oil, and so paid *tribute* to Provence, whilst our own land, with some pains, can be made to grow the olive. He bought cloth, wine, and oranges, and thus paid tribute to Brittany, Medoc, and Hyères, whilst we can cultivate hemp, the vine, and the orange tree with more or less success. He paid *tribute* to the miller and the weaver, whilst our own domestics can weave our linen and grind our wheat." In this way he ruined himself, and spent among strangers that money which he might have spent at home.

Misled by such reasoning, the volatile youth changed his rotation of crops. His land he divided into twenty divisions. In one he planted olives, in another mulberry trees, in a third he sowed flax, in a fourth he had vines, in a fifth wheat, and so on. By this means he succeeded in supplying his family with what they required, and felt himself independent. He no longer drew anything from the general circulation, nor did he add anything to it. Was he the richer for this? No; for the soil was not adapted for the cultivation of the vine, and the climate was not fitted for the successful cultivation of the olive; and he was not long in finding out that his family was less plentifully provided with all the things which they wanted than in the time of his father, who procured them by exchanging his surplus produce.

As regarded his workmen, they had no more employment than formerly. There were five times more fields, but each field was five times smaller; they produced oil, but they produced less wheat; he no longer purchased linens, but he no longer sold rye. Moreover, the farmer could expend in wages only the amount of his capital, and his capital went on constantly diminishing. A great part of it went for buildings, and the various implements needed for the more varied cultivation in which he had engaged. In short, the supply of labour remained the same, but as the means of remunerating that labour fell off, the ultimate result was a forcible reduction of wages.

On a greater scale, this is exactly what takes place in the case of a nation which isolates itself by adopting a prohibitive *regime*. It multiplies its branches of industry, I grant, but they become of diminished importance; it adopts, so to speak, a more complicated *industrial rotation*, but it is not so prolific, because its capital and labour have now to struggle with natural difficulties. A greater proportion of its circulating capital, which forms the wages fund, must be converted into fixed capital. What remains may have more varied employment, but the total mass is not increased. It is like distributing the water of a pond among a multitude of shallow reservoirs—it covers more ground, and presents a greater surface to the rays of the sun, and it is precisely for this reason that it is all the sooner absorbed, evaporated, and lost.

The amount of capital and labour being given, they create a smaller amount of commodities in proportion as they encounter more obstacles. It is beyond doubt, that when international obstructions force capital and labour into channels and localities where they meet with greater difficulties of soil and climate, the general result must be, fewer products created—that is to say, fewer enjoyments for consumers. Now, when there are fewer enjoyments upon the whole, will the workman's share of them be augmented? If it were augmented, as is asserted, then the rich—the men who make the laws—would find their own share not only subject to the general diminution, but that diminished share would be still further reduced by what was added to the labourers' share. Is this possible? Is it credible? I advise you, workmen, to reject such suspicious generosity.*

* See *Harmonies Économiques*, ch. xiv.

XIII. THEORY, PRACTICE.

As advocates of free trade, we are accused of being theorists, and of not taking practice sufficiently into account.

"What fearful prejudices were entertained against M. Say," says M. Ferrier,* "by that long train of distinguished administrators, and that imposing phalanx of authors who dissented from his opinions; and M. Say was not unaware of it. Hear what he says:—'It has been alleged in support of errors of long standing, that there must have been some foundation for ideas which have been adopted by all nations. Ought we not to distrust observations and reasonings which run counter to opinions which have been constantly entertained down to our own time, and which have been regarded as sound by so many men remarkable for their enlightenment and their good intentions? This argument, I allow, is calculated to make a profound impression, and it might have cast doubt upon points which we deem the most incontestable, if we had not seen, by turns, opinions the most false, and now generally acknowledged to be false, received and professed by everybody during a long series of ages. Not very long ago all nations, from the rudest to the most enlightened, and all men, from the street-porter to the *savant*, admitted the existence of four elements. No one thought of contesting that doctrine, which, however, is false; so much so, that even the greenest assistant in a naturalist's class-room would be ashamed to say that he regarded earth, water, and fire as elements.'"

* *De l'Administration Commerciale opposee à Oeconomie Politique, p. 5.*

On this M. Ferrier remarks:—

"If M. Say thinks to answer thus the very strong objection which he brings forward, he is singularly mistaken. That men, otherwise well informed, should have been mistaken for centuries on certain points of natural history is easily understood, and proves nothing. Water, air, earth, and fire, whether elements or not, are not the less useful to man.... Such errors are unimportant: they lead to no popular commotions, no uneasiness in the public mind; they run counter to no pecuniary interest; and this is the reason why without any felt inconvenience they may endure for a thousand years. The physical world goes on as if they did not exist. But of errors in the moral world, can the same thing be said? Can we conceive that a system of administration, found to be absolutely false and therefore hurtful, should be followed out among many nations for centuries, with the general approval of all well-informed men? Can it be explained how such a system could coexist with the constantly increasing prosperity of nations? M. Say admits that the argument which he combats is fitted to make a profound impression. Yes, indeed; and the impression remains; for M. Say has rather deepened than done away with it."

** Might we not say, that it is a "fearful prejudice" against MM. Ferrier and Saint-Chamans, that "economists of all schools, that is to say, everybody who has studied the question, should have arrived at the conclusion, that, after all, liberty is better than constraint, and the laws of God wiser than those of Colbert."*

Let us hear what M. de Saint-Chamans says on the same subject:—

"It was only in the middle of the last century, of that eighteenth century which handed over all subjects and all principles without exception to free discussion, that these *speculative* purveyors of ideas, applied by them to all things without being really applicable to anything, began to write upon political economy. There existed previously a system of political economy, not to be found in books, but which had been put in *practical* operation by governments. Colbert, it is said, was the inventor of it, and it was adopted as a rule by all the nations of Europe. The singular thing is, that in spite of contempt and maledictions, in spite of all the discoveries of the modern school, it still remains in practical operation. This system, which our authors have called the *mercantile system*, was designed to.... impede, by prohibitions or import duties, the entry of foreign products, which might ruin our own manufactures by their competition. Economic writers of all schools* have declared this system untenable, absurd, and calculated to impoverish any country. It has been banished from all their books, and forced to take refuge in the *practical* legislation of all nations. They cannot conceive why, in measures relating to national wealth, governments should not follow the advice and opinions of learned authors, rather than trust to their *experience* of the tried working of a system which has been long in operation. Above all, they cannot conceive why the French government should in economic questions obstinately set itself to resist the progress of enlightenment, and maintain in its *practice* those ancient errors, which all our economic writers have exposed. But enough of this mercantile system, which has nothing in its favour but *facts*, and is not defended by any speculative writer."*

** Du Système de l'Impot, par M. le Vicomte de Saint-Chamans,p. 11.*

Such language as this would lead one to suppose that in demanding for every one *the free disposal of his property*, economists were propounding some new system, some new, strange, and chimerical social order, a sort of *phalanstère*, coined in the mint of their own brain, and without precedent in the annals of the human race. To me it would seem that if we have here anything factitious or contingent, it is to be found, not in liberty, but in protection; not in the free power of exchanging, but in customs duties employed to overturn artificially the natural course of remuneration.

But our business at present is not to compare, or pronounce between, the two systems; but to inquire which of the two is founded on experience.

The advocates of monopoly maintain that *the facts* are on their side, and that we have on our side only *theory*.

They flatter themselves that this long series of public acts, this *old experience* of Europe, which they invoke, has presented itself as something very formidable to the mind of M. Say; and I grant that he has not refuted it with his wonted sagacity. For my own part, I am not disposed to concede to the monopolists the domain of *facts*, for they have only in their favour facts which are forced and exceptional; and we oppose to these, facts which are universal, the free and voluntary acts of mankind at large.

What do we say; and what do they say?

We say,

"You should buy from others what you cannot make for yourself but at a greater expense."

And they say,

"It is better to make things for yourself, although they cost you more than, the price at which you could buy them from others."

Now, gentlemen, throwing aside theory, argument, demonstration, all which seems to affect you with nausea, which of these two assertions has on its side the sanction of *universal practice?*

Visit your fields, your workshops, your forges, your warehouses; look above, below, and around you; look at what takes place in your own houses; remark your own everyday acts; and say what is the principle which guides these labourers, artisans, and merchants; say what is your own personal *practice*.

Does the farmer make his own clothes? Does the tailor produce the corn he consumes? Does your housekeeper continue to have your bread made at home, after she finds she can buy it cheaper from the baker? Do you resign the pen for the brush, to save your paying *tribute* to the shoeblack? Does the entire economy of society not rest upon the separation of employments, the division of labour—in a word, upon *exchange?* And what is exchange, but a calculation which we make with a view to discontinuing direct production in every case in which we find that possible, and in which indirect acquisition enables us to effect a saving in time and in effort?

It is not you, therefore, who are the men of *practice*, since you cannot point to a single human being who acts upon your principle.

But you will say, we never intended to make our principle a rule for individual relations. We perfectly understand that this would be to break up the bond of society, and would force men to live like snails, each in his own shell. All that we contend for is, that our principle regulates *de facto*, the regulations which obtain between the different agglomerations of the human family.

Well, I affirm that this principle is still erroneous. The family, the commune, the canton, the department, the province, are so many agglomerations, which all, without any exception, reject *practically* your principle, and have never dreamt of acting on it. All procure themselves, by means of exchange, those things which it would cost them dearer to procure by means of production. And nations would do the same, did you not hinder them *by force*.

We, then, are the men of practice and of experience; for we oppose to the restriction which you have placed exceptionally on certain international exchanges, the practice and experience of all individuals, and of all agglomerations of individuals, whose acts are voluntary, and can consequently be adduced as evidence. But you begin by *constraining, by hindering*, and then you lay hold of acts which are *forced or prohibited*, as warranting you to exclaim, "We have practice and experience on our side!"

You inveigh against our theory, and even against theories in general. But when you lay down a principle in opposition to ours, you perhaps imagine you are not proceeding on theory? Clear your heads of that idea. You in fact form a theory, as we do; but between your theory and ours there is this difference:

Our theory consists merely in observing universal *facts*, universal opinions; calculations and ways of proceeding which universally prevail; and in classifying these, and rendering them Co-ordinate, with a view to their being more easily understood.

Our theory is so little opposed to practice that it is nothing else but *practice explained.* We observe men acting as they are moved by the instinct of self-preservation and a desire for progress, and what they thus do freely and voluntarily we denominate political or social economy. We can never help repeating, that each individual man is *practically* an excellent economist, producing or exchanging according as he finds it more to his interest to produce or to exchange. Each, by experience, educates himself in this science; or rather the science itself is only this same experience accurately observed and methodically explained.

But on your side, you construct a *theory* in the worst sense of the word. You imagine, you invent, a course of proceeding which is not sanctioned by the practice of any living man under the canopy of heaven; and then you invoke the aid of constraint and prohibition. It is quite necessary that you should have recourse to *force*, for you desire that men should be made to produce those things which they find it *more advantageous* to buy; you desire that they should renounce this *advantage*, and act upon a doctrine which implies a contradiction in terms.

The doctrine which you acknowledge would be absurd in the relations of individuals; I defy you to extend it, even in speculation, to transaction between families, communities, or provinces. By your own admission, it is only applicable to international relations.

This is the reason why you are forced to keep repeating:

"There are no absolute principles, no inflexible rules. What is *good* for an individual, a family, a province, is *bad* for a nation. What is *good* in detail—namely, to purchase rather than produce, when purchasing is more advantageous than producing—that same is *bad* in the gross. The political economy of individuals is not that of nations;" and other nonsense *ejusdèm farino.*

And to what does all this tend? Look at it a little closer. The intention is to prove that we, the consumers, are your property! that we are yours body and soul! that you have an exclusive right over our stomachs and our limbs! that it belongs to you to feed and clothe us on your own terms, whatever be your ignorance, incapacity, or rapacity!

No, you are not men of practice; you are men of abstraction—and of extortion.

XIV. CONFLICT OF PRINCIPLES.

There is one thing which confounds me; and it is this: Sincere publicists, studying the economy of society from the producer's point of view, have laid down this double formula:—

"Governments should order the interests of consumers who are subject to their laws, in such a way as to be favourable to national industry.

"They should bring distant consumers under subjection to their laws, for the purpose of ordering their interests in a way favourable to national industry."

The first of these formulas gets the name of protection; the second we call *debouches*, or the creating of markets, or vents, for our produce.

Both are founded on the *datum* which we denominate the *Balance of Trade.*

"A nation is impoverished when it imports; enriched when it exports."

For if every purchase from a foreign country is a *tribute paid* and a national loss, it follows, of course, that it is right to restrain, and even prohibit, importations.

And if every sale to a foreign country is a *tribute received*, and a national profit, it is quite right and natural to create markets for our products even by force.

The *system of protection* and the *colonial system* are, then, only two aspects of one and the same theory. To *hinder* our fellow-citizens from buying from foreigners, and to *force* foreigners to buy from our fellow-citizens, are only two consequences of one and the same principle.

Now, it is impossible not to admit that this doctrine, if true, makes general utility to repose on *monopoly* or internal spoliation, and on *conquest* or external spoliation.

I enter a cottage on the French side of the Pyrenees.

The father of the family has received but slender wages. His half-naked children shiver in the icy north wind; the fire is extinguished, and there is nothing on the table. There are wool, firewood, and corn on the other side of the mountain; but these good things are forbidden to the poor day-labourer, for the other side of the mountain is not in France. Foreign firewood is not allowed to warm the cottage hearth; and the shepherd's children can never know the taste of Biscayan corn,* and the wool of Navarre can never warm their benumbed limbs. General utility has so ordered it. Be it so; but let us agree that all this is in direct opposition to the first principles of justice. To dispose legislatively of the interests of consumers, and postpone them to the supposed interests of national industry, is to encroach upon their liberty—it is to prohibit an act; namely, the act of exchange, which has in it nothing contrary to good morals; in a word, it is to do them an act of *injustice.*

** The French word employed is meture, probably a Spanish word Gallicized—mestûra, meslin, mixed corn, as wheat and rye.—-Translator.*

And yet this is necessary, we are told, unless we wish to see national labour at a standstill, and public prosperity sustain a fatal shock.

Writers of the protectionist school, then, have arrived at the melancholy conclusion that there is a radical incompatibility between Justice and Utility.

On the other hand, if it be the interest of each nation to *sell*, and not to *buy*, the natural state of their relations must consist in a violent action and reaction, for each will seek to impose its products on all, and all will endeavour to repel the products of each.

A sale, in fact, implies a purchase, and since, according to this doctrine, to sell is beneficial, and to buy is the reverse, every international transaction would imply the amelioration of one people, and the deterioration of another.

But if men are, on the one hand, irresistibly impelled towards what is for their profit, and if, on the other, they resist instinctively what is hurtful, we are forced to conclude that each nation carries in its bosom a natural force of expansion, and a not less natural force of resistance, which forces are equally injurious to all other nations; or, in other words, that antagonism and war are the *natural* state of human society.

Thus the theory we are discussing may be summed up in these two axioms:

Utility is incompatible with Justice at home.

Utility is incompatible with Peace abroad.

Now, what astonishes and confounds me is, that a publicist, a statesman, who sincerely holds an economical doctrine which runs so violently counter to other principles which are incontestable, should be able to enjoy one moment of calm or peace of mind.

For my own part, it seems to me, that if I had entered the precincts of the science by the same gate, if I had failed to perceive clearly that Liberty, Utility, Justice, Peace, are things not only compatible, but strictly allied with each other, and, so to speak, identical, I should have endeavoured to forget what I had learned, and I should have asked:

"How God could have willed that men should attain prosperity only through Injustice and War? How He could have willed that they should be unable to avoid Injustice and War except by renouncing the possibility of attaining prosperity?

"Dare I adopt, as the basis of the legislation of a great nation, a science which thus misleads me by false lights, which has conducted me to this horrible blasphemy, and landed me in so dreadful an alternative? And when a long train of illustrious philosophers have been conducted by this science, to which they have devoted their lives, to more consoling results—when they affirm that Liberty and Utility are perfectly reconcilable with Justice and Peace—that all these great principles run in infinitely extended parallels, and will do so to all eternity, without running counter to each other,—I would ask, Have they not in their favour that presumption which results from all that we know of the goodness and wisdom of God, as manifested in the sublime harmony of the material creation? In the face of such a presumption, and of so many reliable authorities, ought I to believe lightly that God has been pleased to implant antagonism and dissonance in the laws of the moral world? No; before I should venture to conclude that the principles of social order run counter to and neutralize each other, and are in eternal and irreconcilable opposition—before I should venture to impose on my fellow-citizens a system so impious as that to which my reasonings would appear to lead,—I should set myself to reexamine the whole chain of these reasonings, and assure myself that at this stage of the journey I had not missed my way." But if, after a candid and searching examination, twenty times repeated, I arrived always at this frightful conclusion, that we must choose between the Bight and the Good, discouraged, I should reject the science, and bury myself in voluntary ignorance; above all, I should decline all participation in public affairs, leaving to men of another temper and constitution the burden and responsibility of a choice so painful.

XV. RECIPROCITY AGAIN.

M de Saint-Cricq inquires, "Whether it is certain that the foreigner will buy from us as much as he sells?"

M. de Dombasle asks, "What reason we have to believe that English producers will take from us, rather than from some other country of the world, the commodities they have need of, and an amount of commodities equivalent in value to that of their exports to France?"

I wonder how so many men who call themselves *practical* men should have all reasoned without reference to practice!

In practice, does a single exchange take place, out of a hundred, out of a thousand, out of ten thousand perhaps, which represents the direct barter of commodity for commodity? Never since the introduction of money has any agriculturist said: I want to buy shoes, hats, advice, lessons; but only from the shoemaker, the hat-maker, the lawyer, the professor, who will purchase from me corn to an exactly equivalent value. And why should nations bring each other under a yoke of this kind? Practically how are such matters transacted?

Let us suppose a people shut out from external relations. A man, we shall suppose, produces wheat. He sends it to the *home* market, and offers it for the highest price he can obtain. He receives in exchange—what? Coins, which are just so many drafts or orders, varying very much in amount, by means of which he can draw, in his turn, from the national stores, when he judges it proper, and subject to due competition, everything which he may want or desire. Ultimately, and at the end of the operation, he will have drawn from the mass the exact equivalent of what he has contributed to it, and, in value, *his consumption will exactly equal his production.*

If the exchanges of the supposed nation with foreigners are left free, it is no longer to the *national*, but to the *general*, market that each sends his contributions, and, in turn, derives his supplies for consumption. He has no need to care whether what he sends into the market of the world is purchased by a fellow-countryman or by a foreigner; whether the drafts or orders he receives come from a Frenchman or an Englishman; whether the commodities for which he afterwards exchanges these drafts or orders are produced on this or on the other side of the Rhine or the Pyrenees. There is always in each individual case an exact balance between what is contributed and what is received, between what is poured into and what is drawn out of the great common reservoir; and if this is true of each individual, it is true of the nation at large.

The only difference between the two cases is, that in the last each has to face a more extended market both as regards sales and purchases, and has consequently more chances of transacting both advantageously.

This objection may perhaps be urged: If everybody enters into a league not to take from the general mass the commodities of a certain individual, that individual cannot, in his turn, obtain from the mass what he is in want of. It is the same of nations.

The reply to this is, that if a nation cannot obtain what it has need of in the general market, it will no longer contribute anything to that market. It will work for itself. It will be forced in that case to submit to what you want to impose on it beforehand—*isolation.*

And this will realize the ideal of the prohibitive *regime.*

Is it not amusing to think that you inflict upon the nation, now and beforehand, this very *regime*, from a fear that it might otherwise run the risk of arriving at it independently of your exertions?

XVI. OBSTRUCTED NAVIGATION PLEADING FOR THE PROHIBITIONISTS.

Some years ago I happened to be at Madrid, and went to the Cortes. The subject of debate was a proposed treaty with Portugal for improving the navigation of the Douro. One of the deputies rose and said: "If the navigation of the Douro is improved in the way now proposed, the traffic will be carried on at less expense. The grain of Portugal will, in consequence, be sold in the markets of Castile at a lower price, and will become a formidable rival to our *national industry*. I oppose the project, unless, indeed, our ministers will undertake to raise the tariff of customs to the extent required to re-establish the equilibrium." The Assembly found the argument unanswerable.

Three months afterwards I was at Lisbon. The same question was discussed in the Senate. A noble hidalgo made a speech: "Mr President," he said, "this project is absurd. You place guards, at great expense, along the banks of the Douro to prevent Portugal being invaded by Castilian grain; and at the same time you propose, also at great expense, to facilitate that invasion. This is a piece of inconsistency to which I cannot assent. Let us leave the Douro to our children, as it has come to us from our fathers."

Afterwards, when the subject of improving the navigation of the Garonne was discussed, I remembered the arguments of the Iberian orators, and I said to myself, If the Toulouse deputies were as good economists as the Spanish deputies, and the representatives of Bordeaux as acute logicians as those of Oporto, assuredly they would leave the Garonne

"Dormir au bruit flatteur de son onde naissante;"

for the canalisation of the Garonne would favour the invasion of Toulouse products, to the prejudice of Bordeaux, and the inundation of Bordeaux products would do the same thing to the detriment of Toulouse.

XVII. A NEGATIVE RAILWAY.

I have said that when, unfortunately, one has regard to the interest of the producer, and not to that of the consumer, it is impossible to avoid running counter to the general interest, because the demand of the producer, as such, is only for efforts, wants, and obstacles.

I find a remarkable illustration of this in a Bordeaux newspaper.

M. Simiot proposes this question:—

Should the proposed railway from Paris to Madrid offer a solution of continuity at Bordeaux?

He answers the question in the affirmative, and gives a multiplicity of reasons, which I shall not stop to examine, except this one:

The railway from Paris to Bayonne should have a break at Bordeaux, for if goods and passengers are forced to stop at that town, profits will accrue to bargemen, pedlars, commissionaires, hotel-keepers, etc.

Here we have clearly the interest of labour put before the interest of consumers.

But if Bordeaux has a right to profit by a gap in the line of railway, and if such profit is consistent with the public interest, then Angoulême, Poitiers, Tours, Orleans, nay, more, all the intermediate places, Ruffec, Châtellerault, etc., should also demand gaps, as being for the general interest, and, of course, for the interest of national industry; for the more these breaks in the line are multiplied, the greater will be the increase of consignments, commissions, transhipments, etc., along the whole extent of the railway. In this way, we shall succeed in having a line of railway composed of successive gaps, and which may be denominated a *Negative Railway.*

Let the protectionists say what they will, it is not the less certain that *the principle of restriction* is the very same as the *principle of gaps*; the sacrifice of the consumer's interest to that of the producer,—in other words, the sacrifice of the end to the means.

XVIII. THERE ARE NO ABSOLUTE PRINCIPLES.

We cannot wonder enough at the facility with which men resign themselves to continue ignorant of what it is most important that they should know; and we may be certain that such ignorance is incorrigible in those who venture to proclaim this axiom: There are no absolute principles.

You enter the legislative precincts. The subject of debate is whether the law should prohibit international exchanges, or proclaim freedom.

A deputy rises, and says:

If you tolerate these exchanges, the foreigner will inundate you with his products: England with her textile fabrics, Belgium with coals, Spain with wools, Italy with silks, Switzerland with cattle, Sweden with iron, Prussia with corn; so that home industry will no longer be possible.

Another replies:

If you prohibit international exchanges, the various bounties which nature has lavished on different climates will be for you as if they did not exist. You cannot participate in the mechanical skill of the English, in the wealth of the Belgian mines, in the fertility of the Polish soil, in the luxuriance of the Swiss pastures, in the cheapness of Spanish labour, in the warmth of the Italian climate; and you must obtain from a refractory and misdirected production those commodities which, through exchange, would have been furnished to you by an easy production.

Assuredly, one of these deputies must be wrong. But which? We must take care to make no mistake on the subject; for this is not a matter of abstract opinion merely. You have to choose between two roads, and one of them leads necessarily to *poverty.*

To get rid of the dilemma, we are told that there are no absolute principles.

This axiom, which is so much in fashion nowadays, not only countenances indolence, but ministers to ambition.

If the theory of prohibition comes to prevail, or if the doctrine of free trade comes to triumph, one brief enactment will constitute our whole economic code. In the first case, the law will proclaim that *all exchanges with foreign countries are prohibited*; in the second, that *all exchanges with foreign countries are free*; and many grand and distinguished personages will thereby lose their importance.

But if exchange does not possess a character which is peculiar to it,—if it is not governed by any natural law,—if, capriciously, it be sometimes useful and sometimes detrimental,—if it does not find its motive force in the good which it accomplishes, its limit in the good which it ceases to accomplish,—if its consequences cannot be estimated by those who effect exchanges;—in a word, if there be no absolute principles, then we must proceed to weigh, balance, and regulate transactions, we must equalize the conditions of labour, and try to find out the average rate of profits—a colossal task, well deserving the large emoluments and powerful influence awarded to those who undertake it.

On entering Paris, which I had come to visit, I said to myself, Here are a million of human beings, who would all die in a short time if provisions of every kind ceased to flow towards this great metropolis. Imagination is baffled when it tries to appreciate the vast multiplicity of commodities which must enter to-morrow through the barriers in order to preserve the inhabitants from falling a prey to the convulsions of famine, rebellion, and pillage. And yet all sleep at this moment, and their peaceful slumbers are not disturbed for a single instant by the prospect of such a frightful catastrophe. On the other hand, eighty departments have been labouring to-day, without concert, without any mutual understanding, for the provisioning of Paris. How does each succeeding day bring what is wanted, nothing more, nothing less, to so gigantic a market? What, then, is the ingenious and secret power which governs the astonishing regularity of movements so complicated, a regularity in which everybody has implicit faith, although happiness and life itself are at stake? That power is an *absolute principle*, the principle of freedom in transactions. We have faith in that inward light which Providence has placed in the heart of all men, and to which He has confided the preservation and indefinite amelioration of our species, namely, a regard to personal *interest*—since we must give it its right name—a principle so active, so vigilant, so foreseeing, when it is free in its action. In what situation, I would ask, would the inhabitants of Paris be, if a minister should take it into his head to substitute for this power the combinations of his own genius, however superior we might suppose them to be—if he thought to subject to his supreme direction this prodigious mechanism, to hold the springs of it in his hands, to decide by whom, or in what manner, or on what conditions, everything needed should be produced, transported, exchanged, and consumed? Truly, there may be much suffering within the walls of Paris—poverty, despair, perhaps starvation, causing more tears to flow than ardent charity is able to dry up; but I affirm that it is probable, nay, that it is certain, that the arbitrary intervention of government would multiply infinitely those sufferings, and spread over all our fellow-citizens those evils which at present affect only a small number of them.

This faith, then, which we repose in a principle, when the question relates only to our home transactions, why should we not retain, when the same principle is applied to our international transactions, which are undoubtedly less numerous, less delicate, and less complicated? And if it is not necessary that the *prefecture* should regulate our Parisian industries, weigh our chances, balance our profits and losses, see that our circulating medium is not exhausted, and equalize the conditions of our home labour, why should it be necessary that the Customhouse, departing from its fiscal duties, should pretend to exercise a protective action over our external commerce?

XIX. NATIONAL INDEPENDENCE.

Among the arguments which we hear adduced in favour of the restrictive *regime*, we must not forget that which is founded on *national independence.*

"What should we do in case of war," it is said, "if we are placed at the mercy of England for iron and coal?"

English monopolists do not fail to cry out in their turn:

"What would become of Great Britain, in case of war, if she is dependent on France for provisions?"

One thing is overlooked, which is this—that the kind of dependence which results from exchange, from commercial transactions, is a *reciprocal dependence.* We cannot be dependent on the foreigner without the foreigner being dependent on us. Now, this is the very essence of society. To break up natural relations is not to place ourselves in a state of independence, but in a state of isolation.

Remark this: A nation isolates itself looking forward to the possibility of war; but is not this very act of isolating itself the beginning of war? It renders war more easy, less burdensome, and, it may be, less unpopular. Let countries be permanent markets for each other's produce; let their reciprocal relations be such that they cannot be broken without inflicting on each other the double suffering of privation and a glut of commodities; and they will no longer stand in need of naval armaments, which ruin them, and overgrown armies, which crush them; the peace of the world will not then be compromised by the caprice of a Thiers or of a Palmerston; and war will disappear for want of what supports it, for want of resources, inducements, pretexts, and popular sympathy.

I am quite aware that I shall be reproached (it is the fashion of the day) with basing the fraternity of nations on men's personal interest—vile, prosaic self-interest. Better far, it may be thought, that it should have had its basis in charity, in love, even in a little self-abnegation, and that, interfering somewhat with men's material comforts, it should have had the merit of a generous sacrifice.

When shall we be done with these puerile declamations? When will *tartuferie* be finally banished from science? When shall we cease to exhibit this nauseous contradiction between our professions and our practice? We hoot at and execrate personal *interest*; in other words, we denounce what is useful and good (for to say that all men are interested in anything is to say that the thing is good in itself), as if personal interest were not the necessary, eternal, and indestructible mainspring to which Providence has confided human perfectibility. Are we not represented as being all angels of disinterestedness? And does the thought never occur to those who say so, that the public begins to see with disgust that this affected language disfigures the pages of those very writers who axe most successful in filling their own pockets at the public expense? Oh! affectation! affectation! thou art verily the besetting sin of our times!

What! because material prosperity and peace are things correlative, because it has pleased God to establish this beautiful harmony in the moral world, am I not to admire, am I not to adore His ordinances, am I not to accept with gratitude laws which make justice the condition of happiness? You desire peace only in as far as it runs counter to material prosperity; and liberty is rejected because it does not impose sacrifices. If abnegation has indeed so many charms for you, why do you fail to practise it in private life? Society will be grateful to you, for some one, at least, will reap the fruit; but to desire to impose it upon mankind as a principle is the very height of absurdity, for the abnegation of all is the sacrifice of all, which is evil erected into a theory.

But, thank Heaven, one can write or read many of these declamations without the world ceasing on that account to obey the social motive force, which leads us to shun evil and seek after good, and which, whether they like it or not, we must denominate personal interest.

After all, it is singular enough to see sentiments of the most sublime self-denial invoked in support of spoliation itself. See to what this boasted disinterestedness tends! These men who are so fantastically delicate as not to desire peace itself, if it is founded on the vile interest of mankind, put their hand into the pockets of others, and especially of the poor; for what article of the tariff protects the poor? Be pleased, gentlemen, to dispose of what belongs to yourselves as you think proper, but leave us the disposal of the fruit of our own toil, to use it or exchange it as we see best. Declaim on self-sacrifice as much as you choose, it is all very fine and very beautiful, but be at least consistent.

XX. HUMAN LABOUR, NATIONAL LABOUR.

Machine-breaking—prohibition of foreign commodities—are two acts founded on the same doctrine.

We see men who clap their hands when a great invention is introduced, and who nevertheless adhere to the protectionist *regime*. Such men are grossly inconsistent!

With what do they reproach free trade? With encouraging the production by foreigners, more skilled or more favourably situated than we are, of commodities which, but for free trade, would be produced at home. In a word, they accuse free trade of being injurious to *national labour?*

For the same reason, should they not reproach machinery with accomplishing by natural agents what otherwise would have been done by manual labour, and so of being injurious to *human labour?*

The foreign workman, better and more favourably situated than the home workman for the production of certain commodities, is, with reference to the latter, a veritable *economic machine,* crushing him by competition. In like manner, machinery, which executes a piece of work at a lower price than a certain number of men could do by manual labour, is, in relation to these manual labourers, a veritable *foreign competitor*, who paralyzes them by his rivalry.

If, then, it is politic to protect *national labour* against the competition of *foreign labour*, it is not less so to protect *human labour* against the rivalry of *mechanical labour*.

Thus, every adherent of the *regime* of protection, if he is logical, should not content himself with prohibiting foreign products; he should proscribe also the products of the shuttle and the plough.

And this is the reason why I like better the logic of those men who, declaiming against the invasion of foreign merchandise, declaim likewise against the excess of production which is due to the inventive power of the human mind.

Such a man is M. de Saint-Chamans. "One of the strongest arguments against free trade," he says, "is the too extensive employment of machinery, for many workmen are deprived of employment, either by foreign competition, which lowers the price of our manufactured goods, or by instruments which take the place of men in our workshops."*

* *Du Système d'impôts, p. 438.*

M. de Saint-Chamans has seen clearly the analogy, or, we should rather say, the identity, which obtains between imports and machinery. For this reason, he proscribes both; and it is really agreeable to have to do with such intrepid reasoners, who, even when wrong, carry out their argument to its logical conclusion.

But here is the mess in which they land themselves.

If it be true, a priori, that the domain of invention and that of labour cannot be simultaneously extended but at each other's expense, it must be in those countries where machinery most abounds—in Lancashire, for example—that we should expect to find the fewest workmen. And if, on the other hand, we establish the fact that mechanical power and manual labour coexist, and to a greater extent, among rich nations than among savages, the conclusion is inevitable, that these two powers do not exclude each other.

I cannot convince myself how any thinking being can enjoy a moment's repose in presence of the following dilemma: Either the inventions of man are not injurious to manual labour, as general facts attest, since there are more of both in England and France than among the Hurons and Cherokees, and that being so, I am on a wrong road, though I know neither where nor when I missed my way; at all events, I see I am wrong, and I should commit the crime of lese-humanity were I to introduce my error into the legislation of my country.

Or else, the discoveries of the human mind limit the amount of manual labour, as special facts appear to indicate; for I see every day some machine or other superseding twenty or a hundred workmen; and then I am forced to acknowledge a flagrant, eternal, and incurable antithesis between the intellectual and physical powers of man—between his progress and his present wellbeing; and in these circumstances I am forced to say that the Creator of man might have endowed him with reason, or with physical strength, with moral force, or with brute force; but that He mocked him by conferring on him, at the same time, faculties which are destructive of each other.

The difficulty is pressing and puzzling; but you contrive to find your way out of it by adopting the strange apophthegm:

In political economy, there are no absolute principles.

In plain language, this means:

"I know not whether it be true or false; I am ignorant of what constitutes general good or evil. I give myself no trouble about that. The immediate effect of each measure upon my own personal interest is the only law which I can consent to recognise."

There are no principles! You might as well say there are no facts; for principles are merely formulas which classify such facts as are well established.

Machinery, and the importation of foreign commodities, certainly produce effects. These effects may be good or bad; on that there may be difference of opinion. But whatever view we take of them, it is reduced to a formula, by one of these two principles: Machinery is a good; or, machinery is an evil: Importations of foreign produce are beneficial; or, such importations are hurtful. But to assert that there are no principles, certainly exhibits the lowest degree of abasement to which the human mind can descend; and I confess that I blush for my country when I hear such a monstrous heresy proclaimed in the French Chambers, and with their assent; that is to say, in the face and with the assent of the *elite* of our fellow-citizens; and this in order to justify their imposing laws upon us in total ignorance of the real state of the case.

But then I am told to destroy the sophism, by proving that machinery is not hurtful to human labour, nor the importation of foreign products to national labour.

A work like the present cannot well include very full or complete demonstrations. My design is rather to state difficulties than to resolve them; to excite reflection rather than to satisfy doubts. No conviction makes so lasting an impression on the mind as that which it works out for itself. But I shall endeavour nevertheless to put the reader on the right road.

What misleads the adversaries of machinery and foreign importations is, that they judge of them by their immediate and transitory effects, instead of following them out to their general and definitive consequences.

The immediate effect of the invention and employment of an ingenious machine is to render superfluous, for the attainment of a given result, a certain amount of manual labour. But its action does not stop there. For the very reason that the desired result is obtained with fewer efforts, the product is handed over to the public at a lower price; and the aggregate of savings thus realized by all purchasers, enables them to procure other satisfactions; that is to say, to encourage manual labour in general to exactly the extent of the manual labour which has been saved in the special branch of industry which has been recently improved. So that the level of labour has not fallen, while that of enjoyments has risen.

Let us render this evident by an example.

Suppose there are used annually in this country ten millions of hats at 15 shillings; this makes the sum which goes to the support of this branch of industry £7,500,000 sterling. A machine is invented which allows these hats to be manufactured and sold at 10 shillings. The sum now wanted for the support of this industry is reduced to £5,000,000, provided the demand is not augmented by the change. But the remaining sum of £2,500,000 is not by this change withdrawn from the support of *human labour*. That sum, economized by the purchasers of hats, will enable them to satisfy other wants, and, consequently, to that extent will go to remunerate the aggregate industry of the country. With the five shillings saved, John will purchase a pair of shoes, James a book, Jerome a piece of furniture, etc. Human labour, taken in the aggregate, will continue, then, to be supported and encouraged to the extent of £7,500,000; but this sum will yield the same number of hats, plus all the satisfactions and enjoyments corresponding to £2,500,000 that the employment of the machine has enabled the consumers of hats to save. These additional enjoyments constitute the clear profit which the country will have derived from the invention. This is a free gift, a tribute which human genius will have derived from nature. We do not at all dispute, that in the course of the transformation a certain amount of labour will have been *displaced*; but we cannot allow that it has been destroyed or diminished.

The same thing holds of the importation of foreign commodities. Let us revert to our former hypothesis.

The country manufactures ten millions of hats, of which the cost price was 15 shillings. The foreigner sends similar hats to our market, and furnishes them at 10 shillings each. I maintain that the *national labour* will not be thereby diminished.

For it must produce to the extent of £5,000,000, to enable it to pay for 10 millions of hats at 10 shillings.

And then there remains to each purchaser five shillings saved on each hat, or in all, £2,500,000, which will be spent on other enjoyments—that is to say, which will go to support labour in other departments of industry.

Then the aggregate labour of the country will remain what it was, and the additional enjoyments represented by £2,500,000 saved upon hats, will form the clear profit accruing from imports under the system of free trade.

It is of no use to try to frighten us by a picture of the sufferings which, on this hypothesis, the displacement of labour will entail.

For, if the prohibition had never been imposed, the labour would have found its natural place under the ordinary law of exchange, and no displacement would have taken place.

If, on the other hand, prohibition has led to an artificial and unproductive employment of labour, it is prohibition, and not liberty, which is to blame for a displacement which is inevitable in the transition from what is detrimental to what is beneficial.

At all events, let no one pretend that because an abuse cannot be done away with, without inconvenience to those who profit by it, what has been suffered to exist for a time should be allowed to exist for ever.

XXI. RAW MATERIALS.

It is said that the most advantageous of all branches of trade is that which supplies manufactured commodities in exchange for raw materials. For these raw materials are the aliment and support of *national labour.*

Hence the conclusion is drawn:

That the best law of customs is that which gives the greatest possible facility to the importation of raw materials, and which throws most obstacles in the way of importing finished goods.

There is no sophism in political economy more widely disseminated than this. It is cherished not only by the protectionist school, but also, and above all, by the school which dubs itself liberal; and it is unfortunate that it should be so, for what can be more injurious to a good cause than that it should be at the same time vigorously attacked and feebly defended?

Commercial liberty is likely to have the fate of liberty in general; it will only find a place in the statute-book after it has taken possession of men's minds and convictions. But if it be true that a reform, in order to be solidly established, should be generally understood, it follows that nothing can so much retard reform as that which misleads public opinion; and what is more calculated to mislead public opinion than works which, in advocating freedom, invoke aid from the doctrines of monopoly?

Some years ago three of the great towns of France—Lyons, Bordeaux, and Havre—united in a movement against the restrictive *regime.* All Europe was stirred on seeing raised what they took for the banner of liberty. Alas! it proved to be also the banner of monopoly—of a monopoly a little more niggardly and much more absurd than that of which they seemed to desire the overthrow. By the aid of the sophism which I have just endeavoured to expose, the petitioners did nothing more than reproduce the doctrine of protection to national industry, tacking to it an additional inconsistency.

It was, in fact, nothing else than the *regime* of prohibition. Just listen to M. de Saint-Cricq:—

"Labour constitutes the wealth of a nation, because labour alone creates those material objects which our wants demand; and universal ease and comfort consist in the abundance of these things." So much for the principle.

"But this abundance must be produced by *national labour.* If it were the result of foreign labour, national labour would be immediately brought to a stand." Here lies the error. *(See the preceding sophism.)*

"What course should an agricultural and manufacturing country take under such circumstances? Reserve its markets for the products of its own soil and of its own industry." Such is the end and design.

"And for that purpose, restrain by duties, and, if necessary, prohibit importation of the products of the soil and industry of other nations." Such are the means.

Let us compare this system with that which the Bordeaux petition advocates.

Commodities are there divided into three classes:—

"The first includes provisions, and *raw materials upon which no human labour has been bestowed. In principle, a wise economy would demand that this class should be free of duties.* Here we have no labour, no protection.

"The second consists of products which have, *to some extent, been prepared.* This preparation warrants such products being *charged with a certain amount of duty.*" Here protection begins, because here, according to the petitioners, begins *national labour.*

"The third comprises goods and products in their finished and perfect state. These contribute nothing to national labour, and we regard this class as the most taxable." Here labour, and production along with it, reach their maximum.

We thus see that the petitioners profess their belief in the doctrine, that foreign labour is injurious to national labour; and this is the *error* of the prohibitive system.

They demand that the home market should be reserved for home industry. That is the *design* of the system of prohibition.

They demand that foreign labour should be subjected to restrictions and taxes. These are the means employed by the system of prohibition.

What difference, then, can we possibly discover between the Bordeaux petitioners and the Corypheus of restriction? One difference, and one only—the greater or less extension given to the word labour.

M. de Saint-Cricq extends it to everything, and so he wishes to protect all.

"Labour constitutes all the wealth of a people," he says; "to protect agricultural industry, and all agricultural industry; to protect manufacturing industry, and all manufacturing industry, is the cry which should never cease to be heard in this Chamber."

The Bordeaux petitioners take no labour into account but that of the manufacturers; and for that reason they would admit them to the benefits of protection.

"Raw materials are commodities upon which no human labour has been bestowed. In principle, we should not tax them. Manufactured products can no longer serve the cause of national industry, and we regard them as the best subjects for taxation."

It is not our business in this place to inquire whether protection to national industry is reasonable. M. de Saint-Cricq and the Bordeaux gentlemen are at one upon this point, and, as we have shown in the preceding chapters, we on this subject differ from both.

Our present business is to discover whether it is by M. de Saint-Cricq, or by the Bordeaux petitioners, that the word labour is used in a correct sense.

Now, in this view of the question, we think that M. de Saint-Cricq has very much the best of it; and to prove this, we may suppose them to hold some such dialogue as the following:—

M. de Saint-Cricq: You grant that national labour should be protected. You grant that the products of no foreign labour can be introduced into our market without superseding a corresponding amount of our national labour. Only, you contend that there are a multiplicity of products possessed of value (for they sell), but upon which no human labour has been bestowed [vierges de tout travail humain]. And you enumerate, among other things, com, flour, meat, cattle, tallow, salt, iron, copper, lead, coal, wools, hides, seeds, etc.

If you will only prove to me that the value of these things is not due to labour, I will grant that it is useless to protect them.

But, on the other hand, if I demonstrate to you that there is as much labour worked up in a 100 fr. worth of wool as in a 100 fr. worth of textile fabrics, you will allow that the one is as worthy of protection as the other.

Now, why is this sack of wool worth 100 fr.? Is it not because that is its cost price? and what does its cost price represent, but the aggregate wages of all the labour, and profits of all the capital, which have contributed to the production of the commodity?

The Bordeaux Petitioners: Well, perhaps as regards wool you may be right. But take the case of a sack of corn, a bar of iron, a hundredweight of coals,—are these commodities produced by labour? Are they not created by nature?

M. de Saint-Cricq: Undoubtedly nature creates the elements of all these things, but it is labour which produces the value. I was wrong myself in saying that labour created material objects, and that vicious form of expression has led me into other errors. It does not belong to man to create, to make anything out of nothing, be he agriculturist or manufacturer; and if by production is meant creation, all our labour must be marked down as unproductive, and yours, as merchants, more unproductive than all others, excepting perhaps my own.

The agriculturist, then, cannot pretend to have created corn, but he has created value; I mean to say, he has, by his labour, and that of his servants, labourers, reapers, etc., transformed into corn substances which had no resemblance to it whatever. The miller who converts the corn into flour, the baker who converts the flour into bread, do the same thing.

In order that man may be enabled to clothe himself, a multitude of operations are necessary. Prior to all intervention of human labour, the true raw materials of cloth are the air, the water, the heat, the gases, the light, the salts, which enter into its composition. These are the raw materials upon which strictly speaking, no human labour has been employed. They are *vierges de tout travail humain*; and since they have no value, I should never dream of protecting them. But the first application of labour converts these substances into grass and provender, a second into wool, a third into yarn, a fourth into a woven fabric, a fifth into clothing. Who can assert that the whole of these operations, from the first furrow laid open by the plough, to the last stitch of the tailor's needle, do not resolve themselves into labour?

And it is because these operations are spread over several branches of industry, in order to accelerate and facilitate the accomplishment of the ultimate object, which is to furnish clothing to those who have need of it, that you desire, by an arbitrary distinction, to rank the importance of such works in the order in which they succeed each other, so that the first of the series shall not merit even the name of labour, and that the last, being labour *par excellence*, shall be worthy of the favours of protection?

The Petitioners: Yes; we begin to see that corn, like wool, is not exactly a product of which it can be said that no human labour has been bestowed upon it; but the agriculturist has not, at least, like the manufacturer, done everything himself or by means of his workmen; nature has assisted him, and if there is labour worked up in corn, it is not the simple product of labour.

M. de Saint-Cricq: But its value resolves itself exclusively into labour. I am happy that nature concurs in the material formation of grain. I could even wish that it were entirely her work; but you must allow that I have constrained this assistance of nature by my labour, and when I sell you my corn you will remark this, that it is not for the labour of nature that I ask you to pay, but for my own.

But, as you state the case, manufactured commodities are no longer the exclusive products of labour. Is the manufacturer not beholden to nature in his processes? Does he not avail himself of the assistance of the steam-engine, of the pressure of the atmosphere, just as, with the assistance of the plough, I avail myself of its humidity? Has he created the laws of gravitation, of the transmission of forces, of affinity?

The Petitioners: Well, this is the case of the wool over again; but coal is assuredly the work, the exclusive work, of nature. It is indeed a product upon which no human labour has ever been bestowed.

M. de Saint-Cricq: Yes; nature has undoubtedly created the coal, but labour has imparted value to it. For the millions of years during which it was buried 100 fathoms under ground, unknown to everybody, it was destitute of value. It was necessary to search for it—that is labour; it was necessary to send it to market—that is additional labour. Then the price you pay for it in the market is nothing else than the remuneration of the labour of mining and transport.*

** I do not particularize the parts of the remuneration falling to the lessee, the capitalist, etc., for several reasons:—1st, Because, on looking at the thing more closely, you will see that the remuneration always resolves itself into the reimbursement of advances or the payment of anterior labour. 2dly, Because, under the term labour, I include not only the wages of the workmen, but the legitimate recompense of everything which co-operates in the work of production. 3dly (and above all), Because the production of manufactured products is, like that of raw materials, burdened with auxiliary remunerations other than the mere expense of manual labour; and, moreover, this objection, frivolous* *in itself, would apply as much to the most delicate processes of manufacture, as to the rudest operations of agriculture.*

Thus far we see that M. de Saint-Cricq has the best of the argument; that the value of raw materials, like that of manufactured commodities, represents the cost of production, that is to say, the labour worked up in them; that it is not possible to conceive of a product possessing value, which has had no human labour bestowed on it; that the distinction made by the petitioners is futile in theory; that, as the basis of an unequal distribution of favours, it would be iniquitous in practice, since the result would be that one-third of our countrymen, who happened to be engaged in manufactures, would obtain the advantages of monopoly, on the alleged ground that they produce by labour, whilst the other two-thirds—namely, the agricultural population—would be abandoned to competition under the pretext that they produce without labour.

The rejoinder to this, I am quite sure, will be, that a nation derives more advantages from importing what are called raw materials, whether produced by labour or not, and exporting manufactured commodities. This will be repeated and insisted on, and it is an opinion very widely accredited.

"The more abundant raw materials are," says the Bordeaux petition, "the more are manufactures promoted and multiplied."

"Raw materials," says the same document in another place, "open up an unlimited field of work for the inhabitants of the countries into which they are imported."

"Raw materials," says the Havre petition, "constituting as they do the elements of labour, must be submitted to a different treatment, and be gradually admitted at the lowest rate of duty." The same petition expresses a wish that manufactured products should be admitted, not gradually, but after an indefinite lapse of time, not at the lowest rate of duty, but at a duty of 20 per cent.

"Among other articles, the low price and abundance of which are a necessity," says the Lyons petition, "manufacturers include all raw materials."

All this is founded on an illusion.

We have seen that all value represents labour. Now, it is quite true that manufacturing labour increases tenfold, sometimes a hundredfold, the value of the raw material; that is to say, it yields ten times, a hundred times, more profit to the nation. Hence men are led to reason thus: The production of a hundredweight of iron brings in a gain of only fifteen shillings to workmen of all classes. The conversion of this hundredweight of iron into the mainsprings of watches raises their earnings to £500; and will any one venture to say that a nation has not a greater interest to secure for its labour a gain of five hundred pounds than a gain of fifteen shillings? We do not exchange a hundredweight of unwrought iron for a hundredweight of watch-springs, nor a hundredweight of unwashed wool for a hundredweight of cashmere shawls; but we exchange a certain value of one of these materials for an equal value of another. Now, to exchange equal value for equal value is to exchange equal labour for equal labour. It is not true, then, that a nation which sells five pounds' worth of wrought fabrics or watch-springs, gains more than a nation which sells five pounds' worth of wool or iron.

In a country where no law can be voted, where no tax can be imposed, but with the consent of those whose dealings the law is to regulate, and whose pockets the tax is to affect, the public cannot be robbed without first being imposed on and misled.

Our ignorance is the raw material of every extortion from which we suffer, and we may be certain beforehand, that every sophism is the precursor of an act of plunder. My good friends I when you detect a sophism in a petition, button up your breeches-pocket, for you may be sure that this is the mark aimed at.

Let us see, then, what is the real object secretly aimed at by the shipowners of Bordeaux and Havre, and the manufacturers of Lyons, and which is concealed under the distinction which they attempt to draw between agricultural and manufactured commodities.

"It is principally this first class (that which comprises raw materials, upon which no human labour has been bestowed) which affords," say the Bordeaux petitioners, "the principal support to our merchant shipping...." In principle, a wise economy would not tax this class.... The second (commodities partly wrought up) may be taxed to a certain extent. The third (commodities which call for no more exertion of labour) we regard as the fittest subjects of taxation.

The Havre petitioners "consider that it is indispensable to reduce gradually the duty on raw materials to the lowest rate, in order that our manufacturers may gradually find employment for the shipping interest, which furnishes them with the first and indispensable materials of labour."

The manufacturers could not remain behindhand in politeness towards the shipowners. So the Lyons petition asks for the free introduction of raw materials, "in order to prove," as they express it, "that the interests of the manufacturing are not always opposed to those of the maritime towns."

No; but then the interests of both, understood as the petitioners understand them, are in direct opposition to the interests of agriculture and of consumers.

Well, gentlemen, we have come at length to see what you are aiming at, and the object of your subtle economical distinctions. You desire that the law should restrain the transport of finished goods across the ocean, in order that the more costly conveyance of raw and rough materials, bulky, and mixed up with refuse, should afford greater scope for your merchant shipping, and more largely employ your marine resources. This is what you call a wise economy.

On the same principle, why do you not ask that the pines of Russia should be brought to you with their branches, bark, and roots; the silver of Mexico in its mineral state; the hides of Buenos Ayres sticking to the bones of the diseased carcases from which they have been torn?

I expect that railway shareholders, the moment they are in a majority in the Chambers, will proceed to make a law forbidding the manufacture of the brandy which is consumed in Paris. And why not? Would not a law enforcing the conveyance of ten casks of wine for every cask of brandy afford Parisian industry the indispensable materials of its labour, and give employment to our locomotive resources?

How long will men shut their eyes to this simple truth?

Manufactures, shipping, labour—all have for end the general, the public good; to create useless industries, to favour superfluous conveyances, to support a greater amount of labour than is necessary, not for the good of the public, but at the expense of the public—is to realize a true *petitio principii.* It is not labour which is desirable for its own sake; it is consumption. All labour without a commensurate result is a loss.

You may as well pay sailors for pitching stones into the sea as pay them for transporting useless refuse. Thus, we arrive at the result to which all economic sophisms, numerous as they are, conduct us, namely, confounding the means with the end, and developing the one at the expense of the other.

XXII. METAPHORS.

A sophism sometimes expands, and runs through the whole texture of a long and elaborate theory. More frequently, it shrinks and contracts, assumes the guise of a principle, and lurks in a word or a phrase.

May God protect us from the devil and from metaphors! was the exclamation of Paul-Louis. And it is difficult to say which of them has done most mischief in this world of ours. The devil, you will say; for he has put the spirit of plunder into all our hearts. True, but he has left free the means of repressing abuses by the resistance of those who suffer from them. It is the sophism which paralyzes this resistance. The sword which malice puts into the hands of assailants would be powerless, did sophistry not break the buckler which should shield the party assailed. It was with reason, therefore, that Malebranche inscribed on the title-page of his work this sentence: *L'erreur est la cause de la misère des hommes.*

Let us see in what way this takes place. Ambitious men are often actuated by sinister and wicked intentions; their design, for example, may be to implant in the public mind the germ of international hatred. This fatal germ may develop itself, light up a general conflagration, arrest civilization, cause torrents of blood to be shed, and bring upon the country the most terrible of all scourges, invasion. At any rate, and apart from this, such sentiments of hatred lower us in the estimation of other nations, and force Frenchmen who retain any sense of justice to blush for their country. These are undoubtedly most serious evils; and to guard the public against the underhand practices of those who would expose the country to such hazard, it is only necessary to see clearly into their designs. How do they manage to conceal them? By the use of metaphors. They twist, distort, and pervert the meaning of three or four words, and the thing is done.

The word *invasion* itself is a good illustration of this.

A French ironmaster exclaims: Preserve us from the invasion of English iron. An English landowner exclaims in return: Preserve us from the invasion of French corn. And then they proceed to interpose barriers between the two countries. These barriers create isolation, isolation gives rise to hatred, hatred to war, war to invasion. What does it signify? cry the two sophists; is it not better to expose ourselves to an eventual invasion than accept an invasion which is certain? And the people believe them, and the barriers are kept up.

And yet what analogy is there between an exchange and an invasion? What possible similarity can be imagined between a ship of war which comes to vomit fire and devastation on our towns, and a merchant ship which comes to offer a free voluntary exchange of commodities for commodities?

The same thing holds of the use made of the word *inundation.* This word is ordinarily used in a bad sense, for we often see our fields injured, and our harvests carried away by floods. If, however, they leave on our soil something of greater value than what they carry away, like the inundations of the Nile, we should be thankful for them, as the Egyptians are. Before we declaim, then, against the inundations of foreign products—before proceeding to restrain them by irksome and costly obstacles—we should inquire to what class they belong, and whether they ravage or fertilize. What should we think of Mehemet Ali, if, instead of raising, at great cost, bars across the Nile, to extend wider its inundations, he were to spend his money in digging a deeper channel to prevent Egypt being soiled by the foreign slime which descends upon her from the Mountains of the Moon? We display exactly the same degree of wisdom and sense, when we desire, at the cost of millions, to defend our country.... From what? From the benefits which nature has bestowed on other climates.

Among the metaphors which conceal a pernicious theory, there is no one more in use than that presented by the words *tribute and tributary.*

These words have now become so common that they are used as synonymous with *purchase and purchaser*, and are employed indiscriminately.

And yet a tribute is as different from a purchase as a theft is from an exchange; and I should like quite as well to hear it said, Cartouche has broken into my strong-box and purchased a thousand pounds, as to hear one of our deputies repeat, We have paid Germany tribute for a thousand horses which she has sold us.

For what distinguishes the act of Cartouche from a purchase is, that he has not put into my strong-box, and with my consent, a value equivalent to what he has taken out of it.

And what distinguishes our remittance of £20,000 which we have made to Germany from a tribute paid to her is this, that she has not received the money gratuitously, but has given us in exchange a thousand horses, which we have judged to be worth the £20,000.

Is it worth while exposing seriously such an abuse of language? Yes; for these terms are used seriously both in newspapers and in books.

Do not let it be supposed that these are instances of a mere *lapsus linguo* on the part of certain ignorant writers! For one writer who abstains from so using them, I will point you out ten who admit them, and amongst the rest, the D'Argouts, the Dupins, the Villeles—peers, deputies, ministers of state,—men, in short, whose words are laws, and whose sophisms, even the most transparent, serve as a basis for the government of the country.

A celebrated modern philosopher has added to the categories of Aristotle the sophism which consists in employing a phrase which includes a *petitio pinncipii.* He gives many examples of it; and he should have added the word tributary to his list. The business, in fact, is to discover whether purchases made from foreigners are useful or hurtful. They are hurtful, you say. And why? Because they render us tributaries to the foreigner. This is just to use a word which implies the very thing to be proved.

It may be asked how this abuse of words first came to be introduced into the rhetoric of the monopolists?

Money leaves the country to satisfy the rapacity of a victorious enemy. Money also leaves the country to pay for commodities. An analogy is established between the two cases by taking into account only the points in which they resemble each other, and keeping out of view the points in which they differ.

Yet this circumstance—that is to say, the non-reimbursement in the first case, and the reimbursement voluntarily agreed upon in the second—establishes betwixt them such a difference that it is really impossible to class them in the same category. To hand over a hundred pounds by force to a man who has caught you by the throat, or to hand them over voluntarily to a man who furnishes you with what you want, are things as different as light and darkness. You might as well assert that it is a matter of indifference whether you throw your bread into the river, or eat it, for in both cases the bread is destroyed. The vice of this reasoning, like that applied to the word tribute, consists in asserting an entire similitude between two cases, looking only at their points of resemblance, and keeping out of sight the points in which they differ.

CONCLUSION.

All the sophisms which I have hitherto exposed have reference to a single question—the system of restriction. There are other tempting subjects, such as *vested interests, inopportuneness, draining away our money*, etc., etc., with which I shall not at present trouble the reader.

Nor does Social Economy confine herself to this limited circle. *Fourierisme, Saint-Simonisme*, communism, mysticism, sentimentalism, false philanthropy, affected aspirations after a chimerical equality and fraternity; questions relating to luxury, to wages, to machinery, to the pretended tyranny of capital, to colonies, to markets and vents for produce, to conquests, to population, to association, emigration, taxes, and loans,—have encumbered the field of science with a multiplicity of parasitical arguments, of sophisms which afford work to the hoe and the grubber of the diligent economist.

I am quite aware of the inconvenience attending this plan, or rather of this absence of plan. To attack one by one so many incoherent sophisms, which sometimes run foul of each other, and more frequently run into each other, is to enter into an irregular and capricious struggle, and involve ourselves in perpetual repetitions.

How much I should prefer to explain simply the situation in which things are, without occupying myself with the thousand aspects under which ignorance sees them!... To explain the laws under which societies prosper or decay, is to demolish virtually all these sophisms at once. When Laplace described all that was then known of the movements of the heavenly bodies, he dissipated, without even naming them, all the reveries of the Egyptian, Greek, and Hindoo astrologers far more effectually than he could have done by refuting them directly in innumerable volumes. Truth is one, and the work which explains it is an edifice at once durable and imposing:

Il brave les tyrans avides,
Plus hardi que les Pyramides
Et plus durable que l'airain.

Error is multifarious and of an ephemeral nature; and the work which combats it does not carry in itself a principle of greatness and duration.

But if the power, and perhaps the occasion, have been wanting to enable me to proceed in the manner of Laplace and of Say, I cannot help thinking that the form I have adopted has also its modest utility. It seems to me well suited to the wants of our day, and the occasional moments which are set aside for study.

A treatise has no doubt unquestionable superiority, but on one condition—namely, that it is read and carefully pondered and thought over. It is addressed to a select class of readers. Its mission is to fix first of all, and afterwards enlarge, the circle of our acquired knowledge.

A refutation of vulgar errors and prejudices cannot occupy this high position. It aspires merely to clear the road before the march of truth, to prepare men's minds for its reception, to rectify public opinion, and disarm dangerous ignorance.

It is, above all, in the department of Social Economy that this hand-to-hand struggle, that these constantly-recurring battles with popular errors, are of true practical utility.

The sciences may be divided into two classes.

One of these classes may be known only to *savans*. It includes those sciences the application of which constitutes the business of special professions. The vulgar reap the fruit, in spite of their ignorance. A man may find use for a watch, though ignorant of mechanics and astronomy, and he may be carried along by a locomotive or a steamer, trusting to the skill of the engineer and the pilot. We walk according to the laws of equilibrium, although unacquainted with these laws, just as M. Jourdain had talked prose all his life without knowing it.

But there are sciences which exercise on the public mind an influence which is only in proportion to public enlightenment, and derive all their efficacy, not from knowledge accumulated in some gifted minds, but from knowledge diffused over the general masses. Among these we include morals, medicine, social economy, and, in countries where men are their own masters, Politics. It is to such sciences that the saying of Bentham specially applies, "To disseminate them is better than to advance them." What signifies it, that some great man, or even that God himself, should have promulgated the laws of morality, as long as men, imbued with false notions, mistake virtues for vices, and vices for virtues? What matters it that Smith, Say, and, according to M. de Saint-Chamans, economists of all schools, have proclaimed, in reference to commercial transactions, the superiority of liberty over constraint, if the men who make our laws, and for whom our laws are made, think differently?

Those sciences, which have been correctly named social, have also this peculiarity, that being of universal and daily application, no one will confess himself ignorant of them. When the business is to resolve a question in chemistry or geometry, no one pretends to have acquired these sciences by intuition, no one is ashamed to consult M. Thenard, or makes any difficulty about referring to the works of Legendre or Bezout. But in the social sciences, authority is scarcely acknowledged. As each man daily takes charge of his morals, whether good or bad, of his health, of his purse, of his politics, whether sound or absurd, so each man believes himself qualified to discuss, comment, and pronounce judgment on social questions. Are you ill? There is no old woman who will not at once tell you the cause of your ailment, and the remedy for it. "Humours," she will say; "you must take physic." But what are humours? and is there any such disease? About this she gives herself no concern. I cannot help thinking of this old woman when I hear social maladies explained by these hackneyed phrases:—"The superabundance of products," "the tyranny of capital," "an industrial plethora," and other such commonplaces, of which we cannot even say, *Verba et voces, protereaque nihil*, for they are so many pestilent errors.

From what I have said, two things result—1st, That the social sciences must abound more in sophisms than others, because in them each man takes counsel of his own judgment and instincts; 2d, That it is in these sciences that sophisms are especially mischievous, because they mislead public opinion, and in a matter, too, with reference to which public opinion is force, is law.

In these sciences, then, we have need of two sorts of books, those which explain them, and those which further and advance them—those which establish truth, and those which combat error.

It seems to me that the inherent fault of this little work, repetition, is exactly what will make it useful.

In the question I have treated, each sophism has undoubtedly its own formula, and its special bearing, but all may be traced to a common root, which is, *forgetting men's interests as consumers*. To point out that a thousand errors may be traced to this prolific sophism, is to teach the public to detect it, to estimate it at its true worth, and to distrust it, under all circumstances.

After all, the design of my present work is not exactly to implant convictions, but rather to awaken doubts.

I have no expectation that the reader, on laying down the book, will exclaim *I know*; I would much rather that he should say candidly, *I am ignorant!*

"I am ignorant, for I begin to fear that there is something illusory in the flattering promises of scarcity." (Sophism I.)

"I am not so much charmed with obstacles as I once was. (Sophism II.)

"*Effort without result* no longer appears to me so desirable as *result without effort*." (Sophism III.)

"It is very possible that the secret of trade does not consist, like the secret of arms (if we adopt the definition of the bully in the *Bourgeois Gentilhomme*), in giving and not receiving." (Sophism VI.)

"I can understand that a commodity is worth more in proportion as it has had more labour bestowed upon it; but in exchange, will two equal values cease to be equal values, because the one proceeds from the plough, and the other from the loom?" (Sophism XXI.)

"I confess that I begin to think it singular that the human race should be improved by shackles, and enriched by taxes; and, truth to say, I should be relieved of a troublesome weight, I should experience unmitigated satisfaction, were it proved to me, as the author of the *Sophismes* asserts, that there is no incompatibility between thriving circumstances and justice, between peace and liberty, between the extension of labour and the progress of intelligence." (Sophisms XIV. and XX.)

"Then, without being quite convinced by his arguments, to which I know not whether to give the name of reasonings or of paradoxes, I shall apply myself to the acknowledged masters of the science."

Let us conclude this monography of sophism with a final and important observation.

The world is not sufficiently alive to the influence exercised over it by sophisms.

If I must speak my mind, when the *right of the strongest* has been put aside, sophisms have set up in its place *the right of the most cunning*; and it is difficult to say which of these two tryants has been the more fatal to humanity.

Men have an immoderate love of enjoyment, of influence, of consideration, of power—in a word, of wealth.

At the same time, they are urged on by a strong, an overpowering, inclination to procure the things they so much desire, at the expense of other people.

But these other people—in plain language, the public—have an equally strong desire to keep what they have got, if they can, and if they know it.

Spoliation, which plays so great a part in this world's affairs, has, then, only two agents at command, *force and cunning*; and two limits, *courage and intelligence.*

Force employed to effect spoliation forms the groundwork of human annals. To trace back its history, would be to reproduce very nearly the history of all nations—Assyrians, Babylonians, Medes, Persians, Egyptians, Greeks, Romans, Goths, Franks, Huns, Turks, Arabs, Monguls, Tartars; not to speak of Spaniards in America, Englishmen in India, Frenchmen in Africa, Russians in Asia, etc.

But civilized nations, at least, composed of men who produce wealth, have become sufficiently numerous, and sufficiently strong to defend themselves. Does this mean that they are no longer plundered? Not at all; they are plundered as much as ever, and, what is more, they plunder one another.

Only, the agent employed has been changed; it is no longer by *force, but by cunning*, that they seize upon the public wealth.

To rob the public, we must first deceive it. The trick consists in persuading the public that the theft is for its advantage; and by this means inducing it to accept, in exchange for its property, services which are fictitious, and often worse. Hence comes the Sophism,—Sophism theocratic, Sophism economic, Sophism political, Sophism financial. Since; then, force is held in check, the Sophism is not only an evil, but the very genius of evil It must in its turn be held in check also. And for that end we must render the public more cunning than the cunning, as it has already become stronger than the strong.

Good Public! it is under the influence of this conviction that I dedicate to you this first essay—although the preface is strangely transposed, and the dedication somewhat late.

SECOND SERIES.

I. PHYSIOLOGY OF SPOLIATION.

Why should I go on tormenting myself with this dry and dreary science of *Political Economy?*

Why? The question is reasonable. Labour of every kind is in itself sufficiently repugnant to warrant one in asking to what result it leads?

Let us see, then, how it is.

I do not address myself to those philosophers who profess to adore poverty, if not on their own account, at least on the part of the human race.

I speak to those who deem wealth, of some importance. We understand by that word, not the opulence of some classes, but the ease, the material prosperity, the security, the independence, the instruction, the dignity of all.

There are only two means of procuring the necessaries, conveniences, and enjoyments of life: Production and Spoliation.

There are some people who represent Spoliation as an accident, a local and transient abuse, branded by the moralist, denounced by the law, and unworthy of the Economist's attention.

In spite of benevolence, in spite of optimism, we are forced to acknowledge that Spoilation plays too prominent a part in the world, and mingles too largely in important human affairs, to warrant the social sciences, especially Political Economy, in holding it as of no account.

I go further. That which prevents the social order from attaining that perfection of which it is susceptible, is the constant effort of its members to live and enjoy themselves at the expense of each other. So that if Spoliation did not exist, social science would be without object, for society would then be perfect.

I go further still. When Spoliation has once become the recognised means of existence of a body of men united and held together by social ties, they soon proceed to frame a law which sanctions it, and to adopt a system of morals which sanctities it.

It is sufficient to enumerate some of the more glaring forms which Spoliation assumes, in order to show the place which it occupies in human transactions.

There is first of all War. Among savages the conqueror puts to death the vanquished, in order to acquire a right, which, if not incontestable, is, at least, uncontested, to his enemy's hunting grounds.

Then comes Slavery. When man comes to find that the land may be made fertile by means of labour, he says to his brother man, "Thine be the labour, and mine the product."

Next we have Priestcraft. "According as you give or refuse me a portion of your substance, I will open to you the gate of Heaven or of Hell."

Lastly comes Monopoly. Its distinguishing character is to leave in existence the great social law of service for service, but to bring force to bear upon the bargain, so as to impair the just proportion between the service received and the service rendered.

Spoliation bears always in its bosom that germ of death by which it is ultimately destroyed. It is rarely the many who despoil the few. Were it so, the few would soon be reduced to such a state as to be no longer able to satisfy the cupidity of the many, and spoliation would die out for want of support.

It is almost always the majority who are oppressed, but spoliation is not the less on this account subject to an inevitable check.

For, if the agent be Force, as in the cases of War and Slavery, it is natural that Force, in the long run, should pass to the side of the greatest number.

And, if the agent be Cunning, as in the case of Priestcraft and Monopoly, it is natural that the majority should become enlightened, otherwise intelligence would cease to be intelligence.

Another natural law deposits a second germ of death in the heart of spoliation, which is this:

Spoliation not only *displaces* wealth, but always partially *destroys* it.

War annihilates many values.

Slavery paralyzes, to a great extent, men's faculties.

Priestcraft diverts men's efforts towards objects which are puerile or hurtful.

Monopoly transfers wealth from one pocket to another, but much is lost in the transference.

This is an admirable law. Without it, provided there existed an equilibrium between the forces of the oppressors and oppressed, spoliation would have no limits. In consequence of the operation of this law, the equilibrium tends always to be upset; either because the spoliators have the fear of such a loss of wealth, or because, in the absence of such fear, the evil constantly increases, and it is in the nature of anything which constantly gets worse and worse, ultimately to perish and be annihilated.

There comes at last a time when, in its progressive acceleration, this loss of wealth is such that the spoliator finds himself poorer than he would have been had there been no spoliation.

Take, for example, a people to whom the expense of war costs more than the value of the booty.

A master who pays dearer for slave labour than for free labour.

A system of priestcraft, which, renders people so dull and stupid, and destroys their energy to such an extent, that there is no longer anything to be got from them.

A monopoly which increases its efforts at absorption in proportion as there is less to absorb, just as one should endeavour to milk a cow more vigorously in proportion as there is less milk to be got.

Monopoly, it will be seen, is a species of the genus spoliation. There are many varieties; among others, Sinecures, Privileges, Restrictions.

Among the forms which it assumes, there are some which are very simple and primitive. Of this kind are feudal rights. Under this *regime* the masses are despoiled, and they know it. It implies an abuse of force, and goes down when force is wanting.

Others are very complicated. The masses are frequently despoiled without knowing it. They may even imagine that they owe all to spoliation—not only what is left to them, but what is taken from them, and what is lost in the process. Nay more, I affirm that, in course of time, and owing to the ingenious mechanism to which they become accustomed, many men become spoliators without knowing that they are so, or desiring to be so. Monopolies of this kind are engendered by artifice and nourished by error. They disappear only with advancing enlightenment.

I have said enough to show that political economy has an evident practical utility. It is the torch which, by exposing craft and dissipating error, puts an end to this social disorder of spoliation. Some one—I rather think a lady—has rightly described our science as "*la serrure de sûrete du pecule populaire.*"

COMMENTARY.

Were this little book destined to last for three or four thousand years, and, like a new Koran, to be read, re-read, pondered over, and studied sentence by sentence, word by word, letter by letter; if it were destined to a place in all the libraries of the world, and to be explained by avalanches of annotations and paraphrases, I might abandon to their fate the preceding observations, though somewhat obscure from their conciseness; but since they require a gloss, I think it as well to be my own commentator.

The true and equitable law of human transactions is the *exchange, freely bargained for, of service for service.* Spoliation consists in banishing by force or artifice this liberty of bargaining, for the purpose of enabling a man or a class to receive a service without rendering an equivalent service.

Spoliation by force consists in waiting till a man has produced a commodity, and then depriving him of it by the strong hand.

This kind of spoliation is formally forbidden by the decalogue—*Thou shalt not steal.*

When this takes place between individuals, it is called theft, and leads to the hulks; when it takes place between nations, it is called *conquest, and leads to glory.*

Whence this difference? It is proper to search out its caùse, for it will reveal to us the existence of an irresistible power, public opinion, which, like the atmosphere, surrounds and envelops us so thoroughly that we cease to perceive it. Rousseau never said anything truer than this: *Il faut beaucoup de philosophie pour observer les faits qui sont trop près de nous*—"You need much philosophy to observe accurately things which are under your nose."

A thief for the very reason that he does his work secretly, has always public opinion against him. He frightens all who are within his reach. Yet if he has associates, he takes pride in displaying before them his skill and prowess. Here we begin to perceive the force of opinion; for the applause of his accomplices takes away the sense of guilt, and even prompts him to glory in his shame.

The *warrior* lives in a different medium. The public opinion which brands him is elsewhere, among the nations he has conquered, and he does not feel its pressure. The public opinion at home applauds and sustains him. He and his companions in arms feel sensibly the bond which imites them. The country which has created enemies, and brought danger upon herself, feels it necessary to extol the bravery of her sons. She decrees to the boldest, who have enlarged her frontiers, or brought her, in the greatest amount of booty, honours, renown, and glory. Poets sing their exploits, and ladies twine wreaths and garlands for them. And such is the power of public opinion that it takes from spoliation all idea of injustice, and from the spoliator all sense of wrongdoing.

The public opinion which reacts against military spoliation makes itself felt, not in the conquering, but in the conquered, country, and exercises little influence. And yet it is not altogether inoperative, and makes itself the more felt in proportion as nations have more frequent intercourse, and understand each other better. In consequence, we see that the study of languages, and a freer communication between nations, tends to bring about and render predominant a stronger feeling against this species of spoliation.

Unfortunately, it not unfrequently happens that the nations which surround an aggressive and warlike people are themselves given to spoliation when they can accomplish it, and thus become imbued with the same prejudices.

In that case there is only one remedy—time; and nations must be taught by painful experience the enormous evils of mutual spoliation.

We may note another check—a superior and growing morality. But the object of this is to multiply virtuous actions. How then can morality restrain acts of spoliation when public opinion places such acts in the rank of the most exalted virtue? What more powerful means of rendering a people moral than religion? And what religion more favourable to peace than Christianity? Yet what have we witnessed for eighteen hundred years? During all these ages we have seen men fight, not only in spite of their religion, but in name of religion itself.

The wars waged by a conquering nation are not always offensive and aggressive wars. Such a nation is sometimes so unfortunate as to be obliged to send its soldiers into the field to defend the domestic hearth, and to protect its families, its property, its independence, and its liberty. War then assumes a character of grandeur and sacredness. The national banner, blessed by the ministers of the God of peace, represents all that is most sacred in the land; it is followed as the living image of patriotism and of honour; and warlike virtues are extolled above all other virtues. But when the danger is past, public opinion still prevails; and by the natural reaction of a spirit of revenge, which is mistaken for patriotism, the banner is paraded from capital to capital. It is in this way that nature seems to prepare a punishment for the aggressor.

It is the fear of this punishment, and not the progress of philosophy, which retains arms in the arsenals; for we cannot deny that nations the most advanced in civilization go to war, and think little of justice when they have no reprisals to fear, as the Himalaya, the Atlas, and the Caucasus bear witness.

If religion is powerless, and if philosophy is equally powerless, how then are wars to be put an end to?

Political economy demonstrates, that even as regards the nation which proves victorious; war is always made in the interest of the few, and at the expense of the masses. When the masses, then, shall see this clearly, the weight of public opinion, which is now divided, will come to be entirely on the side of peace.

Spoliation by force assumes still another form. No man will engage voluntarily in the business of production in order to be robbed of what he produces. Man himself is therefore laid hold of, robbed of his freedom and personality, and forced to labour. The language held to him is not, "*If you do this for me, I will do that for you;*" *but this,* "*Yours be the fatigue, and mine the enjoyment.*" This is slavery, which always implies abuse of force.

It is important to inquire whether it is not in the very nature of a force which is incontestably dominant to commit abuses. For my own part, I should be loath to trust it, and would as soon expect a stone pitched from a height to stop midway of its own accord, as absolute power to prescribe limits to itself.

I should like, at least, to have pointed out to me a country and an epoch in which slavery has been abolished by the free, graceful, and voluntary act of the masters.

Slavery affords a second and striking example of the insufficiency of religious and philanthropical sentiments, when set in opposition to the powerful and energetic sentiment of self-interest. This may appear a melancholy view of the subject to certain modern schools who seek for the renovating principle of society in self-sacrifice. Let them begin, then, by reforming human nature.

In the West Indies, ever since the introduction of slavery, the masters, from father to son, have professed the Christian religion. Many times a day they repeat these words, "All men are brethren: to love your neighbour is to fulfil the whole law."

And they continue to have slaves. Nothing appears to them more natural and legitimate. Do modern reformers expect that their system of morals will ever be as universally accepted,' as popular, of as great authority, and be as much on men's lips, as the Gospel? And if the Gospel has not been able to penetrate from the lips to the heart, by piercing or surmounting the formidable barrier of self-interest, how can they expect that their system of morals is to work this miracle?

What! is slavery then invulnerable? No; what has introduced it will destroy it, I mean self-interest; provided that, in favouring the special interests which have created this scourge, we do not run counter to the general interests from which we look for the remedy.

It is one of the truths which political economy has demonstrated, that free labour is essentially progressive, and slave labour necessarily stationary. The triumph of the former, therefore, over the latter is inevitable. What has become of the culture of indigo by slave labour?

Free labour directed to the production of sugar will lower its price more and more, and slave property will become less and less valuable to the owners. Slavery would long since have gone down of its own accord in America, if in Europe our laws had not raised the price of sugar artificially. It is for this reason that we see the masters, their creditors, and their delegates working actively to maintain these laws, which are at present the pillars of the edifice.

Unfortunately, they still carry along with them the sympathies of those populations from among whom slavery has disappeared, and this again shows how powerful an agent public opinion is.

If public opinion is sovereign, even in the region of Force, it is very much more so in the region of Craft [*Ruse*], In truth, this is its true domain. Cunning is the abuse of intelligence, and public opinion is the progress of intelligence. These two powers are at least of the same nature. Imposture on the part of the spoliator implies credulity on the part of those despoiled, and the natural antidote to credulity is truth. Hence it follows that to enlighten men's minds is to take away from this species of spoliation what supports and feeds it.

I shall pass briefly in review some specimens of spoliation which are due to craft exercised on a very extensive scale.

The first which presents itself is spoliation by priestcraft [*ruse théocratique*].

What is the object in view? The object is to procure provisions, vestments, luxury, consideration, influence, power, by exchanging fictitious for real services.

If I tell a man, "I am going to render you great and immediate services," I must keep my word, or this man will soon be in a situation to detect the imposture, and my artifice will be instantly unmasked.

But if I say to him, "In exchange for your services I am going to render you immense service, not in this world, but in another; for after this life is ended, your being eternally happy or miserable depends upon me. I am an intermediate being between God and His creature, and I can, at my will, open the gates of heaven or of hell." If this man only believes me, I have him in my power.

This species of imposture has been practised wholesale since the beginning of the world, and we know what plenitude of power was exercised by the Egyptian priests.

It is easy to discover how these impostors proceed. We have only to ask ourselves what we should do were we in their place.

If I arrived among an ignorant tribe with views of this sort, and succeeded by some extraordinary and marvellous act to pass myself off for a supernatural being, I should give myself out for an envoy of God, and as possessing absolute control over the future destinies of man.

Then I should strictly forbid any inquiry into the validity of my titles and pretensions. I should do more. As reason would be my most dangerous antagonist, I should forbid the use of reason itself, unless applied to this formidable subject. In the language of the savages, I should *taboo* this question and everything relating to it. To handle it, or even think of it, should be declared an unpardonable sin.

It would be the very triumph of my art to guard with a *taboo* barrier every intellectual avenue which could possibly lead to a discovery of my imposture; and what better security than to declare even doubt to be sacrilege?

And still to this fundamental security I should add others. For example, effectually to prevent enlightenment ever reaching the masses, I should appropriate to myself and my accomplices the monopoly of all knowledge, which I would conceal under the veil of a dead language and hieroglyphic characters; and in order that I should never be exposed to any danger, I would take care to establish an institution which would enable me, day after day, to penetrate the secrets of all consciences.

It would not be amiss that I should at the same time satisfy some of the real wants of my people, especially if, in doing so, I could increase my influence and authority. Thus, as men have great need of instruction, and of being taught morals, I should constitute myself the dispenser of these. By this means I should direct as I saw best the minds and hearts of my people. I should establish an indissoluble connexion between morals and my authority. I should represent them as incapable of existing, except in this state of union; so that, if some bold man were to attempt to stir a tabooed question, society at large, which could not dispense with moral teaching, would feel the earth tremble under its feet, and would turn with rage against this frantic innovator.

When things had come to this pass, it is obvious that the people would become my property in a stricter sense than if they were my slaves. The slave curses his chains—they would hug theirs; and I should thus succeed in imprinting the brand of servitude, not on their foreheads, but on their innermost consciences.

Public opinion alone can overturn such an edifice of iniquity; but where can it make a beginning, when every stone of the edifice is tabooed? It is obviously an affair of time and the printing-press.

God forbid that I should desire to shake the consoling religious convictions which connect this life of trial with a life of felicity. But that our irresistible religious aspirations have been abused, is what no one, not even the head of the Church himself, can deny. It appears to me that there is a sure test by which a people can discover whether they are duped or not. Examine Religion and the Priest, in order to discover whether the priest is the instrument of religion, or whether religion is not rather the instrument of the priest.

If the priest is the instrument of religion, if his sole care is to spread over the country morals and blessings, he will be gentle, tolerant, humble, charitable, full of zeal; his life will be a reflection of his Divine Model; he will preach liberty and equality among men, peace and fraternity between nations; he will repel the seductions of temporal power, desiring no alliance with what of all things in the world most requires to be kept in check; he will be a man of the people, a man of sound counsels, a man of consolation, a man of public opinion, a man of the Gospel.

If, on the contrary, *religion is the instrument of the priest*, he will treat it as we treat an instrument, which we alter, bend, and twist about in all directions, so as to make it available for the purpose we have in view. He will increase the number of questions which are tabooed; his morals will change with times, men, and circumstances. He will endeavour to impose upon people by gestures and studied attitudes; and will mumble a hundred times a day words, the meaning of which has evaporated, and which have come to be nothing better than a vain conventionalism. He will traffic in sacred things, but in such a way as not to shake men's faith in their sacredness; and he will take care, when he meets with acute, clear-sighted people, not to carry on this traffic so openly or actively as in other circumstances. He will mix himself up with worldly intrigues; and he will take the side of men in power, provided they embrace his side. In a word, in all his actions, we shall discover that his object is not to advance the cause of religion through the clergy, but the cause of the clergy through religion; and as so many efforts must have an object, and as this object, on our hypothesis, can be nothing else than wealth and power, the most incontestable sign of the people having been duped is that the priest has become rich and powerful.

It is quite evident that a true religion may be abused as well as a false religion. The more respectable its authority is, the more is it to be feared that the proofs of that respectability will be pressed too far. But the results will be widely different. Abuses have a tendency to excite the sound, enlightened, and independent portion of the population to rebellion. And it is a much more serious thing to shake public belief in a true than in a false religion.

Spoliation by such means, and the intelligence of a people, are always in an inverse ratio to each other; for it is of the nature of abuses to be carried as far only as safety permits. Not that in the midst of the most ignorant people pure and devoted priests are never to be found; but the question is, how can we prevent a knave from assuming the cassock, and ambition from encircling his brow with a mitre? Spoliators obey the Malthusian law: they multiply as the means of existence increase; and a knave's means of existence is the credulity of his dupes. Public opinion must be enlightened. There is no other remedy.

Another variety of spoliation by craft and artifice is to be found in what are called *commercial frauds*, an expression, as it appears to me, not sufficiently broad; for not only is the merchant who adulterates his commodities, or uses a false measure, guilty of fraud, but the physician who gets paid for bad advice, and the advocate who fans and encourages lawsuits. In an exchange between two services, one of them may be of bad quality; but here, the services received being stipulated for beforehand, spoliation must evidently recede before the advance of public enlightenment.

Next in order come abuses of *public services*—a vast field of spoliation, so vast that we can only glance at it.

Had man been created a solitary animal, each man would work for himself. Individual wealth would, in that case, be in proportion to the services rendered by each man to himself.

But, man being a sociable animal, services are exchanged for other services; a proposition which you may, if you choose, construe backwards [*à rebours*].

There exist in society wants so general, so universal, that its members provide for them by organizing public services. Such, for example, is the need of security. We arrange, we club together, to remunerate by services of various kinds those who render us the service of watching over the general security.

There is nothing which does not come within the domain of political economy. Do this for me, and I will do that for you. The essence of the transaction is the same, the remunerative process alone is different; but this last is a circumstance of great importance.

In ordinary transactions, each man is the judge, both of the service he receives and the service he renders. He can always refuse an exchange, or make it elsewhere; whence the necessity of bringing to market services which will be willingly accepted.

It is not so in state matters, especially before the introduction of representative government. Whether we have need of such services as the government furnishes or not, whether they are good or bad, we are forced always to accept them such as they are, and at the price at which the government estimates them.

Now it is the tendency of all men to see through the small end of the telescope the services which they render, and through the large end the services which they receive. In private transactions, then, we should be led a fine dance, if we were without the security afforded by *a price freely and openly bargained for.*

Now this guarantee we have either not at all or to a very limited extent in public transactions. And yet the government, composed of men (although at the present day they would persuade us that legislators are something more than men), obeys the universal tendency. The government desires to render us great service, to serve us more than we need, and to make us accept, as true services, services which are sometimes very far from being so, and to exact from us in return other services or contributions.

In this way the state is also subject to the Malthusian law. It tends to pass the level of its means of existence, it grows great in proportion to these means, and these means consist of the people's substance. Woe, then, to those nations who are unable to set bounds to the action of the government! Liberty, private enterprise, wealth, thrift, independence, all will be wanting in such circumstances.

For there is one circumstance especially which it is very necessary to mark—it is this: Among the services which we demand from the government, the principal one is security. To ensure this there is needed a force which is capable of overcoming all other forces, individual or collective, internal or external, which can be brought against it. Combined with that unfortunate disposition, which we discover in men to live at other people's expense, there is here a danger which is self-evident.

Just consider on what an immense scale, as we learn from history, spoliation has been exercised through the abuse and excess of the powers of government. Consider what services have been rendered to the people, and what services the public powers have exacted from them, among the Assyrians, the Babylonians, Egyptians, Romans, Persians, Turks, Chinese, Russians, English, Spaniards, Frenchmen. Imagination is startled at the enormous disproportion.

At length, representative government has been instituted, and we should have thought, *a priori*, that these disorders would have disappeared as if by enchantment.

In fact, the principle of representative government is this: "The people themselves, by their representatives, are to decide on the nature and extent of the functions which they judge it right to regard as public services, and the amount of remuneration to be attached to such services."

The tendency to appropriate the property of others, and the tendency to defend that property, being thus placed in opposite scales, we should have thought that the second would have outweighed the first.

I am convinced that this is what must ultimately happen, but it has not happened hitherto.

Why? For two very simple reasons. Governments have had too much, and the people too little, sagacity.

Governments are very skilful. They act with method and consistency, upon a plan well arranged, and constantly improved by tradition and experience. They study men, and their passions. If they discover, for example, that they are actuated by warlike impulses, they stimulate this fatal propensity, and add fuel to the flame. They surround the nation with dangers through the action of diplomacy, and then they very naturally demand more soldiers, more sailors, more arsenals and fortifications; sometimes they have not even to solicit these, but have them offered; and then they have rank, pensions, and places to distribute. To meet all this, large sums of money are needed, and taxes and loans are resorted to.

If the nation is generous, government undertakes to cure all the ills of humanity; to revive trade, to make agriculture flourish, to develop manufactures, encourage arts and learning, extirpate poverty, etc., etc. All that requires to be done is to create offices, and pay functionaries.

In short, the tactics consist in representing restraints as effective services; and the nation pays, not for services, but for disservices. Governments, assuming gigantic proportions, end by eating up half the revenues they exact. And the people, wondering at being obliged to work so hard, after hearing of inventions which are to multiply products *ad infinitum*.... continue always the same overgrown children they were before.

While the government displays so much skill and ability, the people display scarcely any. When called upon to elect those whose province it is to determine the sphere and remuneration of governmental action, whom do they choose? The agents of the government. Thus, they confer on the executive the power of fixing the limits of its own operations and exactions. They act like the *Bourgeois Gentilhomme*, who, in place of himself deciding on the number and cut of his coats, referred the whole thing—to his tailor.

And when matters have thus gone on from bad to worse, the people at length have their eyes opened, not to the remedy—(they have not got that length yet)—but to the evil.

To govern is so agreeable a business, that every one aspires to it. The counsellors of the people never cease telling them: We see your sufferings, and deplore them. It would be very different if we governed you.

In the meantime, and sometimes for a long period, there are rebellions and *emeutes*. When the people are vanquished, the expense of the war only adds to their burdens. When they are victorious, the *personnel* of the government is changed, and the abuses remain unreformed.

And this state of things will continue until the people shall learn to know and defend their true interests—so that we always come back to this, that there is no resource but in the progress of public intelligence.

Certain nations seem marvellously disposed to become the prey of government spoliation; those especially where the people, losing sight of their own dignity and their own energy, think themselves undone if they are not *governed and controlled* in everything. Without having travelled very much, I have seen countries where it is believed that agriculture can make no progress unless experimental farms are maintained by the government; that there would soon be no horses but for the state *haras*; and that fathers of families would either not educate their children, or have them taught immorality, if the state did not prescribe the course of education, etc., etc. In such a country, revolutions succeed each other, and the governing powers are changed in rapid succession. But the governed continue nevertheless to be governed on the principle of mercy and compassion (for the tendency which I am here exposing is the very food upon which governments live), until at length the people perceive that it is better to leave the greatest possible number of services in the category of those which the parties interested exchange at *a price fixed by free and open bargaining*.

We have seen that an exchange of services constitutes society; and it must be an exchange of good and loyal services. But we have shown also that men have a strong interest, and consequently an irresistible bent, to exaggerate the relative value of the services which they render. And, in truth, I can perceive no other cure for this evil but the free acceptance or the free refusal of those to whom these services are offered.

Whence it happens that certain men have recourse to the law in order that it may control this freedom in certain branches of industry. This kind of spoliation is called Privilege or Monopoly. Mark well its origin and character.

Everybody knows that the services which he brings to the general market are appreciated and remunerated in proportion to their rarity. The intervention of law is invoked to drive out of the market all those who come to offer analogous services; or, which comes to the same thing, if the assistance of an instrument or a machine is necessary to enable such services to be rendered, the law interposes to give exclusive possession of it.

This variety of spoliation being the principal subject of the present volume, I shall not enlarge upon it in this place, but content myself with one remark.

When monopoly is an isolated fact, it never fails to enrich the man who is invested with it. It may happen, then, that other classes of producers, in place of waiting for the downfall of this monopoly, demand for themselves similar monopolies. This species of spoliation, thus erected into a system, becomes the most ridiculous of mystifications for everybody; and the ultimate result is, that each man believes himself to be deriving greater profit from a market which is impoverished by all.

It is unnecessary to add, that this strange *regime* introduces a universal antagonism among all classes, all professions, and all nations; that it calls for the interposition (constant, but always uncertain) of government action; that it gives rise to all the abuses we have enumerated; that it places all branches of industry in a state of hopeless insecurity; and that it accustoms men to rely upon the law, and not upon themselves, for their means of subsistence. It would be difficult to imagine a more active cause of social perturbation.

But it may be said, Why make use of this ugly term, Spoliation? It is coarse, it wounds, irritates, and turns against you all calm and moderate men—it envenoms the controversy.

To speak plainly, I respect the persons, and I believe in the sincerity of nearly all the partisans of protection; I claim no right to call in question the personal probity, the delicacy, the philanthropy, of any one whatsoever. I again repeat that protection is the fruit, the fatal fruit, of a common error, of which everybody, or at least the majority of men, are at once the victims and the accomplices. But with all this I cannot prevent things being as they are.

Figure Diogenes putting his head out of his tub, and saying, "Athenians, you are served by slaves. Has it never occurred to you, that you thereby exercise over your brethren the most iniquitous species of spoliation?"

Or, again, figure a tribune speaking thus in the forum: "Romans, you derive all your means of existence from the pillage of all nations in succession."

JUSTIFICATION.

In saying so, they would only speak undoubted truth. But are we to conclude from this that Athens and Rome were inhabited only by bad and dishonest people, and hold in contempt Socrates and Plato, Cato and Cincinnatus?

Who could entertain for a moment any such thought? But these great men lived in a social medium which took away all consciousness of injustice. We know that Aristotle could not even realize the idea of any society existing without slavery.

Slavery in modern times has existed down to our own day without exciting many scruples in the minds of planters. Armies serve as the instruments of great conquests, that is to say, of great spoliations. But that is not to say that they do not contain multitudes of soldiers and officers personally of as delicate feelings as are usually to be found in industrial careers, if not indeed more so; men who would blush at the very thought of anything dishonest, and would face a thousand deaths rather than stoop to any meanness.

We must not blame individuals, but rather the general movement which carries them along, and blinds them to the real state of the case; a movement for which society at large is responsible.

The same thing holds of monopoly. I blame the system, and not individuals—society at large, and not individual members of society. If the greatest philosophers have been unable to discover the iniquity of slavery, how much more easily may agriculturists and manufacturers have been led to take a wrong view of the nature and effects of a system of restriction!

II. TWO PRINCIPLES OF MORALITY.

Having reached, if he has reached, the end of the last chapter, I fancy I hear the reader exclaim:

"Well, are we wrong in reproaching economists with being dry and cold? What a picture of human nature! What! Is spoliation, then, to be regarded as an inevitable, almost normal, force, assuming all forms, at work under all pretexts, by law and without law, jobbing and abusing things the most sacred, working on feebleness and credulity by turns, and making progress just in proportion as these are prevalent! Is there in the world a more melancholy picture than this?"

The question is not whether the picture be melancholy, but whether it is true. History will tell us.

It is singular enough that those who decry political economy (or *economisme*, as they are pleased to call it), because that science studies man and the world as they are, are themselves much further advanced in pessimism, at least as regards the past and the present, than the economists whom they disparage. Open their books and their journals; and what do you find? Bitterness, hatred of society, carried to such a pitch that the very word civilization is in their eyes the synonym of injustice, dis-order, and anarchy. They go the length even of denouncing liberty, so little confidence have they in the development of the human race as the natural result of its organization. Liberty! it is liberty, as they think, which is impelling us nearer and nearer to ruin.

True, these writers are optimists in reference to the future. For if the human race, left to itself, has pursued a wrong road for six thousand years, a discoverer has appeared, who has pointed out the true way of safety; and however little the flock may regard the pastor's crook, they will be infallibly led towards the promised land, where happiness, without any effort on their part, awaits them, and where order, security, and harmony are the cheap reward of improvidence.

The human race have only to consent to these reformers changing (to use Rousseau's expression) *its physical and moral constitution.*

It is not the business of political economy to inquire what society might have become had God made man otherwise than He has been pleased to make him. It may perhaps be a subject of regret that in the beginning, Providence should have forgotten to call to its counsels some of our modern *organisateurs*. And as the celestial mechanism would have been very differently constructed had the Creator consulted Alphonsus the Wise, in the same way had He only taken the advice of Fourrier, the social order would have had no resemblance to that in which we are forced to breathe, live, and move. But since we are here—since *in eo vivimus, movemur, et minus*—all we have to do is to study and make ourselves acquainted with the laws of the social order in which we find ourselves, especially if its amelioration depends essentially on our knowledge of these laws.

We cannot prevent the human heart from being the seat of insatiable desires.

We cannot so order it that these desires should be satisfied without labour.

We cannot so order it that man should not have as much repugnance to labour as desire for enjoyment.

We cannot so order it that from this organization there should not result a perpetual effort on the part of certain men to increase their own share of enjoyments at the expense of others; throwing over upon them, by force or cunning, the labour and exertion which are the necessary condition of such enjoyments being obtained.

It is not for us to go in the face of universal history, or stifle the voice of the past, which tells us that such has been the state of things from the beginning. We cannot deny that war, slavery, thraldom, priestcraft, government abuses, privileges, frauds of every kind, and monopolies, have been the incontestable and terrible manifestations of these two sentiments combined in the heart of man—*desire of enjoyments, and repugnance to fatigue.*

In the sweat of thy face shalt thou eat bread. Yes, but every one desires to have the greatest possible quantity of bread, with the least possible amount of sweat. Such is the testimony of history.

But let us be thankful that history also shows us that the diffusion of enjoyments and of efforts has a tendency to become more and more equal among men.

Unless we shut our eyes to the light of the sun, we must admit that society has in this respect made progress.

If this be so, there must be in society a natural and providential force, a law which repels more and more the principle of dishonesty, and realizes more and more the principle of justice.

We maintain that this force exists in society, and that God has placed it there. If it did not exist, we should be reduced, like Utopian dreamers, to seek for it in artificial arrangements, in arrangements which imply a previous alteration in the physical and moral constitution of man; or rather, we should conclude that the search was useless and vain, for the simple reason that we cannot understand the action of a lever without its fulcrum.

Let us try, then, to describe the beneficent force which tends gradually to surmount the mischievous and injurious force to which we have given the name of spoliation, and the presence of which is only too well explained by reasoning, and established by experience.

Every injurious or hurtful act has necessarily two terms: the point whence it comes, and the point to which it tends—the *terminus a quo, and the terminus ad quern*—the man who acts, and the man acted upon; or, in the language of the schoolmen, the *agent and the patient.*

We may be protected, then, from an injurious act in two ways: by the voluntary abstention of the agent; or by the resistance of the patient.

These two moral principles, far from running counter to each other, concur in their action, namely, the religious or philosophical moral principle, and the moral principle which I shall venture to term economic.

The religious moral principle, in order to ensure the suppression of an injurious act, addresses its author, addresses man in his capacity of agent, and says to him: "Amend your life; purify your conduct; cease to do evil; learn to do well; subdue your passions; sacrifice self-interest; oppress not your neighbour, whom it is your duty to love and assist; first of all, be just, and be charitable afterwards." This species of moral principle will always be esteemed the most beautiful and touching, that which best displays the human race in its native majesty, which will be most extolled by the eloquent, and call forth the greatest amount of admiration and sympathy.

The economic moral principle aspires at attaining the same result; but addresses man more especially in the capacity of patient. It points out to him the effects of human actions, and by that simple explanation, stimulates him to react against those who injure him, and honour those who are useful to him. It strives to disseminate among the oppressed masses enough of good sense, information, and well-founded distrust, to render oppression more and more difficult and dangerous.

We must remark, too, that the economic principle of morality does not fail to act likewise on the oppressor. An injurious act is productive of both good and evil; evil for the man who is subject to it, and good for the man who avails himself of it; without which indeed it would not have been thought of. But the good and the evil are far from compensating each other. The sum total of evil always and necessarily preponderates over the good; because the very fact that oppression is present entails a loss of power, creates dangers, provokes reprisals, and renders, costly precautions necessary. The simple explanation of these effects, then, not only provokes reaction on the part of the oppressed, but brings over to the side of justice all whose hearts are not perverted, and disturbs the security of the oppressors themselves.

But it is easy to understand that this economic principle of morality, which is rather virtual than formal; which is only, after all, a scientific demonstration, which would lose its efficacy if it changed its character; which addresses itself not to the heart, but to the intellect; which aims at convincing rather than persuading; which does not give advice, but furnishes proofs; whose mission is not to touch the feelings, but enlighten the judgment, which obtains over vice no other victory than that of depriving it of support; it is easy, I say, to understand why this principle of morality should be accused of being dry and prosaic.

The reproach is well founded in itself, without being just in its application. It just amounts to saying that political economy does not discuss everything, that it does not comprehend everything—that it is not, in short, universal science. But who ever claimed for it this character, or put forward on its behalf so exorbitant a pretension?

The accusation would be well founded only if political economy presented its processes as exclusive, and had the presumption, if we may so speak, to deny to philosophy and religion their own proper and peculiar means of working for the cultivation and improvement of man.

Let us admit, then, the simultaneous action of morality, properly so called, and of political economy; the one branding the injurious act in its motive, and exposing its unseemliness, the other discrediting it in our judgment, by a picture of its effects.

Let us admit even that the triumph of the religious moralist, when achieved, is more beautiful, more consoling, more fundamental But we must at the same time acknowledge that the triumph of the economist is more easy and more certain.

In a few lines, which are worth many large volumes, J. B. Say has said that, to put an end to the disorder introduced into an honourable family by hypocrisy there are only two alternatives: to *reform Tartuffe, or sharpen the wits of Orgon*. Molière, that great painter of the human heart, appears constantly to have regarded the second of these processes as the more efficacious.

It is the same thing in real life, and on the stage of the world.

Tell me what Cæsar did, and I will tell you what the character was of the Romans of his time.

Tell me what modern diplomacy accomplishes, and I will tell you what is the moral condition of the nations among whom it is exercised.

We should not be paying nearly two milliards [£80,000,000 sterling] of taxes, if we did not empower those who live upon them to vote them.

We should not have been landed in all the difficulties and charges to which the African question has given rise, had we had our eyes open to the fact that *two and two make four, in political economy, as well as in arithmetic.*

M. Guizot would not have felt himself authorized to say that *France is rich enough to pay for her glory*, if France had never been smitten with the love of false glory.

The same statesman would never have ventured to say that liberty is too precious a thing for France to stand higgling about its price, had France only reflected that a *heavy budget and liberty are incompatible.*

It is not by monopolists, but by their victims, that monopolies are maintained.

In the matter of elections, it is not because there are parties who offer bribes that there are parties open to receive them, but the contrary; and the proof of this is, that it is the parties who receive the bribes who, in the long run, defray the cost of corruption. Is it not their business to put an end to the practice?

Let the religious principle of morality, if it can, touch the hearts of the Tartuffes, the Cæsars, the planters of colonies, the sinecurists, the monopolists, etc. The clear duty of political economy is to enlighten their dupes.

Of these two processes, which exercises the more efficacious influence on social progress? I feel it almost unnecessary to say, that I believe it is the second; and I fear we can never exempt mankind from the necessity of learning first of all *defensive morality.*

After all I have heard and read and observed, I have never yet met with an instance of an abuse which had been in operation on a somewhat extensive scale, put an end to by the voluntary renunciation of those who profit by it.

On the other hand, I have seen many abuses put down by the determined resistance of those who suffered from them.

To expose the effects of abuses, then, is the surest means of putting an end to them. And this holds especially true of abuses like the policy of restriction, which, whilst inflicting real evils on the masses, are productive of nothing to those who imagine they profit by them but illusion and deception!

After all, can the kind of morality we are advocating of itself enable us to realize all that social perfection which the sympathetic nature of the soul of man and its noble faculties authorize us to look forward to and hope for? I am far from saying so. Assume the complete diffusion of defensive morality, it resolves itself simply into the conviction that men's interests, rightly understood, are always in accord with justice and general utility. Such a society, although certainly well ordered, would not be very attractive. There would be fewer cheats simply because there would be fewer dupes. Vice always lurking in the background, and starved, so to speak, for want of support, would revive the moment that support was restored to it.

The prudence of each would be enforced by the vigilance of all; and reform, confining itself to the regulation of external acts, and never going deeper than the skin, would fail to penetrate men's hearts and consciences. Such a society would remind us of one of those exact, rigorous, and just men, who are ready to resent the slightest invasion of their rights, and to defend themselves on all sides from attacks.

You esteem them; you perhaps admire them; you would elect them as deputies; but you would never make them your friends.

But the two principles of morality I have described, instead of running counter to each other, work in concert, attacking vice from opposite directions. Whilst the economists are doing their part, sharpening the wits of the Orgons, eradicating prejudices, exciting just and necessary distrust, studying and explaining the true nature of things and of actions, let the religious moralist accomplish on his side his more attractive, although more difficult, labours. Let him attack dishonesty in a hand-to-hand fight; let him pursue it into the most secret recesses of the heart; let him paint in glowing colours the charms of beneficence, of self-sacrifice, of devotion; let him open up the fountains of virtue, where we can only dry up the fountains of vice. This is his duty, and a noble duty it is. But why should he contest the utility of the duty which has devolved upon us?

In a society which, without being personally and individually virtuous, would nevertheless be well ordered through the action of the economic principle of morality (which means a knowledge of the economy of the social body), would not an opening be made for the work of the religious moralist?

Habit, it is said, is a second nature.

A country might still be unhappy, although for a long time each man may have been unused to injustice through the continued resistance of an enlightened public. But such a country, it seems to me, would be well prepared to receive a system of teaching more pure and elevated. We get a considerable way on the road to good, when we become unused to evil. Men can never remain stationary. Diverted from the path of vice, feeling that it leads only to infamy, they would feel so much the more sensibly the attractions of virtue.

Society must perhaps pass through this prosaic state of transition, in which men practise virtue from motives of prudence, in order to rise afterwards to that fairer and more poetic region where such calculating motives are no longer wanted.

III. THE TWO HATCHETS.

Petition of Jacques Bonhomme, Carpenter, to M. Cunin-Gridaine, Minister of Commerce.

Monsieur le Fabricant-Ministre,

I am a carpenter to trade, as was St Joseph of old; and I handle the hatchet and adze, for your benefit.

Now, while engaged in hewing and chopping from morning to night upon the lands of our Lord the King, the idea has struck me that my labour may be regarded as *national*, as well as yours.

And, in these circumstances, I cannot see why protection should not visit my woodyard as well as your workshop.

For, sooth to say, if you make cloths I make roofs; and both, in their own way, shelter our customers from cold and from rain.

And yet I run after customers; and customers run after you. You have found out the way of securing them by hindering them from supplying themselves elsewhere, while mine apply to whomsoever they think proper.

What is astonishing in all this? Monsieur Cunin, the Minister of State, has not forgotten M. Cunin, the manufacturer—all quite natural. But, alas! my humble trade has not given a Minister to France, although practised, in Scripture times, by far more august personages.

And in the immortal code which I find embodied in Scripture, I cannot discover the slightest expression which could be quoted by carpenters, as authorizing them to enrich themselves at the expense of other people.

You see, then, how I am situated. I earn fifteen pence a day, when it is not Sunday or holiday. I offer you my services at the same time as a Flemish carpenter offers you his, and, because he abates a halfpenny, you give him the preference.

But I desire to clothe myself; and if a Belgian weaver presents his cloth alongside of yours, you drive him and his cloth out of the country.

So that, being forced to frequent your shop, although the dearest, my poor fifteen pence go no further in reality than fourteen.

Nay, they are not worth more than thirteen! for in place of expelling the Belgian weaver at your own cost (which was the least you could do), you, for your own ends, make me pay for the people you set at his heels.

And as a great number of your co-legislators, with whom you are on a marvellously good footing, take each a halfpenny or a penny, under pretext of protecting iron, or coal, or oil, or corn, I find, when everything is taken into account, that of my fifteen pence, I have only been able to save seven pence or eight pence from pillage.

You will no doubt tell me that these small halfpence, which pass in this way from my pocket to yours, maintain workpeople who reside around your castle, and enable you to live in a style of magnificence. To which I will only reply, that if the pence had been left with me, the person who earned them, they would have maintained workpeople in my neighbourhood.

Be this as it may, Monsieur le Ministre-fabricant, knowing that I should be but ill received by you, I have not come to require you, as I had good right to do, to withdraw the restriction which you impose on your customers. I prefer following the ordinary course, and I approach you to solicit a little bit of protection for myself.

Here, of course, you will interpose a difficulty. "My good friend," you will say, "I would protect you and your fellow-workmen with all my heart; but how can I confer customhouse favours on carpenter-work? What use would it be to prohibit the importation of houses by sea or by land?"

That would be a good joke, to be sure; but, by dint of thinking, I have discovered another mode of favouring the children of St Joseph; which you will welcome the more willingly, I hope, as it differs in nothing from that which constitutes the privilege which you vote year after year in your own favour.

The means of favouring us, which I have thus marvellously discovered, is to prohibit the use of sharp axes in this country.

I maintain that such a restriction would not be in the least more illogical or more arbitrary than the one to which you subject us in the case of your cloth.

Why do you drive away the Belgians? Because they sell cheaper than you. And why do they sell cheaper than you? Because they have a certain degree of superiority over you as manufacturers.

Between you and a Belgian, therefore, there is exactly the same difference as in my trade there would be between a blunt and a sharp axe.

And you force me, as a tradesman, to purchase from you the product of the blunt hatchet?

Regard the country at large as a workman who desires, by his labour, to procure all things he has want of, and, among others, cloth.

There are two means of effecting this.

The first is to spin and weave the wool.

The second is to produce other articles, as, for example, French clocks, paper-hangings, or wines, and exchange them with the Belgians for the cloth wanted.

Of these two processes, the one which gives the best result may be represented by the sharp axe, and the other by the blunt one.

You do not deny that at present, in France, we obtain a piece of stuff by the work of our own looms (that is the blunt axe) *with more labour* than by producing and exchanging wines (that is the sharp axe). So far are you from denying this, that it is precisely because of this *excess of labour* (in which you make wealth to consist) that you recommend, nay, that you *compel* the employment of the worse of the two hatchets.

Now, only be consistent, be impartial, and if you mean to be just, treat the poor carpenters as you treat yourselves.

Pass a law to this effect:

"*No one shall henceforth be permitted to employ any beams or rafters, but such as are produced and fashioned by blunt hatchets.*"

And see what will immediately happen.

Whereas at present we give a hundred blows of the axe, we shall then give three hundred. The work which we now do in an hour will then require three hours. What a powerful encouragement will thus be given to labour! Masters, journeymen, apprentices! our sufferings are now at an end. We shall be in demand; and, therefore, well paid. Whoever shall henceforth desire to have a roof to cover him must comply with our exactions, just as at present whoever desires clothes to his back must comply with yours.

And should the theoretical advocates of free trade ever dare to call in question the utility of the measure, we know well where to seek for reasons to confute them Your Inquiry of 1834 is still to be had. With that weapon, we shall conquer; for you have there admirably pleaded the cause of restriction, and of blunt axes, which are in reality the same thing.

IV. LOWER COUNCIL OF LABOUR.

What! you have the face to demand for all citizens a right to sell, buy, barter, and exchange; to render and receive service for service, and to judge for themselves, on the single condition that they do all honestly, and comply with the demands of the public treasury? Then you simply desire to deprive our workmen of employment, of wages, and of bread?"

This is what is said to us. I know very well what to think of it; but what I wish to know is, what the workmen themselves think of it.

I have at hand an excellent instrument of inquiry. Not those Upper Councils of Industry, where extensive proprietors who call themselves labourers, rich shipowners who call themselves sailors, and wealthy shareholders who pass themselves off for workmen, turn their philanthropy to account in a way which we all know.

No; it is with workmen, who are workmen in reality, that we have to do—joiners, carpenters, masons, tailors, shoemakers, dyers, blacksmiths, innkeepers, grocers, etc., etc.,—and who, in my village, have founded a friendly society.

I have transformed this friendly society, at my own hand, into a Lower Council of Labour, and instituted an inquiry which will be found of great importance, although it is not crammed with figures, or inflated to the bulk of a quarto volume, printed at the expense of the State.

My object was to interrogate these plain, simple people as to the manner in which they are, or believe themselves to be, affected by the policy of protection. The president pointed out that this would be infringing to some extent on the fundamental conditions of the Association. For in France, this land of liberty, people who associate give up their right to talk politics—in other words, their right to discuss their common interests. However, after some hesitation, he agreed to include the question in the order of the day.

They divided the assembly into as many committees as there were groups of distinct trades, and delivered to each committee a schedule to be filled up after fifteen days' deliberation.

On the day fixed, the worthy president (we adopt the official style) took the chair, and there were laid upon the table (still the official style) fifteen reports, which he read in succession.

The first which was taken into consideration was that of the tailors. Here is an exact and literal copy of it:—

EFFECTS OF PROTECTION.—REPORT OF THE TAILORS.

Inconveniences.

1st, In consequence of the policy of protection, we pay dearer for bread, meat, sugar, firewood, thread, needles, etc., which is equivalent in our case to a considerable reduction of wages.

2d, In consequence of the policy of 'protection, our customers also pay dearer for everything, and this leaves them less to spend upon clothing; whence it follows that we have less employment, and, consequently, smaller returns.

3d, In consequence of the policy of protection, the stuffs which we make up are dear, and people on that account wear their clothes longer, or dispense with part of them. This, again, is equivalent to a diminution of employment, and forces us to offer our services at a lower rate of remuneration.

Advantages.

None.

Note.—After all our inquiries, deliberations, and discussions, we have been quite unable to discover that in any respect whatever the policy of protection has been of advantage to our trade.

Here is another report:—

Inconveniences.

1st, The policy of protection imposes a tax upon us every time we eat, drink, or warm or clothe ourselves, and this tax does not go to the treasury.

2d, It imposes a like tax upon all our fellow-citizens who are not of our trade, and they, being so much the poorer, have recourse to cheap substitutes for our work, which deprives us of the employment we should otherwise have had. None.

3d, It keeps up iron at so high a price, that it is not employed in the country for ploughs, grates, gates, balconies, etc.; and our trade, which might furnish employment to so many other people who are in want of it, no longer furnishes employment to ourselves.

4th, The revenue which the treasury fails to obtain from commodities which are not imported is levied upon the salt we use, postages, etc.

All the other reports (with which it is unnecessary to trouble the reader) are to the same tune. Gardeners, carpenters, shoemakers, clogmakers, boatmen, millers, all give vent to the same complaints.

I regret that there are no agricultural labourers in our association. Their report would assuredly have been very instructive.

But, alas! in our country of the Landes, the poor labourers, protected though they be, have not the means of joining an association, and, having insured their cattle, they find they cannot themselves become members of a friendly society. The boon of protection does not hinder them from being the parias of our social order. What shall I say of the vine-dressers?

What I remark, especially, is the good sense displayed by our villagers in perceiving not only the direct injury which the policy of protection does them, but the indirect injury, which, although in the first instance affecting their customers, falls back, *par ricochet*, upon themselves.

This is what the economists of the *Moniteur Industriel* do not appear to understand.

And perhaps those men whose eyes a dash of protection has fascinated, especially our agriculturists, would be willing to give it up, if they were enabled to see this side of the question.

In that case they might perhaps say to themselves, "Better far to be self-supported in the midst of a set of customers in easy circumstances, than to be protected in the midst of an impoverished clientèle."

For to desire to enrich by turns each separate branch of industry by creating a void round each in succession, is as vain an attempt as it would be for a man to try to leap over his own shadow.

V. DEARNESS-CHEAPNESS.

I think it necessary to submit to the reader some theoretical remarks on the illusions to which the words dearness and cheapness give rise. At first sight, these remarks may, I feel, be regarded as subtle, but the question is not whether they are subtle or the reverse, but whether they are true. Now, I not only believe them to be perfectly true, but to be well fitted to suggest matter of reflection to men (of whom there are not a few) who have sincere faith in the efficacy of a protectionist policy.

The advocates of Liberty and the defenders of Restriction are both obliged to employ the expressions, dearness, cheapness. The former declare themselves in favour of cheapness with a view to the interest of the consumer; the latter pronounce in favour of dearness, having regard especially to the interest of the producer. Others content themselves with saying, The producer and consumer are one and the same person; which leaves undecided the question whether the law should promote cheapness or dearness.

In the midst of this conflict, it would seem that the law has only one course to follow, and that is to allow prices to settle and adjust themselves naturally. But then we are attacked by the bitter enemies of *laissez faire.* At all hazards they want the law to interfere, without knowing or caring in what direction. And yet it lies with those who desire to create by legal intervention an artificial dearness or an unnatural cheapness, to explain the grounds of their preference. The *onus probandi* rests upon them exclusively. Liberty is always esteemed good, till the contrary is proved; and to allow prices to settle and adjust themselves naturally, is liberty.

But the parties to this dispute have changed positions. The advocates of dearness have secured the triumph of their system, and it lies with the defenders of natural prices to prove the goodness of their cause. On both sides, the argument turns on two words; and it is therefore very essential to ascertain what these two words really mean.

But we must first of all notice a series of facts which are fitted to disconcert the champions of both camps.

To engender dearness, the restrictionists have obtained protective duties, and a cheapness, which is to them inexplicable, has come to deceive their hopes.

To create cheapness, the free-traders have occasionally succeeded in securing liberty, and, to their astonishment, an elevation of prices has been the consequence.

For example, in France, in order to favour agriculture, a duty of 22 per cent has been imposed on foreign wool, and it has turned out that French wool has been sold at a lower price after the measure than before it.

In England, to satisfy the consumer, they lowered, and ultimately removed, the duty on foreign wool; and it has come to pass that in that country the price of wool is higher than ever.

And these are not isolated facts; for the price of wool is governed by precisely the same laws which govern the price of everything else. The same result is produced in all analogous cases. Contrary to expectation, protection has, to some extent, brought about a fall, and competition, to some extent, a rise of prices.

When the confusion of ideas thence arising had reached its height, the protectionists began saying to their adversaries, "It is our system which brings about the cheapness of which you boast so much." To which the reply was, "It is liberty which has induced the dearness which you find so useful."*

At this rate, would it not be amusing to see cheapness become the watch-word of the Rue Hauteville, and dearness the watchword of the Rue Choiseul?

Evidently there is in all this a misconception, an illusion, which it is necessary to clear up; and this is what I shall now endeavour to do.

Put the case of two isolated nations, each composed of a million of inhabitants. Grant that, *coteris paribus*, the one possesses double the quantity of everything,—corn, meat, iron, furniture, fuel, books, clothing, etc.,—which the other possesses.

It will be granted that the one is twice as rich as the other.

And yet there is no reason to affirm that a difference in *actual money prices*** exists in the two countries. Nominal prices may perhaps be higher in the richer country. It may be that in the United States everything is nominally dearer than in Poland, and that the population of the former country should, nevertheless, be better provided with all that they need; whence we infer that it is not the nominal price of products, but their comparative abundance, which constitutes wealth. When, then, we desire to pronounce an opinion on the comparative merits of restriction and free-trade, we should not inquire which of the two systems engenders dearness or cheapness, but which of the two brings abundance or scarcity.

* *Recently, M. Duchâtel, who had formerly advocated free trade, with a view to low prices, said to the Chamber: It would not be difficult for me to prove that protection leads to cheapness.*

***The expression, prix absolus (absolute prices), which the author employs here and in chap. xi. of the First Series (ante), is not, I think, used by English economists, and from the context in both instances I take it to mean actual money prices; or what Adam Smith terms nominal prices,—Translator.*

For, observe this, that products being exchanged for each other, a relative scarcity of all, and a relative abundance of all, leave the nominal prices of commodities in general at the same point; but this cannot be affirmed of the relative condition of the inhabitants of the two countries.

Let us dip a little deeper still into this subject.

When we see an increase and a reduction of duties produce effects so different from what we had expected, depreciation often following taxation, and enhancement following free trade, it becomes the imperative duty of political economy to seek an explanation of phenomena so much opposed to received ideas; for it is needless to say that a science, if it is worthy of the name, is nothing else than a faithful statement and a sound explanation of facts.

Now the phenomenon we are here examining is explained very satisfactorily by a circumstance of which we must never lose sight.

Dearness is due to two causes, and not to one only.

The same thing holds of cheapness.

It is one of the least disputed points in political economy that price is determined by the relative state of supply and demand.

There are then two terms which affect price—supply and demand. These terms are essentially variable. They may be combined in the same direction, in contrary directions, and in infinitely varied proportions. Hence the combinations of which price is the result are inexhaustible.

High price may be the result, either of diminished supply, or of increased demand.

Low price may be the result of increased supply, or of diminished demand.

Hence there are two kinds of dearness, and two kinds of cheapness.

There is a *dearness* of an injurious kind, that which proceeds from a diminution of supply, for that implies scarcity, privation (such as has been felt this year* from the scarcity of corn); and there is a dearness of a beneficial kind, that which results from an increase of demand, for the latter presupposes the development of general wealth.

* *This was written in 1847.—Translator.*

In the same way, there is a *cheapness* which is desirable, that which has its source in abundance; and an injurious cheapness, that has for its cause the failure of demand, and the impoverishment of consumers.

Now, be pleased to remark this; that restriction tends to induce, at the same time, both the injurious cause of dearness, and the injurious cause of cheapness: injurious dearness, by diminishing the supply, for this is the avowed object of restriction; and injurious cheapness, by diminishing also the demand; seeing that it gives a false direction to labour and capital, and fetters consumers with taxes and trammels.

So that, as regards price, these two tendencies neutralize each other; and this is the reason why the restrictive system, restraining, as it does, demand and supply at one and the same time, does not in the long run realize even that dearness which is its object.

But, as regards the condition of the population, these causes do not at all neutralize each other; on the contrary, they concur in making it worse.

The effect of freedom of trade is exactly the opposite. In its general result, it may be that it does not realize the cheapness it promises; for it has two tendencies, one towards desirable cheapness through the extension of supply, or abundance; the other towards appreciable dearness by the development of demand, or general wealth. These two tendencies neutralize each other in what concerns nominal price, but they concur in what regards the material prosperity of the population.

In short, under the restrictive system, in as far as it is operative, men recede towards a state of things, in which both demand and supply are enfeebled. Under a system of freedom, they progress towards a state of things in which both are developed simultaneously, and without necessarily affecting nominal prices. Such prices form no good criterion of wealth. They may remain the same whilst society is falling into a state of the most abject poverty, or whilst it is advancing towards a state of the greatest prosperity.

We shall now, in a few words, show the practical application of this doctrine.

A cultivator of the south of France believes himself to be very rich, because he is protected by duties from external competition. He may be as poor as Job; but he nevertheless imagines that sooner or later he will get rich by protection. In these circumstances, if we ask him the question which was put by the Odier Committee in these words,—

"Do you desire—yes or no—to be subject to foreign competition?" His first impulse is to answer "No," and the Odier Committee proudly welcome his response.

However, we must go a little deeper into the matter. Unquestionably, foreign competition—nay, competition in general—is always troublesome; and if one branch of trade alone could get quit of it, that branch of trade would for some time profit largely.

But protection is not an isolated favour; it is a system. If, to the profit of the agriculturist, protection tends to create a scarcity of corn and of meat, it tends likewise to create, to the profit of other industries, a scarcity of iron, of cloth, of fuel, tools, etc.,—a scarcity, in short, of everything.

Now, if a scarcity of corn tends to enhance its price through a diminution of supply, the scarcity of all other commodities for which corn is exchanged tends to reduce the price of corn by a diminution of demand, so that it is not at all certain that ultimately corn will be a penny dearer than it would have been under a system of free trade. There is nothing certain in the whole process but this—that as there is upon the whole less of every commodity in the country, each man will be less plentifully provided with everything he has occasion to buy.

The agriculturist should ask himself whether it would not be more for his interest that a certain quantity of corn and cattle should be imported from abroad, and that he should at the same time find himself surrounded by a population in easy circumstances, able and willing to consume and pay for all sorts of agricultural produce.

Suppose a department in which the people are clothed in rags, fed upon chesnuts, and lodged in hovels. How can agriculture flourish in such a locality? What can the soil be made to produce with a well-founded expectation of fair remuneration? Meat? The people do not eat it. Milk? They must content themselves with water. Butter? It is regarded as a luxury. Wool? The use of it is dispensed with as much as possible. Does any one imagine that all the ordinary objects of consumption can thus be put beyond the reach of the masses, without tending to lower prices as much as protection is tending to raise them?

What has been said of the agriculturist holds equally true of the manufacturer. Our manufacturers of cloth assure us that external competition will lower prices by increasing the supply. Granted; but will not these prices be again raised by an increased demand? Is the consumption of cloth a fixed and invariable quantity? Has every man as much of it as he would wish to have? And if general wealth is advanced and developed by the abolition of all these taxes and restrictions, will the first use to which this emancipation is turned by the population not be to dress better?

The question,—the constantly-recurring question,—then, is not to find out whether protection is favourable to any one special branch of industry, but whether, when everything is weighed, balanced, and taken into account, restriction is, in its own nature, more productive than liberty.

Now, no one will venture to maintain this. On the contrary, we are perpetually met with the admission, "You are right in principle."

If it be so, if restriction confers no benefit on individual branches of industry without doing a greater amount of injury to general wealth, we are forced to conclude that actual money prices, considered by themselves, only express a relation between each special branch of industry and industry in general, between supply and demand; and that, on this account, a remunerative price, which is the professed object of protection, is rather injured than favoured by the system.

SUPPLEMENT.*

** What follows appeared in the Libre Échange of 1st August 1847.—Editor.*

The article which we have published under the title of Dearness, Cheapness, has brought us several letters. We give them, along with our replies:—

Mr Editor,—You upset all our ideas. I endeavoured to aid the cause of free trade, and found it necessary to urge the consideration of cheapness. I went about everywhere, saying, "When freedom of trade is accorded, bread, meat, cloth, linen, iron, fuel, will go on falling in price." This displeased those who sell, but gave great pleasure to those who buy these commodities. And now you throw out doubts as to whether free trade will bring us cheapness or not. What, then, is to be gained by it? What gain will it be to the people if foreign competition, which may damage their sales, does not benefit them in their purchases?

Mr Free-trader,—Allow us to tell you that you must have read only half the article which has called forth your letter. We said that free trade acts exactly in the same way as roads, canals, railways, and everything else which facilitates communication by removing obstacles. Its first tendency is to increase the supply of the commodity freed from duty, and consequently to lower its price. But by augmenting at the same time the supply of all other commodities for which this article is exchanged, it increases the demand, and the price by this means rises again. You ask what gain this would be to the people? Suppose a balance with several scales, in each of which is deposited a certain quantity of the articles you have enumerated. If you add to the corn in one scale it will tend to fall; but if you add a little cloth, a little iron, a little fuel, to what the other scales contained, you will redress the equilibrium. If you look only at the beam, you will find nothing changed. But if you look at the people for whose use these articles are produced, you will find them better fed, clothed, and warmed.

Mr Editor,—I am a manufacturer of cloth, and a protectionist. I confess that your article on dearness and cheapness has made me reflect. It contains something specious which would require to be well established before we declare ourselves converted.

Mr Protectionist,—We say that your restrictive measures have an iniquitous object in view, namely, artificial dearness. But we do not affirm that they always realize the hopes of those who promote them. It is certain that they inflict on the consumer all the injurious consequences of scarcity. It is not certain that they always confer a corresponding advantage on the producer. Why? Because if they diminish the supply, they diminish also the demand.

This proves that there is in the economic arrangement of this world a moral force, a *vis medieatrix*, which causes unjust ambition in the long run to fall a prey to self-deception.

Would you have the goodness, Sir, to remark that one of the elements of the prosperity of each individual branch of industry is the general wealth of the community. The value of a house is not always in proportion to what it has cost, but likewise in proportion to the number and fortune of the tenants. Are two houses exactly similar necessarily of the same value? By no means, if the one is situated in Paris and the other in Lower Brittany. Never speak of price without taking into account collateral circumstances, and let it be remembered that no attempt is so bootless as to endeavour to found the prosperity of parts on the ruin of the whole. And yet this is what the policy of restriction pretends to do.

Consider what would have happened at Paris, for example, if this strife of interests had been attended with success.

Suppose that the first shoemaker who established himself in that city had succeeded in ejecting all others; that the first tailor, the first mason, the first printer, the first watchmaker, the first physician, the first baker, had been equally successful.

Paris would at this moment have been still a village of 1200 or 1500 inhabitants. It has turned out very differently. The market of Paris has been open to all (excepting those whom you still keep out), and it is this freedom which has enlarged and aggrandized it. The struggles of competition have been bitter and long continued, and this is what has made Paris a city of a million of inhabitants. The general wealth has increased, no doubt; but has the individual wealth of the shoemakers and tailors been diminished? This is the question you have to ask. You may say that according as the number of competitors increased, the price of their products would go on falling. Has it done so? No; for if the supply has been augmented, the demand has been enlarged.

The same thing will hold good of your commodity, cloth; let it enter freely. You will have more competitors in the trade, it is true; but you will have more customers, and, above all, richer customers. Is it possible you can never have thought of this, when you see nine-tenths of your fellow-citizens underclothed in winter, for want of the commodity which you manufacture?

If you wish to prosper, allow your customers to thrive. This is a lesson which you have* been very long in learning. When it is thoroughly learnt, each man will seek his own interest in the general good; and then jealousies between man and man, town and town, province and province, nation and nation, will no longer trouble the world.

VI. TO ARTISANS AND WORKMEN.

Many journals have attacked me in your presence and hearing. Perhaps you will not object to read my defence?

I am not suspicious. When a man writes or speaks, I take for granted that he believes what he says.

And yet, after reading and re-reading the journals to which I now reply, I seem unable to discover any other than melancholy tendencies.

Our present business is to inquire which is more favourable to your interests,—liberty or restriction.

I believe that it is liberty,—they believe that it is restriction. It is for each party to prove his own thesis.

Was it necessary to insinuate that we free-traders are the agents of England, of the south of France, of the government?

On this point, you see how easy recrimination would be.

We are the agents of England, they say, because some of us employ the words meeting and free-trader!

And do they not make use of the words drawback and budget?

We, it would seem, imitate Cobden and the English democracy!

And do they not parody Lord George Bentinck and the British aristocracy?

We borrow from perfidious Albion the doctrine of liberty!

And do they not borrow from the same source the quibbles of protection?

We follow the lead of Bordeaux and the south!

And do they not avail themselves of the cupidity of Lille and the north?

We favour the secret designs of the ministry, whose object is to divert public attention from their real policy!

And do they not act in the interest of the civil list, which profits most of all from the policy of protection?

You see, then, very clearly, that if we did not despise this war of disparagement, arms would not be wanting to carry it on. But this is beside the question.

The question, and we must never lose sight of it, is this: *Whether is it better for the working classes to be free, or not to be free to purchase foreign commodities?*

Workmen! they tell you that "If you are free to purchase from the foreigner those things which you now produce yourselves, you will cease to produce them; you will be without employment, without wages, and without bread; it is therefore for your own good to restrain your liberty."

This objection returns upon us under two forms:—They say, for example, "If we clothe ourselves with English cloth; if we make our ploughs of English iron; if we cut our bread with English knives; if we wipe our hands with English towels,—what will become of French workmen, what will become of national labour?"

Tell me, workmen! if a man should stand on the quay at Boulogne, and say to every Englishman who landed, "If you will give me these English boots, I will give you this French hat;" or, "If you will give me that English horse, I will give you this French tilbury;" or ask him, "Will you exchange that machine made at Birmingham, for this clock made at Paris?" or, again, "Can you arrange to barter this Newcastle coal against this champagne wine?" Tell me whether, assuming this man to make his proposals with discernment, any one would be justified in saying that our national labour, taken in the aggregate, would suffer in consequence?

Nor would it make the slightest difference in this respect were we to suppose twenty such offers to be made in place of one, or a million such barters to be effected in place of four; nor would it in any respect alter the case were we to assume the intervention of merchants and money, whereby such transactions would be greatly facilitated and multiplied.

Now, when one country buys from another wholesale, to sell again in retail, or buys in retail, to sell again in the lump, if we trace the transaction to its ultimate results, we shall always find that *commerce resolves itself into barter, products for products, services for services. If, then, barter does no injury to national labour, since it implies as much national labour given as foreign labour received, it follows that a hundred thousand millions of such acts of barter would do as little injury as one.*

But who would profit? you will ask. The profit consists in turning to most account the resources of each country, so that the same amount of labour shall yield everywhere a greater amount of satisfactions and enjoyments.

There are some who in your case have recourse to a singular system of tactics. They begin by admitting the superiority of the free to the prohibitive system, in order, doubtless, not to have the battle to fight on this ground.

Then they remark that the transition from one system to another is always attended with some displacement of labour.

Lastly, they enlarge on the sufferings, which, in their opinion, such displacements must always entail. They exaggerate these sufferings, they multiply them, they make them the principal subject of discussion, they present them as the exclusive and definitive result of reform, and in this way they endeavour to enlist you under the banners of monopoly.

This is just the system of tactics which has been employed to defend every system of abuse; and one thing I must plainly avow, that it is this system of tactics which constantly embarrasses those who advocate reforms, even those most useful to the people. You will soon see the reason of this.

When an abuse has once taken root, everything is arranged on the assumption of its continuance. Some men depend upon it for subsistence, others depend upon them, and so on, till a formidable edifice is erected.

Would you venture to pull it down? All cry out, and remark this—the men who bawl out appear always at first sight to be in the right, because it is far easier to show the derangements which must accompany a reform than the arrangements which must follow it.

The supporters of abuses cite particular instances of sufferings; they point out particular employers who, with their workmen, and the people who supply them with materials, are about to be injured; and the poor reformer can only refer to the general good which must gradually diffuse itself over the masses. That by no means produces the same sensation.

Thus, when the question turns on the abolition of slavery. "Poor men!" is the language addressed to the negroes, "who is henceforth to support you. The manager handles the lash, but he likewise distributes the cassava."

The slaves regret to part with their chains, for they ask themselves, "Whence will come the cassava?"

They fail to see that it is not the manager who feeds them, but their own labour—which feeds both them and the manager.

When they set about reforming the convents in Spain, they asked the beggars, "Where will you now find food and clothing? The prior is your best friend. Is it not very convenient to be in a situation to address yourselves to him?"

And the mendicants replied, "True; if the prior goes away, we see very clearly that we shall be losers, and we do not see at all so clearly who is to come in his place."

They did not take into account that if the convents bestowed alms, they lived upon them; so that the nation had more to give away than to receive.

In the same way, workmen! monopoly, quite imperceptibly, saddles you with taxes, and then, with the produce of these taxes, finds you employment.

And your sham friends exclaim, "But for monopolies, where would you find employment?"

And you, like the Spanish beggars, reply, "True, true; the employment which the monopolists find us is certain. The promises of liberty are of uncertain fulfilment."

For you do not see that they take from you in the first instance the money with part of which they afterwards afford you employment.

You ask, Who is to find you employment? And the answer is, that you will give employment to one another! With the money of which he is no longer deprived by taxation, the shoemaker will dress better, and give employment to the tailor. The tailor will more frequently renew his *chaussure*, and afford employment to the shoemaker; and the same thing will take place in all other departments of trade.

It has been said that under a system of free trade we should have fewer workmen in our mines and spinning-mills.

I do not think so. But if this happened, we should necessarily have a greater number of people working freely and independently, either in their own houses or at out-door employment.

For if our mines and spinning-factories are not capable of supporting themselves, as is asserted, without the aid of taxes levied from the *public at large*, the moment these taxes are repealed *everybody* will be by so much in better circumstances; and it is this improvement in the general circumstances of the community which lends support to individual branches of industry.

Pardon my dwelling a little longer on this view of the subject; for my great anxiety is to see you all ranged on the side of liberty.

Suppose that the capital employed in manufactures yields 5 per cent, profit. But Mondor has an establishment in which he employs £100,000, at a loss, instead of a profit, of 5 per cent. Between the loss and the gain supposed there is a difference of £10,000. What takes place? A small tax of £10,000 is coolly levied from the public, and handed over to Mondor. You don't see it, for the thing is skilfully disguised. It is not the tax-gatherer who waits upon you to demand your share of this burden; but you pay it to Mondor, the ironmaster, every time that you purchase your trowels, hatchets, and planes. Then they tell you that unless you pay this tax, Mondor will not be able to give employment; and his workmen, James and John, must go without work. And yet, if they gave up the tax, it would enable you to find employment for one another, independently of Mondor.

And then, with a little patience, after this smooth pillow of protection has been taken from under his head, Mondor, you may depend upon it, will set his wits to work, and contrive to convert his loss into a profit, and James and John will not be sent away, in which case there will be profit for everybody.

You may still rejoin, "We allow that, after the reform, there will be more employment, upon the whole, than before; in the meantime, James and John are starving."

To which I reply:

1st, That when labour is only displaced, to be augmented, a man who has a head and hands is seldom left long in a state of destitution.

2d, There is nothing to hinder the State's reserving a fund to meet, during the transition, any temporary want of employment, in which, however, for my own part, I do not believe.

3d, If I do not misunderstand the workmen, they are quite prepared to encounter any temporary suffering necessarily attendant on a transfer of labour from one department to another, by which the community are more likely to be benefited and have justice done them. I only wish I could say the same thing of their employers!

What! will it be said that because you are workmen you are for that reason unintelligent and immoral? Your pretended friends seem to think so. Is it not surprising that in your hearing they should discuss such a question, talking exclusively of wages and profits without ever once allowing the word justice to pass their lips? And yet they know that restriction is unjust. Why have they not the courage to admit it, and say to you, "Workmen! an iniquity prevails in this country, but it is profitable to you, and we must maintain it." Why? because they know you would disclaim it.

It is not true that this injustice is profitable to you. Give me your attention for a few moments longer, and then judge for yourselves.

What is it that we protect in France? Things which are produced on a great scale by rich capitalists and in large establishments, as iron, coal, cloth, and textile fabrics;

and they tell you that this is done, not in the interest of employers, but in yours, and in order to secure you employment.

And yet whenever *foreign labour* presents itself in our markets, in such a shape that it may be injurious to you, but advantageous for your employers, it is allowed to enter without any restriction being imposed.

Are there not in Paris thirty thousand Germans who make clothes and shoes? Why are they permitted to establish themselves alongside of you while the importation of cloth is restricted? Because cloth is manufactured in grand establishments which belong to manufacturing legislators. But clothes are made by workmen in their own houses. In converting wool into cloth, these gentlemen desire to have no competition, because that is their trade; but in converting cloth into coats, they allow it, because that is your trade.

In making our railways, an embargo was laid on English rails, but English workmen were brought over. Why was this? Simply because English rails came into competition with the iron produced in our great establishments, while the English labourers were only your rivals.

We have no wish that German tailors and English navvies should be kept out of France. What we ask is, that the entry of cloth and rails should be left free. We simply demand justice and equality before the law, for all.

It is a mockery to tell us that customs restrictions are imposed for your benefit. Tailors, shoemakers, carpenters, masons, blacksmiths, shopkeepers, grocers, watchmakers, butchers, bakers, dressmakers! I defy you all to point out a single way in which restriction is profitable to you, and I shall point out, whenever you desire it, four ways in which it is hurtful to you.

And, after all, see how little foundation your journalists have for attributing self-abnegation to the monopolists.

I may venture to denominate the rate of wages which settles and establishes itself naturally under a regime of freedom, the *natural rate of wages*. When you affirm, therefore, that restriction is profitable to you, it is tantamount to affirming that it adds an *overplus to your natural* wages. Now, a surplus of wages beyond the natural rate must come from some quarter or other; it does not fall from the skies, but comes from those who pay it.

You are landed, then, in this conclusion by your pretended friends, that the policy of protection has been introduced in order that the interests of capitalists should be sacrificed to those of the workmen.

Do you think this probable?

Where is your place, then, in the Chamber of Peers? When did you take your seat in the Palais Bourbon? Who has consulted you? And where did this idea of establishing a policy of protection take its rise?

I think I hear you answer, "It is not we who have established it. Alas! we are neither Peers, nor Deputies, nor Councillors of State. The capitalists have done it all."

Verily, they must have been in a good humour that day! What! these capitalists have made the law; they have established a policy of prohibition for the express purpose of enabling you to profit at their expense!

But here is something stranger still.

How does it come to pass that your pretended friends, who hold forth to you on the goodness, the generosity, and the self-abnegation of capitalists, never cease condoling with you on your being deprived of your political rights? From their point of view, I would ask what you could make of such rights if you had them? The capitalists have a monopoly of legislation;—granted. By means of this monopoly, they have adjudged themselves a monopoly of iron, of cloth, of textile fabrics, of coal, of wood, of meat,—granted likewise. But here are your pretended friends, who tell you that in acting thus, capitalists have impoverished themselves, without being under any obligation to do so, in order to enrich you who have no right to be enriched! Assuredly, if you were electors and deputies tomorrow, you could not manage your affairs better than they are managed for you; you could not manage them so well.

If the industrial legislation under which you live is intended for your profit, it is an act of perfidy to demand for you political rights; for these new-fashioned democrats never can get quit of this dilemma—the law made by the bourgeoisie either gives you more, or it gives you less than your natural wages. If that law gives you less, they deceive you, in soliciting you to maintain it. If it gives you more, they still deceive you, by inviting you to demand political rights at the very time when the bourgeoisie are making sacrifices for you, which, in common honesty, you could not by your votes exact, even if you had the power.

Workmen! I should be sorry indeed if this address should excite in your minds feelings of irritation against the rich. If self-interest, ill understood, or too apt to be alarmed, still maintains monopoly, let us not forget that monopoly has its root in errors which are common to both capitalists and labourers.

Instead of exciting the one class against the other, let us try to bring them together. And for that end what ought we to do? If it be true that the natural social tendencies concur in levelling inequalities among men, we have only to allow these tendencies to act, remove artificial obstructions which retard their operation, and allow the relations of the various classes of society to be established on principles of Justice—principles always mixed up, in my mind at least, with the principle of Liberty.

VII. A CHINESE STORY.

We hear a great outcry against the cupidity and the egotism of the age!

For my own part, I see the world, Paris especially, peopled with Deciuses.

Open the thousand volumes, the thousand newspapers of all sorts and sizes, which the Parisian press vomits forth every day on the country—are they not all the work of minor saints?

How vividly they depict the vices of the times! How touching the tenderness they display for the masses! How liberally they invite the rich to share with the poor, if not the poor to share with the rich! How many plans of social reforms, social ameliorations, and social organizations! What shallow writer fails to devote himself to the wellbeing of the working classes? We have only to contribute a few shillings to procure them leisure to deliver themselves up to their humane lucubrations.

And then they declare against the egotism and individualism of our age!

There is nothing which they do not pretend to enlist in the service of the working classes—there is positively no exception, not even the Customhouse. You fancy, perhaps, that the Customhouse is merely an instrument of taxation, like the *octroi* or the toll-bar? Nothing of the kind. It is essentially an institution for promoting the march of civilization, fraternity, and equality. What would you be at? It is the fashion to introduce, or affect to introduce, sentiment and sentimentalism everywhere, even into the toll-gatherer's booth.

The Customhouse, we must allow, has a very singular machinery for realizing philanthropical aspirations.

It includes an army of directors, sub-directors, inspectors, sub-inspectors, comptrollers, examiners, heads of departments, clerks, supernumeraries, aspirant-supernumeraries, not to speak of the officers of the active service; and the object of all this complicated machinery is to exercise over the industry of the people a negative action, which is summed up in the word obstruct.

Observe, I do not say that the object is to tax, but to obstruct. To prevent, not acts which are repugnant to good morals or public order, but transactions which are in themselves not only harmless, but fitted to maintain peace and union among nations.

And yet the human race is so flexible and elastic that it always surmounts these obstructions. And then we hear of the labour market being glutted.

If you hinder a people from obtaining its subsistence from abroad, it will produce it at home. The labour is greater and more painful, but subsistence must be had. If you hinder a man from traversing the valley, he must cross the hills. The road is longer and more difficult, but he must get to his journey's end.

This is lamentable, but we come now to what is ludicrous. When the law has thus created obstacles, and when, in order to overcome them, society has diverted a corresponding amount of labour from other employments, you are no longer permitted to demand a reform. If you point to the obstacle, you are told of the amount of labour to which it has given employment. And if you rejoin that this labour is not created, but displaced, you are answered, in the words of the *Esprit Public*, "The impoverishment alone is certain and immediate; as to our enrichment, it is more than problematical."

This reminds me of a Chinese story, which I shall relate to you.

There were in China two large towns, called *Tchin* and *Tchan.*

A magnificent canal united them. The Emperor thought fit to order enormous blocks of stone to be thrown into it, for the purpose of rendering it useless.

On seeing this, Kouang, his first mandarin, said to him:

"Son of Heaven! this is a mistake."

To which the Emperor replied:

"Kouang! you talk nonsense."

I give you only the substance of their conversation.

At the end of three months, the Celestial Emperor sent again for the mandarin, and said to him:

"Kouang, behold!"

And Kouang opened his eyes, and looked.

And he saw at some distance from the canal a multitude of men at work. Some were excavating, others were filling up hollows, levelling, and paving; and the mandarin, who was very knowing, said to himself, They are making a highway.

When other three months had elapsed, the Emperor again sent for Kouang, and said to him:

"Look!"

And Kouang looked.

And he saw the road completed, and from one end of it to the other he saw here and there inns for travellers erected. Crowds of pedestrians, carts, palanquins, came and went, and innumerable Chinese, overcome with fatigue, carried backwards and forwards heavy burdens from Tchin to Tchan, and from Tchan to Tchin; and Kouang said to himself, It is the destruction of the canal which gives employment to these poor people. But the idea never struck him that their labour was simply *diverted from other employments.*

Three months more passed, and the Emperor said to Kouang: "Look!"

And Kouang looked.

And he saw that the hostelries were full of travellers, and that to supply their wants there were grouped around them butchers' and bakers' stalls, shops for the sale of edible birds' nests, etc. He also saw that, the artisans having need of clothing, there had settled among them tailors, shoemakers, and those who sold parasols and fans; and as they could not sleep in the open air, even in the Celestial Empire, there were also masons, carpenters, and slaters. Then there were officers of police, judges, fakirs; in a word, a town with its faubourgs had risen round each hostelry.

And the Emperor asked Kouang what he thought of all this. And Kouang said that he never could have imagined that the destruction of a canal could have provided employment for so many people; for the thought never struck him that this was not employment created, but *labour diverted* from other employments, and that men would have eaten and drank in passing along the canal as well as in passing along the highroad.

However, to the astonishment of the Chinese, the Son of Heaven at length died and was buried.

His successor sent for Kouang, and ordered him to have the canal cleared out and restored.

And Kouang said to the new Emperor:

"Son of Heaven! you commit a blunder."

And the Emperor replied:

"Kouang, you talk nonsense."

But Kouang persisted, and said: "Sire, what is your object?"

"My object is to facilitate the transit of goods and passengers between Tchin and Tchan, to render carriage less expensive, in order that the people may have tea and clothing cheaper."

But Kouang was ready with his answer. He had received the night before several numbers of the Moniteur Industriel, a Chinese newspaper. Knowing his lesson well, he asked and obtained permission to reply, and after having prostrated himself nine times, he said:

"Sire, your object is, by increased facility of transit, to reduce the price of articles of consumption, and bring them within reach of the people; and to effect that, you begin by taking away from them all the employment to which the destruction of the canal had given rise. Sire, in political economy, nominal cheapness-" *The Emperor*: "I believe you are repeating by rote." *Kouang*: "True, Sire; and it will be better to read what I have to say." So, producing the *Esprit Public*, he read as follows: "In political economy, the nominal cheapness of articles of consumption is only a secondary question. The problem is to establish an equilibrium between the price of labour and that of the means of subsistence. The abundance of labour constitutes the wealth of nations; and the best economic system is that which supplies the people with the greatest amount of employment. The question is not whether it is better to pay four or eight cash for a cup of tea, or five or ten tales for a shirt. These are puerilities unworthy of a thinking mind. Nobody disputes your proposition. The question is whether it is better to pay dearer for a commodity you want to buy, and have, through the abundance of employment and the higher price of labour, the means of acquiring it; or whether, it is better to limit the sources of employment, and with them the mass of the national production—to transport, by improved means of transit, the objects of consumption, cheaper, it is true, but taking away at the same time from classes of our population the means of purchasing these objects even at their reduced price."

Seeing the Emperor still unconvinced, Kouang added, "Sire, deign to give me your attention. I have still another quotation from the *Moniteur Industriel* to bring under your notice."

But the Emperor said:

"I don't require your Chinese journals to enable me to find out that to create *obstacles* is to divert and misapply labour. But that is not my mission. Go and clear out the canal; and we shall reform the Customhouse afterwards."

And Kouang went away tearing his beard, and appealing to his God, "O Fo! take pity on thy people; for we have now got an Emperor of the English school, and I see clearly that in a short time we shall be in want of everything, for we shall no longer require to do anything."

VIII. POST HOC, ERGO PROPTER HOC.

This is the greatest and most common fallacy in reasoning.

Real sufferings, for example, have manifested themselves in England.*

* *This was written in January 1848.—Translator.*

These sufferings come in the train of two other phenomena:

1st, The reformed tariff;

2d, Two bad harvests in succession.

To which of these two last circumstances are we to attribute the first?

The protectionists exclaim:

It is this accursed free-trade which does all the harm. It promised us wonderful things; we accepted it; and here are our manufactures at a standstill, and the people suffering: *Cum hoc, ergo propter hoc.*

Free-trade distributes in the most uniform and equitable manner the fruits which Providence accords to human labour. If we are deprived of part of these fruits by natural causes, such as a succession of bad seasons, free-trade does not fail to distribute in the same manner what remains. Men are, no doubt, not so well provided with what they want; but are we to impute this to free-trade, or to the bad harvests?

Liberty acts on the same principle as insurances. When an accident, like a fire, happens, insurance spreads over a great number of men, and a great number of years, losses which, in the absence of insurance, would have fallen all at once upon one individual. But will any one undertake to affirm that fire has become a greater evil since the introduction of insurance?

In 1842, 1843, and 1844, the reduction of taxes began in England. At the same time the harvests were very abundant; and we are led to conclude that these two circumstances concurred in producing the unparalleled prosperity which England enjoyed during that period.

In 1845, the harvest was bad; and in 1846, worse still.

Provisions rose in price; and the people were forced to expend their resources on first necessaries, and to limit their consumption of other commodities. Clothing was less in demand, manufactories had less work, and wages tended to fall.

Fortunately, in that same year, the barriers of restriction were still more effectually removed, and an enormous quantity of provisions reached the English market. Had this not been so, it is nearly certain that a formidable revolution would have taken place.

And yet free-trade is blamed for disasters which it tended to prevent, and in part, at least, to repair!

A poor leper lived in solitude. Whatever he happened to touch, no one else would touch. Obliged to pine in solitude, he led a miserable existence. An eminent physician cured him, and now our poor hermit was admitted to all the benefits of *free-trade, and had full liberty to effect exchanges*. What brilliant prospects were opened to him! He delighted in calculating the advantages which, through his restored intercourse with his fellow-men, he was able to derive from his own vigorous exertions. He happened to break both his arms, and was landed in poverty and misery. The journalists who were witnesses of that misery said, "See to what this liberty of making exchanges has reduced him! Verily, he was less to be pitied when he lived alone." "What!" said the physician, "do you make no allowance for his broken arms? Has that accident nothing to do with his present unhappy state? His misfortune arises from his having lost the use of his hands, and not from his having been cured of his leprosy. He would have been a fitter subject for your compassion had he been lame, and leprous into the bargain."

Post hoc, ergo propter hoc. Beware of that sophism.

IX. THE PREMIUM THEFT.

This little book of Sophisms is found to be too theoretical, scientific, and metaphysical. Be it so. Let us try the effect of a more trivial and hackneyed, or, if you will, a ruder style. Convinced that the public is duped in this matter of protection, I have endeavoured to prove it. But if outcry is preferred to argument, let us vociferate,

"King Midas has a snout, and asses' ears."*

* *"Auriculas asini Mida rex habet."—Persius, sat. i. The line as given in the text is from Dryden's translation.— Translator.*

A burst of plain speaking has more effect frequently than the most polished circumlocution. You remember Oronte, and the difficulty which the *Misanthrope* had in convincing him of his folly.*

Alceste. On s'expose à jouer un mauvais personnage.

Oronte. Est-ce que vous voulez me declarer par là que j'ai tort de vouloir....

Alceste. Je ne dis pas cela.

Mais....

Oronte. Est-ce que j'ecris mal?

Alceste. Je ne dis pas cela.

Mais enfin....

Oronte. Mais ne puis-je savoir ce que dans mon sonnet?...

Alceste. Franchement, il est bon à mettre au Cabinet.

To speak plainly, Good Public! *you are robbed.* This is speaking bluntly, but the thing is very evident. (*C'est cru, mais c'est clair*).

The words *theft, to steal, robbery*, may appear ugly words to many people. I ask such people, as Harpagon asks Elise,** "Is it the word or the thing which frightens you?"

* *See Molière's play of The Misanthrope.—Translator.*

** *See Molière's play of Oevare.—Translator.*

"Whoever has possessed himself fraudulently of a thing which does not belong to him is guilty of theft." (C. Pen., art. 379.)

To steal: To take by stealth or by force. (*Dictionnaire de l'Academie.*)

Thief: He who exacts more than is due to him. (75.)

Now, does the monopolist, who, by a law of his own making, obliges me to pay him 20 francs for what I could get elsewhere for 15, not take from me fraudulently 5 francs which belonged to me?

Does he not take them by stealth or by force?

Does he not exact more than is due to him?

He takes, purloins, exacts, it may be said; but not by stealth or by force, which are the characteristics of theft.

When our bulletins de contributions have included in them 5 francs for the premium which the monopolist takes, exacts, or abstracts, what can be more stealthy for the unsuspecting? And for those who are not dupes, and who do suspect, what savours more of force, seeing that on the first refusal the tax-gather's bailiff is at the door?

But let monopolists take courage. Premium thefts, tariff thefts, if they violate equity as much as theft à l'Americaine, do not violate the law; on the contrary, they are perpetrated according to law; and if they are worse than common thefts, they do not come under the cognizance of *la correctionnelle.*

Besides, right or wrong, we are all robbed or robbers in this business. The author of this volume might very well cry "Stop thief!" when he buys; and with equal reason he might have that cry addressed to him when he sells;* and if he is in a situation different from that of many of his countrymen, the difference consists in this, that he knows that he loses more than he gains by the game, and they don't know it. If they knew it, the game would soon be given up.

* *Possessing some landed property, on which he lives, he belongs to the protected class. This circumstance should disarm criticism. It shows that if he uses hard words, they are directed against the thing itself, and not against men's intentions or motives.*

Nor do I boast of being the first to give the thing its right name. Adam Smith said, sixty years ago, that "when manufacturers hold meetings, we may be sure a plot is hatching against the pockets of the public." Can we be surprised at this, when the public winks at it?

Well, then, suppose a meeting of manufacturers deliberating formally, under the title of *conseils generaux*. What takes place, and what is resolved upon?

Here is an abridged report of one of their meetings:—

"Shipowner: Our merchant shipping is at the lowest ebb. (Dissent) That is not to be wondered at. I cannot construct ships without iron. I can buy it in the market of the world at 10 francs; but by law the French ironmaster forces me to pay him 15 francs, which takes 5 francs out of my pocket. I demand liberty to purchase iron wherever I see proper.

"Ironmaster: In the market of the world I find freights at 20 francs. By law I am obliged to pay the French shipowner 30; he takes 10 francs out of my pocket. He robs me, and I rob him; all quite right.

"Statesman: The shipowner has arrived at a hasty conclusion. Let us cultivate union as regards that which constitutes our strength. If we give up a single point of the theory of protection, the whole theory falls to the ground.

"Shipowner: For us shipowners protection has been a failure. I repeat that the merchant marine is at its lowest ebb.

"Shipmaster: Well, let us raise the *surtaxe*, and let the shipowner who now exacts 30 francs from the public for his freight, charge 40.

"A Minister: The government will make all the use they can of the beautiful mechanism of the *surtaxe*; but I fear that will not be sufficient.

"A Government Functionary: You are all very easily frightened. Does the tariff alone protect you? and do you lay taxation out of account? If the consumer is kind and benevolent, the taxpayer is not less so. Let us heap taxes upon him, and the shipowner will be satisfied. I propose a premium of five francs to be levied from the public taxpayers, to be handed over to the shipbuilder for each ton of iron he shall employ.

"Confused voices: Agreed! agreed! An agriculturist: Three francs premium upon the hectolitre of corn for me! A manufacturer: Two francs premium on the yard of cloth for me! etc., etc.

"The President: This then is what we have agreed upon. Our session has instituted a system of *premiums*, and it will be to our eternal honour. What branch of industry can possibly henceforth be a loser, since we have two means, and both so very simple, of converting our losses into gains—the tariff and the premium? The sitting is adjourned."

I really think some supernatural vision must have foreshadowed to me in a dream the near approach of the premium (who knows but I may have first suggested the idea to M. Dupin?) when six months ago I wrote these words:—

"It appears evident to me that protection, without changing its nature or the effects which it produces, might take the form of a direct tax, levied by the state, and distributed in premiums of indemnification among privileged branches of industry."

And after comparing a protective duty to a premium, I added, "I confess candidly my preference for the last system. It seems to me juster, more economical, and more fair. Juster, because if society desires to make presents to some of its members, all ought to bear the expense; more economical, because it would save a great deal in the cost of collection, and do away with many of the trammels with which trade is hampered; more fair, because the public would see clearly the nature of the operation, and act accordingly."*

* *Sophismes Economiques, first series, ch. v. ante.*

Since the occasion presents itself to us so opportunely, let us study this system of *plunder by premium*; for all we say of it applies equally to the system of plunder by tariff;

and as the latter is a little better concealed, the direct may help us to detect and expose the indirect system of cheating. The mind will thus be led from what is simple to what is more complicated.

But it may be asked, Is there not a species of theft which is more simple still? Undoubtedly; there is *highway robbery*, which wants only to be legalized, and made a monopoly of, or, in the language of the present day, *organized.*

I have been reading what follows in a book of travels:—

"When we reached the kingdom of A., all branches of industry declared themselves in a state of suffering. Agriculture groaned, manufactures complained, trade murmured, the shipping interest grumbled, and the government were at a loss what to do. First of all, the idea was to lay a pretty smart tax on all the malcontents, and afterwards to divide the proceeds among them after retaining its own quota; this would have been on the principle of the Spanish lottery. There are a thousand of you, and the State takes a piastre from each; then by sleight of hand, it conveys away 250 piastres, and divides the remaining 750 in larger and smaller proportions among the ticket-holders. The gallant Hidalgo who gets three-fourths of a piastre, forgetting that he had contributed a whole piastre, cannot conceal his delight, and rushes off to spend his fifteen reals at the alehouse. This is very much the same thing as we see taking place in France. But the government had overrated the stupidity of the population when it endeavoured to make them accept such a species of protection, and at length it lighted upon the following expedient.

"The country was covered with a network of highroads. The government had these roads accurately measured; and then it announced to the agriculturist, 'All that you can steal from travellers between these two points is yours; let that serve as a *premium* for your protection and encouragement.' Afterwards it assigned to each manufacturer, to each shipowner, a certain portion of road, to be made available for their profit, according to this formula:—

Dono tibi et concedo Virtutem et puissantiam Yolandi,
Pillandi,
Derobandi,
Filoutandi,
Et escroqtĩïndi,
Impunè per totam istam Viam."

Now it has come to pass that the natives of the kingdom of A. have become so habituated to this system, that they take into account only what they are enabled to steal, not what is stolen from them, being so determined to regard pillage only from the standpoint of the thief, that they look upon the sum total of individual thefts as a national gain, and refuse to abandon a system of protection, without which they say no branch of industry could support itself.

You demur to this. It is not possible, you exclaim, that a whole people should be led to ascribe a redundancy of wealth to mutual robbery.

And why not? We see that this conviction pervades France, and that we are constantly organizing and improving the system of *reciprocal robbery* under the respectable names of premiums and protective tariffs.

We must not, however, be guilty of exaggeration. As regards the mode of levying, and other collateral circumstances, the system adopted in the kingdom of A. may be worse than ours; but we must at the same time admit that, as regards the principle and its necessary consequences, there is not an atom of difference between these two species of theft; which are both organized by law for the purpose of supplementing the profits of particular branches of industry.

Remark also, that if *highway robbery* presents some inconveniences in its actual perpetration, it has likewise some advantages which we do not find in *robbery by tariff.*

For example, it is possible to make an equitable division among all the producers. It is not so in the case of customs duties. The latter are incapable of protecting certain classes of society, such as artisans, shopkeepers, men of letters, lawyers, soldiers, labourers, etc.

It is true that the robbery by premium assumes an infinite number of shapes, and in this respect is not inferior to highway robbery; but, on the other hand, it leads frequently to results so whimsical and awkward that the natives of the kingdom of A. may well laugh at us.

What the victim of a highway robbery loses, the thief gains, and the articles stolen remain in the country. But under the system of robbery by premium, what the tax exacts from the Frenchman is conferred frequently on the Chinese, on the Hottentots, on the Caffres, etc., and here is the way in which this takes place:

A piece of cloth, we shall suppose, is worth 100 francs at Bordeaux. It cannot be sold below that price without a loss. It is impossible to sell it above that price because the competition of merchants prevents the price rising. In these circumstances, if a Frenchman desires to have the cloth, he must pay 100 francs, or want it. But if it is an Englishman who wants the cloth, the government steps in, and says to the merchant, "Sell your cloth, and we will get you 20 francs from the taxpayers." The merchant who could not get more than 100 francs for his cloth, sells it to the Englishman for 80. This sum, added to the 20 francs produced by the premium theft, makes all square. This is exactly the same case as if the taxpayers had given 20 francs to the Englishmen, upon condition of his buying French cloth at 20 francs discount, at 20 francs below the cost of production, at 20 francs below what it has cost ourselves. The robbery by premium, then, has this peculiarity, that the people robbed are resident in the country which tolerates it, while the people who profit by the robbery are scattered over the world.

Verily, it is marvellous that people should persist in maintaining that *all which an individual steals from the masses is a general gain.* Perpetual motion, the philosopher's stone, the quadrature of the circle, are antiquated problems; but the theory of *progress by plunder* is still held in honour. *A priori*, we should have thought that, of all imaginable puerilities, it was the least likely to survive.

Some people will say, You are partisans, then, of the *laissez passer?*—economists of the school of Smith and Say? You do not desire the organization of labour. Yes, gentlemen, organize labour as much as you choose, but have the goodness not to organize theft.

Another, and a more numerous, set keep repeating, premiums, tariffs, all that has been exaggerated. We should use them without abusing them. A judicious liberty, combined with a moderate protection, that is what discreet and practical men desire. Let us steer clear of fixed principles and inflexible rules.

This is precisely what the traveller tells us takes place in the kingdom of A. "Highway robbery," say the sages, "is neither good nor bad in itself; that depends upon circumstances. All we are concerned with is to weigh things, and see our functionaries well paid for the work of weighing. It may be that we have given too great latitude to pillage; perhaps we have not given enough. Let us examine and balance the accounts of each man employed in the work of pillage. To those who do not earn enough, let us assign a larger portion of the road. To those who gain too much, we must limit the days or months of pillage."

Those who talk in this way gain a great reputation for moderation, prudence, and good sense. They never aspire to the highest offices in the state.

Those who say, Repress all injustice, whether on a greater or a smaller scale, suffer no dishonesty, to however small an extent, are marked down for *ideologues*, idle dreamers, who keep repeating over and over again the same thing. The people, moreover, find their arguments too clear, and why should they be expected to believe what is so easily understood?

X. THE TAXGATHERER.

Jacques Bonhomme, a Vinedresser.

M. Lasouche, Taxgatherer.

L.: You have secured twenty tuns of wine?

J.: Yes; by dint of my own skill and labour.

L.: Have the goodness to deliver up to me six of the best.

J.: Six tuns out of twenty! Good Heaven! you are going to ruin me. And, please, Sir, for what purpose do you intend them?

L.: The first will be handed over to the creditors of the State. When people have debts, the least thing they can do is to pay interest upon them.

J.: And what becomes of the capital?

L.: That is too long a story to tell you at present. One part used to be converted into cartridges, which emitted the most beautiful smoke in the world. Another went to pay the men who had got crippled in foreign wars. Then, when this expenditure brought invasion upon us, our polite friend, the enemy, was unwilling to take leave of us without carrying away some of our money as a *soutenir*, and this money had to be borrowed.

J.: And what benefit do I derive from this now?

L.: The satisfaction of saying—

Que je suis fier d'être Français

Quand je regarde la colonne!

J.: And the humiliation of leaving to my heirs an estate burdened with a perpetual rent-charge. Still, it is necessary to pay one's debts, whatever foolish use is made of the proceeds. So much for the disposal of one tun; but what about the five others?

L.: One goes to support the public service, the civil list, the judges who protect your property when your neighbour wishes wrongfully to appropriate it, the gendarmes who protect you from robbers when you are asleep, the cantonnier who maintains the highways, the cure who baptizes your children, the schoolmaster who educates them, and, lastly, your humble servant, who cannot be expected to work exactly for nothing.

J.: All right; service for service is quite fair, and I have nothing to say against it. I should like quite as well, no doubt, to deal directly with the rector and the schoolmaster on my own account; but I don't stand upon that. This accounts for the second tun—but we have still other four to account for.

L.: Would you consider two tuns as more than your fair contribution to the expense of the army and navy?

J.: Alas! that is a small affair, compared with what the two services have cost me already, for they have deprived me of two sons whom I dearly loved.

L.: It is necessary to maintain the balance of power.

J.: And would that balance not be quite as well maintained if the European powers were to reduce their forces by one-half or three -fourths? We should preserve our children and our money. All that is requisite is to come to a common understanding.

L.: Yes; but they don't understand one another.

J.: It is that which fills me with astonishment, for they suffer from it in common.

L.: It is partly your own doing, Jacques Bonhomme.

J.: You are joking, Mr Taxgatherer. Have I any voice in the matter?

L.: Whom did you vote for as deputy?

J.: A brave general officer, who will soon be a marshal, if God spares him.

L.: And upon what does the gallant general live?

J.: Upon my six tuns, I should think.

L.: What would happen to him if he voted a reduction of the army, and of your contingent?

J.: Instead of being made a marshal, he would be forced to retire.

L.: Do you understand now that you have yourself....

J.: Let us pass on to the fifth tun, if you please.

L.: That goes to Algeria.

J.: To Algeria! And yet they tell us that all the Mussulmans are wine-haters, barbarians as they are! I have often inquired whether it is their ignorance of claret which has made them infidels, or their infidelity which has made them ignorant of claret. And then, what service do they render me in return for this nectar which has cost me so much toil?

L.: None at all; nor is the wine destined for the Mussulman, but for good Christians who spend their lives in Barbary.

J.: And what service do they render me?

L.: They make *razzias*, and suffer from them in their turn; they kill and are killed; they are seized with dysentery and sent to the hospital; they make harbours and roads, build villages, and people them with Maltese, Italians, Spaniards, and Swiss, who live upon your wine; for another supply of which, I can tell you, I will soon come back to you.

J.: Good gracious! that is too much. I shall give you a flat refusal A vinedresser who could be guilty of such folly would be sent to Bicetre. To make roads over Mount Atlas—good Heavens! when I can scarcely leave my house for want of roads! To form harbours in Barbary, when the Garonne is silted up! To carry off my children whom I love, and send them to torment the Kabyles! To make me pay for houses, seed, and cattle, to be handed over to Greeks and Maltese, when we have so many poor people to provide for at home!

L.: The poor! Just so; they rid the country of the *trop plein*, and prevent a redundant population.

J.: And we are to send after them to Algeria the capital on which they could live at home!

L.: But then you are laying the foundations of a great empire, you carry civilization into Africa, thus crowning your country with immortal glory.

J.: You are a poet, Mr Taxgatherer. I am a plain vinedresser, and I refuse your demand.

L.: But think, that in the course of some thousands of years, your present advances will be recouped and repaid a hundredfold to your descendants. The men who direct the enterprise assure us that it will be so.

J.: In the meantime, in order to defray the expense, they ask me first of all for one cask of wine, then for two, then for three, and now I am taxed by the tun! I persist in my refusal.

L.: Your refusal comes too late. Your *representative* has stipulated for the whole quantity I demand.

J.: Too true. Cursed weakness on my part! Surely, in making him my proxy, I was guilty of a piece of folly; for what is there in common between a general officer and a poor vinedresser?

L.: Oh, yes; there is something in common, namely, the wine, which he has voted to himself in your name.

J.: You may well laugh at me, Mr Taxgatherer, for I richly deserve it. But be reasonable. Leave me at least the sixth tun. You have already secured payment of the interest of the debt, and provided for the civil list and the public service, besides perpetuating the war in Africa. What more would you have?

L.: It is needless to higgle with me. Communicate your views to Monsieur le General, your representative. For the present, he has voted away your vintage.

J.: Confound the fellow! But tell me what you intend to make of this last cask, the best of my whole stock? Stay, taste this wine. How ripe, mellow, and full-bodied it is!

L.: Excellent! delicious! It will suit Mons. D., the cloth-manufacturer, admirably.

J.: Mons. D., the cloth-manufacturer? What do you mean?

L.: That he will reap the benefit.

J.: How? What? I'll be hanged if I understand you!

L.: Don't you know that Mons. D. has set on foot a grand undertaking, which will prove most useful to the country, but which, when everything is taken into account, causes each year a considerable pecuniary loss?

J.: I am sorry to hear it, but what can I do?

L.: The Chamber has come to the conclusion that, if this state of things continues, Mons. D. will be under the necessity of either working more profitably, or of shutting up his manufacturing establishment altogether.

J.: But what have these losing speculations of Mons. D. to do with my wine?

L.: The Chamber has found out that, by making over to Mons. D. some wine taken from your cellar, some corn taken from your neighbour's granaries, some money kept off the workmen's wages, the losses of that enterprising patriot may be converted into profits.

J.: The recipe is as infallible as it is ingenious. But, zounds! it is awfully iniquitous. Mons. D., forsooth, is to make up his losses by laying hold of my wine?

L.: Not exactly of the wine, but of its price. This is what we denominate *premiums of encouragement*, or bounties. Don't you see the great service you are rendering to the country?

J.: You mean to Mons. D.?

L.: To the country. Mons. D. assures us that his manufacture prospers in consequence of this arrangement, and in this way he considers the country is enriched. He said so the other day in the Chamber, of which he is a member.

J.: This is a wretched quibble! A speculator enters into a losing trade, and dissipates his capital; and then he extorts from me and from my neighbours wine and corn of sufficient value, not only to repair his losses, but afford him a profit, and this is represented as a gain to the country at large.

L.: Your representative having come to this conclusion, you have nothing more to do but to deliver up to me the six tuns of wine which I demand, and sell the remaining fourteen tuns to the best advantage.

J.: That is my business.

L.: It will be unfortunate if you do not realize a large price

J.: I will think of it.

L.: The higher price will enable you to procure more of other things.

J.: I am aware of that, Sir.

L.: In the first place, if you purchase iron to renew your ploughs and your spades, the law decrees that you must pay the ironmaster double what the commodity is worth.

J.: Yes, this is very consolatory.

L.: Then you have need of coal, of butchers' meat, of cloth, of oil, of wool, of sugar; and for each of these commodities the law makes you pay double.

J.: It is horrible, frightful, abominable!

L.: Why should you indulge in complaints? You yourself, through your representative...

J.: Say nothing more of my representative. I am singularly represented, it is true. But they will not impose upon me a second time. I shall be represented by a good and honest peasant.

L.: Bah! you will re-elect the gallant General.

J.: Shall I re-elect him, to divide my wine among Africans and manufacturers?

L.: I tell you, you will re-elect him.

J,: This is too much. I am free to re-elect him or not, as I choose.

L.: But you will so choose.

J.: Let him come forward again, and he will find whom he has to deal with.

L.: Well, we shall see. Farewell. I carry away your six tuns of wine, to be distributed as your friend, the General, has determined.

XI. THE UTOPIAN FREE-TRADER.

If I were but one of His Majesty's ministers!...

"Well, what would you do?"

"I should begin by—by—faith, by being very much at a loss. For it is clear I could only be a minister in consequence of having the majority in my favour; I could only have the majority in my favour by securing the popular suffrage; and I could attain that end, honestly at least, only by governing in accordance with public opinion. If I should attempt to carry out my own opinions, I should no longer have the majority; and if I lost the favour of the majority, I should be no longer one of His Majesty's ministers."

"But suppose yourself already a minister, and that you experience no opposition from the majority, what would you do?"

"I should inquire on what side *justice* lay."

"And then?"

"I should inquire on what side *utility* lay."

"And then?"

"I should inquire whether justice and utility were in harmony, or ran counter to one another."

"And if you found they were not in harmony?"

"Je dirais au roi Philippe:

Reprenez votre portefeuille.

La rime n'est pas riche et le style en est vieux;

Mais ne voyez-vous pas que cela vaut bien mieux,

Que ces transactions dont le bon sens murmure,

Et que l'honnêtete parle là toute pure."

"But if you found that the just and the useful were one and the same thing?"

"Then I should go straight forward."

"True; but to realize utility by means of justice, a third thing is needed."

"What?"

"Possibility."

"You granted me that."

"When?"

"Just now."

"How?"

"In assuming that I had the majority on my side."

"A most dangerous concession, I fear; for it implies that the majority see clearly what is just, see clearly what is useful, and see clearly that both are in perfect harmony."

"And if they see clearly all this, good results will work themselves out, so to speak, of their own accord."

"You always bring me back to this, that no reform is possible apart from the progress of general intelligence."

"Assuming this progress, every needed reform will infallibly follow."

"True; but this presupposed progress is a work of time. Suppose it accomplished, what would you do? I am anxious to see you actually and practically at work."

"I should begin by reducing the rate of postage to a penny."

"I have heard you speak of a halfpenny."*

* *See chap. xii. of Sophismes, second series, post.*

"Yes, but as I have other reforms in view, I should proceed prudently, in the first instance, to avoid any risk of a deficit."

"Fine prudence, to be sure! You have already landed yourself in a deficit of 30 millions of francs."

"Then I should reduce the salt-tax to 10 francs."

"Good. Then you land yourself in a deficit of other thirty millions. You have doubtless invented a new tax?"

"Heaven forbid! And besides, I do not flatter myself with possessing an inventive genius."

"It will be very necessary, however.... Ah! I see. What was I thinking of? You intend simply to reduce the expenditure. I did not think of that."

"You are not singular. I shall come to that; but for the present, that is not the resource on which I depend."

"What! you are to diminish the revenue without reducing the expenditure, and withal avoid a deficit!"

"Yes; by diminishing other taxes at the same time."

(Here the interlocutor, raising the forefinger of the right hand to his forehead, tossed his head, as if beating about for ideas.)

"By my faith! a most ingenious process. I pay over 100 francs to the Treasury; you relieve me to the extent of 5 francs upon salt, and 5 francs upon postages; and in order that the Treasury may still receive 100 francs, you relieve me to the extent of 10 francs on some other tax."

"Exactly; I see you understand what I mean."

"The thing seems so strange that I am not quite sure that I even heard you distinctly."

"I repeat, I balance one *degrèvement* by another."

"Well, I happen to have a few minutes to spare, and I should like much to hear you explain this paradox."

"Here is the whole mystery. I know a tax which costs the taxpayer 20 francs, and of which not one farthing ever reaches the Treasury. I relieve you of one-half, and I see that the other half finds its way to the *Hôtel des Finances*."

"Truly you are an unrivalled financier. And what tax, pray, do I pay which does not reach the Treasury?"

"How much does this coat cost you?"

"100 francs."

"And if you procured the cloth from Verviers, how much would it cost you?"

"80 francs."

"Why, then, did you not order it from Verviers?"

"Because that is forbidden."

"And why is it forbidden?"

"In order that the coat may cost 100 instead of 80 francs."

"This prohibition, then, costs you 20 francs."

"Undoubtedly."

"And where do these 20 francs go to?"

"Where should they go to, but into the pocket of the cloth-manufacturer?"

"Well, then, give me 10 francs for the Treasury, I will abrogate the prohibition, and you will still be a gainer of 10 francs."

"Oh! I begin to follow you. The account with the Treasury will then stand thus: The revenue loses 5 francs upon salt, and 5 upon postages, and gains 10 francs upon cloth. The one balances the other."

"And your own account stands thus: You gain 5 francs upon salt, 5 francs upon postages, and 10 francs upon cloth."

"Total, 20 francs. I like your plan; but what comes of the poor cloth-manufacturer?"

"Oh! I have not lost sight of him. I manage to give him compensation likewise by means of *degrèvements* which are profitable to the revenue; and what I have done for you as regards cloth, I do for him as regards wool, coals, machinery, etc., so that he is enabled to reduce his price without being a loser."

"But are you sure that the one will balance the other?"

"The balance will be in his favour. The 20 francs which I enable you to gain upon cloth, will be augmented by the amount I enable you to save upon corn, meat, fuel, etc. This will amount to a large sum; and a similar saving will be realized by each of your 35 millions of fellow-countrymen. In this way, you will find the means of consuming all the cloth produced at Verviers and Elbeuf. The nation will be better clothed; that is all."

"I shall think over it; for all this, I confess, confuses my head somewhat."

"After all, as regards clothing, the main consideration is to be clothed. Your limbs are your own, and not the property of the manufacturer. To protect them from the cold is your business and not his! If the law takes his part against you, the law is unjust; and we have been reasoning hitherto on the hypothesis that what is unjust is injurious."

"Perhaps I make too free with you; but I beg you to complete the explanation of your financial plan."

"I shall have a new law of Customs."

"In two volumes folio?"

"No, in two articles."

"For once, then, we may dispense with repeating the famous axiom, 'No one is supposed to be ignorant of the law'—*Nul n'est cerne ignorer la loi*; which is a fiction. Let us see, then, your proposed tariff."

"Here it is:

"'Art. 1st.—All imported merchandise shall pay a duty of 5 per cent. *ad valorem*.'"

"Even raw materials?"

"Except those which are destitute of value."

"But they are all possessed of value, less or more."

"In that case they must pay duty, less or more."

"How do you suppose that our manufacturers can compete with foreign manufacturers who have their raw materials free?"

"The expenditure of the State being given, if we shut up this source of revenue, we must open another. That will not do away with the relative inferiority of our manufactures, and we shall have an additional staff of officials to create and to pay for."

"True. I reason as if the problem were to do away with taxation, and not to substitute one tax for another. I shall think over it. What is your second article?"

"'Art. 2d.—All merchandise exported shall pay a duty of 5 per cent, *ad valorem*.'"

"Good gracious! Monsieur l'Utopiste. You are going to get yourself pelted, and, if necessary, I myself will cast the first stone."

"We have taken for granted that the majority are enlightened."

"Enlightened! Can you maintain that export duties will not be onerous?"

"All taxes are onerous; but this will be less so than others."

"The carnival justifies many eccentricities. Please to render plausible, if that be possible, this new paradox."

"How much do you pay for this wine?"

"One franc the litre."

"How much would you have paid for it outside the barrier?"

"Half a franc."

"What is the reason of this difference?"

"Ask the octroi, which has imposed a tax of half a franc upon it."

"And who established the octroi?"

"The Commune of Paris, to enable them to pave and light the streets."

"It resolves itself, then, into an import duty. But if the neighbouring communes had erected the octroi for their profit, what would have been the consequence?"

"I should not the less have paid one franc for wine worth half a franc, and the other half franc would have gone to pave and light Montmartre and the Batignoles."

"So that, in effect, it is the consumer who pays the tax."

"That is beyond all doubt."

"Then, in imposing an export duty, you make the foreigner contribute to your expenditure."

"Pardon me, that is *unjust*."

"Why? Before any commodity can be produced in a country, we must presuppose as existing in that country education, security, roads, which are all things that cost money. Why then should not the foreigner bear the charges necessary to the production of the commodity of which ultimately he is the consumer?"

"That is contrary to received ideas."

"Not in the least. The last buyer must bear the whole cost of production, direct and indirect."

"It is in vain that you argue on this subject. It is self-evident that such a measure would paralyze trade, and shut all markets against us."

"This is a mistake. If you paid this tax over and above all others, you might be right. But if the 100 millions levied by this means relieved the taxpayer to a corresponding extent of other burdens, you would reappear in the foreign market with all your advantages, and even with greater advantages, if this tax shall have given rise to less complication and expense."

"I shall think over it. And now that we have put salt, postages, and customs duties on a new footing, does this end your projected reform?"

"On the contrary, we are only beginning."

"Pray give me some account of your other utopian schemes."

"We have already given up 60 millions of francs on salt and postages. The Customhouse affords compensation, but it gives also something far more precious."

"And what is that, if you please?"

"International relations founded on justice, and a probability of peace nearly equal to a certainty. I disband the army."

"The whole army?"

"Excepting the special arms, which will be recruited voluntarily like all other professions. You thus see the conscription abolished."

"Be pleased, Sir, to use the word recruitment."

"Ah! I had forgotten; how easy it is in some countries to perpetuate and hand down the most unpopular things by changing their names!"

"Thus, *droits reunis* have become *contributions indirectes*."

"And *gendarmes* have taken the name of *gardes municipaux*."

"In short, you would disarm the country on the faith of a utopian theory."

"I said that I should disband the army—not that I would disarm the country. On the contrary, I intend to give it invincible force."

"And how can you give consistency to this mass of contradictions?"

"I should call upon all citizens to take part in the service."

"It would be well worth while to dispense with the services of some of them, in order to enrol all."

"You surely have not made me a minister in order to leave things as they are. On my accession to power, I should say, like Richelieu, 'State maxims are changed.' And my first maxim, the one I should employ as the basis of my administration, would be this: Every citizen must prepare for two things—to provide for his own subsistence, and to defend his country."

"It appears to me, at first sight, that there is some show of common sense in what you say."

"Consequently, I should base the law of national defence on these two enactments:

"'Art. 1st.—Every able-bodied citizen shall remain *sous les drapeaux* for four years—namely, from 21 to 25—for the purpose of receiving military instruction.'"

"A fine economy, truly! You disband four hundred thousand soldiers to create ten millions."

"Listen to my second article:

"'Art. 2d.—Unless it is proved that at 21 years of age he knows perfectly the platoon drill.'"

"Nor do I stop here. It is certain that in order to get quit of four years' service, there would be a terrible emulation among our youth to learn the *par le flanc droit and the charge en douze temps*. The idea is whimsical."

"It is better than that. For without bringing families to grief, without encroaching on equality, would it not secure to the country, in a simple and inexpensive manner, 10 millions of defenders capable of setting at defiance all the standing armies of the world?"

"Really, if I were not on my guard, I should end with taking a serious interest in your conceits."

Utopian free-trader getting excited. "Thank Heaven! here is my Budget relieved of 200 millions. I suppress the octroi. I remodel indirect contributions. I..."

"Oh! Monsieur l'Utopiste!"

Utopian free-trader getting more and more excited. "I should proclaim freedom of worship, freedom of teaching, and new resources. I would buy up the railways, pay off the public debtr and starve out stockjobbers."

"Monsieur l'Utopiste!"

"Set free from a multiplicity of cares, I should concentrate all the powers of government in the repression of fraud, and in the administration of prompt and cheap justice; I....

"Monsieur l'Utopiste, you undertake too many things; the nation will not support you!"

"You have granted me a majority."

"I withdraw it."

"Be it so. Then I am no longer a minister, and my projects will continue to be what they were—*Utopias*."

XII. THE SALT-TAX, RATES OF POSTAGE, AND CUSTOMHOUSE DUTIES.

We expected some time ago to see our representative machinery produce an article quite new, the manufacture of which had not as yet been attempted—namely, *the relief of the taxpayer.*

All was expectation. The experiment was interesting, as well as new. The motion of the machine disturbed nobody. In this respect, its performance was admirable, no matter at what time, in what place, or under what circumstances it was set agoing.

But as regarded those reforms which were to simplify, equalize, and lighten the public burdens, no one has yet been able to find out what has been accomplished.

It was said: You shall soon see; wait a little; this popular result involves the labours of four sessions. The year 1842 gave us railways; 1846 is to give us the reduction of the salt-tax and of the rates of postage; in 1850 we are to have a reformation of the tariff and of indirect taxation. The fourth session is to be the jubilee of the taxpayer.

Men were full of hope, for everything seemed to favour the experiment. The *Moniteur* had announced that the revenue would go on increasing every quarter, and what better use could be made of these unlooked-for returns than to give the villager a little more salt to his *eau tiede*, and an additional letter now and then from the battle-field, where his son was risking his life?

But what has happened? Like the two preparations of sugar which are said to hinder each other from crystallizing, or the Kilkenny cats, which fought so desperately that nothing remained of them but their tails, the two promised reforms have swallowed up each other. Nothing remains of them but the tails; that is to say, we have *projets de lois, exposes des motifs*, reports, statistical returns, and schedules, in which we have the comfort of seeing our sufferings philanthropically appreciated and homeopathically reckoned up. But as to the reforms themselves, they have not crystallized. Nothing has come out of the crucible, and the experiment has been a failure.

The chemists will by-and-by come before the jury and explain the causes of the breakdown.

One will say, "I proposed a postal reform; but the Chamber wished first of all to rid us of the salt-tax, and I gave it up."

Another will say, "I voted for doing away with the salt-tax, but the Minister had proposed a postal reform, and my vote went for nothing."

And the jury, finding these reasons satisfactory, will begin the experiment of new on the same data, and remit the work to the same chemists.

This proves that it would be well for us, notwithstanding the sources from which it is derived, to adopt the practice introduced half a century ago on the other side of the Channel, of prosecuting only one reform at a time. It is slow, it is wearisome; but it leads to some result.

Here we have a dozen reforms on the anvil at the same time. They hustle one another, like the ghosts at the Gate of Oblivion, where no one enters.

"Ohimè! che lasso Î

Una a la volta, per carità."

Here is what Jacques Bonhomme said, in a dialogue with John Bull, and it is worth being reported:—

Jacques Bonhomme, John Bull.

Jacques Bonhomme: Oh! who will deliver me from this hurricane of reforms? My head is in a whirl. A new one seems to be invented every day: university reform, financial reform, sanitary reform, parliamentary reform, electoral reform, commercial reform, social reform, and, last of all, comes postal reform!

John Bull: As regards the last, it is so easy and so useful, as we have found by experience, that I venture to give you some advice upon the subject.

Jacques: We are told that postal reform has turned out ill in England, and that the Exchequer has lost half a million.

John: And has benefited the public by ten times that sum.

Jacques: No doubt of that.

John: We have every sign by which the public satisfaction can be testified. The nation, following the lead of Sir Robert Peel and Lord John Russell, have given Rowland Hill, in true British fashion, substantial marks of the public gratitude. Even the poorer classes testify their satisfaction by sealing their letters with wafers bearing this inscription: "Public gratitude for postal reform." The leaders of the Anti-Corn-Law League have proclaimed aloud in their place in Parliament that without cheap postage thirty years would have been required to accomplish their great undertaking, which had for object the removal of duties on the food of the poor. The officers of the Board of Trade have declared it unfortunate that the English coin does not admit of a still greater reduction! What more proofs would you have?

Jacques: But the Treasury?

John: Do not the Treasury and the public sail in the same boat?

Jacques: Not quite. And then, is it quite clear that our postal system has need to be reformed?

John: That is the question. Let us see how matters now stand. What is done with the letters that are put into the post-office?

Jacques: The routine is very simple. The postmaster opens the letter-box at a certain hour, and takes out of it, say, a hundred letters.

John: And then?

Jacques: Then he inspects them one by one. With a geographical table before him, and a letter-weigher in his hand, he assigns each letter to its proper category, according to weight and distance. There are only eleven postal zones or districts, and as many degrees of weight.

John: That constitutes simply 121 combinations for each letter.

Jacques: Yes; and we must double that number, because the letter may, or may not, belong to the *service rural.*

John: There are, then, 24,200 things to be inquired into with reference to every hundred letters. And how does the postmaster then proceed?

Jacques: He marks the weight on one corner of the letter, and the postage in the middle of the address, by a hieroglyphic agreed upon at headquarters.

John: And then?

Jacques: He stamps the letters, and arranges them in ten parcels corresponding with the other post-offices with which he is in communication. He adds up the total postages of the ten parcels.

John: And then?

Jacques: Then he enters the ten sums in a register, with counterfoils.

John: And then?

Jacques: Then he writes a letter to each of his ten correspondent postmasters, telling them with what sums he debits them.

John: And if the letters are prepaid?

Jacques: Then, I grant you, the service becomes somewhat complicated. He must in that case receive the letter, weigh it, and consign it to its proper category as before, receive payment and give change, select the appropriate stamp among thirty others, mark on the letter its number, weight, and postage; transcribe the full address, first in one register, then in a second, then in a third, then on a detached slip; wrap up the letter in the slip; send the whole, well secured by a string, to the correspondent postmaster; and enter each of these details in a dozen columns, selected from fifty other columns, which indicate the letter-bag in which prepaid letters are put.

John: And all this for forty centimes (4d.)!

Jacques: Yes, on an average.

John: I see now that the despatch of letters is simple enough. Let us see now what takes place on their arrival.

Jacques: The postmaster opens the post-bag.

John: And then?

Jacques: He reads the ten invoices of his correspondents.

John: And after that?

Jacques: He compares the totals of the invoices with the totals brought out by each of the ten parcels of letters.

John: And after that?

Jacques: He brings the whole to a grand total to find out with what sum, *en bloc*, he is to debit each letter-carrier.

John: And after that?

Jacques: After that, with a table of distances and letter-weigher in hand, he verifies or rectifies the postage of each letter.

John: And after that?

Jacques: He enters in register after register, and in column after column, the greater or less results he has found.

John: And after that?

Jacques: He puts himself in communication with the ten postmasters, his correspondents, to advise them of errors of 10 or 20 centimes (a penny or twopence).

John: And then?

Jacques: He collects and arranges all the letters he has received, to hand them to the postman.

John: And after that?

Jacques: He states the total postages that each postman is charged with.

John: And after that?

Jacques: The postman verifies, or discusses, the signification of the hieroglyphics. The postman finally advances the amount, and sets out.

John: Go on.

Jacques: The postman goes to the party to whom a letter is addressed, and knocks at the door. A servant opens. There are six letters for that address. The postages are added up, separately at first, then altogether. They amount to 2 francs 70 centimes (2s. 3d.).

John: Go on.

Jacques: The servant goes in search of his master. The latter proceeds to verify the hieroglyphics. He mistakes the threes for twos and the nines for fours. He has doubts about the weights and distances. In short, he has to ask the postman to walk upstairs, and on the way he tries to find out the signatures of the letters, thinking it may be prudent to refuse some of them.

John: Go on.

Jacques: The postman when he has got upstairs pleads the cause of the post-office. They argue, they examine, they weigh, they calculate distances—at length the party agrees to receive five of the letters, and refuses one.

John: Go on.

Jacques: What remains is to pay the postage. The servant is sent to the grocer for change. After a delay of twenty minutes he returns, and the postman is at length set free, and rushes from door to door, to go through the same ceremony at each.

John: Go on.

Jacques: He returns to the post-office. He counts and recounts with the postmaster. He returns the letters refused, and gets repayment of his advances for these. He reports the objections of the parties with reference to weight and distance.

John: Go on.

Jacques: The postmaster has to refer to the registers, letter-bags, and special slips, in order to make up an account of the letters which have been refused.

John: Go on, if you please.

Jacques: I am thankful I am not a postmaster. We now come to accounts in dozens and scores at the end of the month; to contrivances invented not only to establish, but to check and control a minute responsibility, involving a total of 50 millions of francs, made up of postages amounting on an average to 43 centimes each (less than 4d.), and of 116 millions of letters, each of which may belong to one or other of 242 categories.

John: A very complicated simplicity truly! The man who has resolved this problem must have a hundred times more genius than your Mons. Piron or our Rowland Hill.

Jacques: Well, you seem to laugh at our system. Would you explain yours to me?

John: In England, the government causes to be sold all over the country, wherever it is judged useful, stamps, envelopes, and covers at a penny apiece.

Jacques: And after that?

John: You write your letter, fold it, put it in the envelope, and throw it into the post-office.

Jacques: And after that?

John: "After that"—why, that is the whole affair. We have nothing to do with distances, bulletins, registers, control, or accounting; we have no money to give or to receive, and no concern with hieroglyphics, discussions, interpretations, etc., etc.

Jacques: Truly this is very simple. But is it not too much so? An infant might understand it. But such reforms as you describe stifle the genius of great administrators. For my own part, I stick to the French mode of going to work. And then your *uniform rate* has the greatest of all faults. It is unjust.

John: How so?

Jacques: Because it is unjust to charge as much for a letter addressed to the immediate neighbourhood, as for one which you carry three hundred miles.

John: At all events you will allow that the injustice goes no further than to the extent of a penny.

Jacques: No matter—it is still injustice.

John: Besides, the injustice, which at the outside cannot extend beyond a penny in any particular case, disappears when you take into account the entire correspondence of any individual citizen who sends his letters sometimes to a great distance and sometimes to places in the immediate vicinity.

Jacques: I adhere to my opinion. The injustice is lessened—infinitely lessened, if you will; it is inappreciable, infinitesimal, homoeopathic; but it exists.

John: Does your government make you pay dearer for an ounce of tobacco which you buy in the Rue de Clichy than for the same quantity retailed on the Quai d'Orsay?

Jacques: What connexion is there between the two subjects of comparison?

John: In the one case as in the other, the cost of transport must be taken into account. Mathematically, it would be just that each pinch of snuff should be dearer in the Rue de Clichy than on the Quai d'Orsay by the millionth part of a farthing.

Jacques: True; I don't dispute that it may be so.

John: Let me add, that your postal system is just only in appearance. Two houses stand side by side, but one of them happens to be within, and the other just outside, the zone or postal district. The one pays a penny more than the other, just equal to the entire postage in England. You see, then, that with you injustice is committed on a much greater scale than with us.

Jacques: That is so. My objection does not amount to much; but the loss of revenue still remains to be taken into account.

Here I ceased to listen to the two interlocutors. It turned out, however, that Jacques Bonhomme was entirely converted; for some days afterwards, the Report of M. Vuitry having made its appearance, Jacques wrote the following letter to that honourable legislator:—

"J. Bonhomme to M. de Vuitry, Deputy, Reporter of the Commission charged to examine the *projet de loi* relative to the Postage of Letters.

"Monsieur,—Although I am not ignorant of the extreme discredit into which one falls by making oneself the advocate of an absolute theory, I think it my duty not to abandon the cause of a uniform rate of postage, reduced to simple remuneration for the service actually rendered.

"My addressing myself to you will no doubt be regarded as a good joke. On the one side appears a heated brain, a closet-reformer, who talks of overturning an entire system all at once and without any gradual transition; a dreamer, who has never, perhaps, cast his eye on that mass of laws, ordinances, tables, schedules, and statistical details which accompany your report,—in a word, a theorist. On the other appears a grave, prudent, moderate-minded legislator, who has weighed, compared, and shown due respect for the various interests involved, who has rejected all systems, or, which comes to the same thing, has constructed a system of his own, borrowed from all the others. The issue of such a struggle cannot be doubtful.

"Nevertheless, as long as the question is pending, every one has a right to state his opinions. I know that mine are sufficiently decided to expose me to ridicule. All I can expect from the reader of this letter is not to throw ridicule away (if, indeed, there be room for ridicule), before, in place of after, having heard my reasons.

"For I, too, can appeal to experience. A great people has made the experiment. What has been the result? We cannot deny that that people is knowing in such matters, and that its opinion is entitled to weight.

"Very well, there is not a man in England whose voice is not in favour of postal reform. Witness the subscription which has been opened for a testimonial to Mr Rowland Hill. Witness the manner in which John Bull testifies his gratitude. Witness the oft-repeated declaration of the Anti-Corn-Law League:

'Without the penny postage we should never have had developed that public opinion which has overturned the system of protection." All this is confirmed by what we read in a work emanating from an official source:—

"' The rates of postage should be regulated, not with a view to revenue, but for the sole purpose of covering the expense.'

"To which Mr Macgregor adds:—

"'It is true that the rate having come down to our smallest coin, we cannot lower it further, although it does yield some revenue. But this source of revenue, which will go on constantly increasing, must be employed to improve the service, and to develop our system of mail steamers all over the world.'

"This brings me to examine the leading idea of the commission, which is, on the other hand, that the rate of postage should be a source of revenue to government.

"This idea runs through your entire report, and I allow that, under the influence of this prejudice, you could arrive at nothing great or comprehensive, and you are fortunate if, in trying to reconcile the two systems, you have not fallen into the errors and drawbacks of both.

"The first question we have to consider is this: Is the correspondence which passes between individual citizens a proper subject of taxation?

"I shall not fall back on abstract principles, or remind you that the very essence of society being the communication of ideas, the object of every government, should be to facilitate and not impede this communication.

"Let us look to actual facts.

"The total length of our highways and departmental and country roads extends to a million of kilomètres (625,000 miles). Supposing that each has cost 100,000 francs

(£4000), this makes a capital of 100 milliards (£4,000,000,000) expended by the State to facilitate the transport of passengers and goods.

"Now, put the question, if one of your honourable colleagues asked leave of the Chamber to bring in a bill thus conceived:

"'From and after 1st January next, the Government will levy upon all travellers a tax sufficient not only to cover the expense of maintaining the highways, but to bring back to the Exchequer four or five times the amount of that expense....

"Would you not feel such a proposal to be anti-social and monstrous?

"How is it that this consideration of profits, nay, of simple remuneration, never presents itself to our minds when the question regards the circulation of commodities, and yet appears so natural when the question regards the circulation of ideas?

"Perhaps it is the result of habit. If we had a postal system to create, it would most assuredly appear monstrous to establish it on a principle of revenue.

"And yet remark that oppression is more glaring in this case than in the other.

"When Government has opened a new road it forces no one to make use of it (It would do so undoubtedly if the use of the road were taxed.) But while the Post-office regulations continue to be enforced, no one can send a letter through any other channel, were it to his own mother.

"The rate of postage, then, in principle, ought to be remunerative, and, for the same reason, uniform.

"If we set out with this idea, what marvellous beauty, facility, and simplicity does not the reform I am advocating present!

"Here is the whole thing nearly put into the form of a law.

"'Article 1. From and after 1st January next there will be exposed to sale, in every place where the Government judges it expedient, stamped envelopes and covers, at the price of a halfpenny or a penny.

"'2. Every letter put into one of these envelopes, and not exceeding the weight of half an ounce, every newspaper or print put into one of these covers, and not exceeding the weight of... will be transmitted, and delivered without cost at its address.

"'3. All Post-office accounting is entirely suppressed.

"'4. All pains and penalties with reference to the conveyance of letters are abolished.'

"That is very simple, I admit—much too simple; and I anticipate a host of objections.

"That the system I propose may be attended with drawbacks is not the question; but whether yours is not attended with more.

"In sober earnest, can the two (except as regards revenue) be put in comparison for a moment?

"Examine both. Compare them as regards facility, convenience, despatch, simplicity, order, economy, justice, equality, multiplication of transactions, public satisfaction, moral and intellectual development, civilizing tendency; and tell me honestly if it is possible to hesitate a moment.

"I shall not stop to enlarge on each of these considerations—I give you the headings of twelve chapters, which I leave blank, persuaded that no one can fill them up better than yourself.

"But since there is one objection—namely, revenue—I must say a word on that head.

"You have constructed a table in order to show that even at twopence the revenue would suffer a loss of £880,000.

"At a penny, the loss Would be £1,120,000, and at a halfpenny, of £1,320,000; hypotheses so frightful that you do not even formulate them in detail.

"But allow me to say that the figures in your report dance about with a little too much freedom. In all your tables, in all your calculations, you have the tacit reservation of *coteris paribus*. You assume that the cost will be the same under a simple as under a complicated system of administration—the same number of letters with the present average postage of 4 1/2d. as with the uniform rate of twopence. You confine yourself to this rule of three: if 87 millions of letters at 4d. yield so much, then at 2d. the same number will yield so much; admitting, nevertheless, certain distinctions when they militate against our proposed reform.

"In order to estimate the real sacrifice of revenue, we must, first of all, calculate the economy in the service which will be effected; then in what proportion the amount of correspondence will be augmented. We take this last datum solely into account, because we cannot suppose that the saving of cost which will be realized will not be met by an increased personnel rendered necessary by a more extended service.

"Undoubtedly, it is impossible to fix the exact amount of increase in the circulation of letters which the reduction of postage would cause, but in such matters a reasonable analogy has always been admitted.

"You yourself admit that in England a reduction of seven-eighths in the rate has caused an increase of correspondence to the extent of 360 per cent.

"Here, the lowering to 5 centimes (a halfpenny) of the rate which is at present at an average of something less than 4 1/2d., would constitute likewise a reduction of seven-eighths. We may therefore be allowed to expect the same result—that is to say, 417 millions of letters, in place of 116 millions.

"But let us count on 300 millions.

"Is there any exaggeration in assuming that with a rate of postage one half less, we shall reach an average of 8 letters to each inhabitant when in England they have reached 13.

Now 300 millions of letters, at 5 centimes, give, 15

100 millions of journals and prints, at 5 centimes, give 5

The present expense (which may diminish) is.

31 Deducting for mail steamers,....5

There remains for despatches, travellers, and money parcels,....26

Net product,......2

At present the net product is.....19

"Now I ask whether the Government, which makes a positive sacrifice of 800 millions (£32,000,000) per annum in order to facilitate the gratuitous transport of passengers, should not make a negative sacrifice of 17 millions, in order not to make a gain upon the transmission and circulation of ideas?

"But the Treasury, I am aware, has its own habits, and with whatever complacence it sees its receipts increase, it feels proportional disappointment in seeing them diminished by a single farthing. It seems to be provided with those admirable valves which in the human framc allow the blood to flow in one direction, but prevent its return. Be it so. The Treasury is perhaps a little too old for us to quicken its pace. We have no hope, therefore, that it will give in to us. But what will be said if I, Jacques Bonhomme, show it a way which is simple, easy, convenient, and essentially practical, of doing a great service to the country without its costing a single farthing?

"The Post-office yields a gross return to the Treasury of.....50 millions

Total yield of these three services, 280 millions.

"Now, bring down postages to the uniform rate of 5 centimes (a halfpenny).

"Lower the salt-tax to 10 francs (8s.) the hundredweight, as the Chamber has already voted.

"Give me power to modify the customs tariff in such a way that I shall be peremptorily prohibited from increasing any duty, but that I may lower duties at pleasure.

"And I, Jacques Bonhomme, guarantee you a revenue, not of 280 millions, but of 300 millions. Two hundred French bankers will be my sureties, and all I ask for my reward is as much as these three taxes will produce over and above 300 millions.

"Is it necessary for me to enumerate the advantages of my proposal?

"1. The people will receive all the advantage resulting from cheapness in the price of an article of the first necessity—salt.

"2. Fathers will be able to write to their sons, and mothers to their daughters. Nor will men's affections and sentiments, and the endearments of love and friendship, be stemmed and driven back into their hearts, as at present, by the hand of the tax-gatherer.

"3. To carry a letter from one friend to another will no longer be inscribed in our code as a crime.

"4. Trade will revive with liberty, and our merchant shipping will recover from its humiliation.

"5. The Treasury will gain at first twenty millions, afterwards it will gain all that shall accrue to the revenue from other sources through the saving realized by each citizen on salt, postages, and other things, the duties on which have been lowered.

"If my proposal is rejected, what am I to conclude? Provided the bankers I represent offer sufficient security, under what pretext can my proposal be refused acceptance? It is impossible to invoke the equilibrium of budgets. It would indeed be upset, but upset in such a way that the receipts should exceed the expenses. This is no affair of theory, of system, of statistics, of probability, of conjecture; it is an offer, an offer like that of a company which solicits the concession of a line of railway. The Treasury tells me what it derives from postages, salt-tax, and customs. I offer to give it more. The objection, then, cannot come from the Treasury. I offer to reduce the tariff of salt, postages, and customs; I engage not to raise it; the objection, then, cannot come from the taxpayers. From whom does it come, then? From monopolists? It remains to be seen whether their voice shall be permitted in France to drown the voice of the Government and the people. To assure us of this, I beg you to transmit my proposal to the Council of Ministers. Jacques Bonhomme.

"P.S.—Here is the text of my offer:—

"I, Jacques Bonhomme, representing a company of bankers and capitalists, ready to give all guarantees and deposit whatever security may be necessary.

"Having learnt that the Government derives only 280 millions of francs from customs duties, postages, and salt-tax, by means of the duties at present fixed;

"I offer to give the Government 300 millions from the gross produce of these three sources of revenue;

"And this while reducing the salt-tax from 30fr. to l0fr.;

"Reducing the rate of postage from 42 1/2 centimes, at an average, to a uniform rate of from 5 to 10 centimes,

"On the single condition that I am permitted not to raise (which will be formally prohibited), but to lower as much as I please the duties of customs. Jacques Bonhomme."

"You are a fool," said I to Jacques Bonhomme, when he read me his letter. "You can do nothing with moderation. The other day you cried out against the hurricane of reforms, and here I find you demanding three, making one of them the condition of the other two. You will ruin yourself."

"Be quiet," said he, "I have made all my calculations; I only wish they may be accepted. But they will not be accepted." Upon this we parted, our heads full, his of figures, mine of reflections which I forbear to inflict upon the reader.

XIII. PROTECTION; OR, THE THREE CITY MAGISTRATES. DEMONSTRATION IN FOUR

Tableaux.

Scene I.—House of Master Peter.—Window looking out on a fine park.—Three gentlemen seated near a good fire.

Peter: Bravo! Nothing like a good fire after a good dinner. It does feel so comfortable. But, alas! how many honest folks, like the Boi d'Yvetot,

"Soufflent, faute de bois,

Dans leurs doigts."

Miserable creatures! A charitable thought has just come into my head. You see these fine trees; I am about to fell them, and distribute the timber among the poor.

Paul and John: What! gratis?

Peter: Not exactly. My good works would soon have an end were I to dissipate my fortune. I estimate my park as worth £1000. By cutting down the trees I shall pocket a good sum.

Paul: Wrong. Your wood as it stands is worth more than that of the neighbouring forests, for it renders you services which they cannot render. When cut down it will be only good for firewood, like any other, and will not bring a penny more the load.

Peter: Oh! oh! Mr Theorist, you forget that I am a practical man. My reputation as a speculator is sufficiently well established, I believe, to prevent me from being taken for a noodle. Do you imagine I am going to amuse myself by selling my timber at the price of float-wood?

Paul: It would seem so.

Peter: Simpleton! And what if I can hinder float-wood from being brought into Paris?

Paul: That alters the case. But how can you manage it?

Peter: Here is the whole secret. You know that float-wood, on entering the city, pays 5d. the load. To-morrow, I induce the commune to raise the duty to £4, £8, £12,—in short, sufficiently high to prevent the entry of a single log. Now, do you follow me? If the good people are not to die of cold, they have no alternative but to come to my woodyard. They will bid against each other for my wood, and I will sell it for a high price; and this act of charity, successfully carried out, will put me in a situation to do other acts of charity.

Paul: A fine invention, truly! It suggests to me another of the same kind.

John: And what is that? Is philanthropy to be again brought into play?

Paul: How do you like this Normandy butter?

John: Excellent.

Paul: Hitherto I have thought it passable. But do you not find that it takes you by the throat? I could make better butter in Paris. I shall have four or five hundred cows, and distribute milk, butter, and cheese among the poor.

Peter and John: What! in charity?

Paul: Bah! let us put charity always in the foreground. It is so fine a figure that its very mask is a good passport. I shall give my butter to the people, and they will give me their money. Is that what is called selling?

John: No; not according to the Bourgeois Gentilhomme. But, call it what you please, you will ruin yourself. How can Paris ever compete with Normandy in dairy produce?

Paul: I shall be able to save the cost of carriage.

John: Be it so. Still, while paying that cost, the Normans can beat the Parisians.

Paul: To give a man something at a lower price—is that what you call beating him?

John: It is the usual phrase; and you will always find yourself beaten.

Paul: Yes; as Don Quixote was beaten. The blows will fall upon Sancho. John, my friend, you forget the octroi.

John: The octroi! What has that to do with your butter?

Paul: To-morrow, I shall demand *protection*, and induce the commune to prohibit butter being brought into Paris from Normandy and Brittany. The people must then either dispense with it, or purchase mine, and at my own price, too.

John: Upon my honour, gentlemen, your philanthropy has quite made a convert of me.

"On apprend à hurler, dit l'autre, avec les loups."

My mind is made up. I shall not be thought unworthy of my colleagues. Peter, this sparkling fire has inflamed your soul. Paul, this butter has lubricated the springs of your intelligence. I, too, feel stimulated by this piece of powdered pork; and tomorrow I shall vote, and cause to be voted, the exclusion of swine, dead and alive. That done, I shall construct superb sheds in the heart of Paris,

"Pour l'animal immonde aux Hebreux defendu."

I shall become a pig-driver and pork-butcher. Let us see how the good people of Paris can avoid coming to provide themselves at my shop.

Peter: Softly, my good friends; if you enhance the price of butter and salt meat to such an extent, you cut down beforehand the profit I expect from my wood.

Paul: And my speculation will be no longer so wondrously profitable, if I am overcharged for my firewood and bacon.

John: And I, what shall I gain by overcharging you for my sausages, if you overcharge me for my faggots and bread and butter?

Peter: Very well, don't let us quarrel Let us rather put our heads together and make reciprocal concessions. Moreover, it is not good to consult one's self-interest exclusively—we must exercise humanity, and see that the people do not want fuel.

Paul: Very right; and it is proper that the people should have butter to their bread.

John: Undoubtedly; and a bit of bacon for the pot.

All: Three cheers for charity; three cheers for philanthropy; and to-morrow we take the octroi by assault.

Peter: Ah! I forgot. One word more; it is essential. My good friends, in this age of egotism the world is distrustful, and the purest intentions are often misunderstood. Paul, you take the part of pleading for the wood; John will do the same for the butter; and I shall devote myself to the home-bred pig. It is necessary to prevent malignant suspicions.

Paul and John (leaving): Upon my word, that is a clever fellow.

Scene II.—Council Chamber.

Paul: *Mes chers collègues*, Every day there are brought to Paris great masses of firewood, which drain away large sums of money. At this rate, we shall all be ruined in three years, and what will become of the poorer classes? (Cheers) We must prohibit foreign timber. I don't speak for myself, for all the wood I possess would not make a tooth-pick. In what I mean to say, then, I am entirely free from any personal interest or bias. (Hear, hear) But here is my friend Peter, who possesses a park, and he will guarantee an adequate supply of fuel to our fellow-citizens, who will no longer be dependent on the charcoal-burners of the Yonne. Have you ever turned your attention to the risk which we run of dying of cold, if the proprietors of forests abroad should take it into their heads to send no more firewood to Paris? Let us put a prohibition, then, on bringing in wood. By this means we shall put a stop to the draining away of our money, create an independent interest charged with supplying the city with firewood, and open up to workmen a new source of employment and remuneration. (Cheers)

John: I support the proposal of my honourable friend, the preceding speaker, which is at once so philanthropic, and, as he himself has explained, so entirely disinterested. It is indeed high time that we should put an end to this insolent *laissez passer*, which has brought immoderate competition into our markets, and to such an extent that there is no province which possesses any special facility for providing us with a product, be it what it may, which does not immediately inundate us, undersell us, and bring ruin on the Parisian workman. It is the duty of Government to equalize the conditions of production by duties wisely adapted to each case, so as not to allow to enter from without anything which is not dearer than in Paris, and so relieve us from an unequal struggle. How, for example, can we possibly produce milk and butter in Paris, with Brittany and Normandy at our door? Remember, gentlemen, that the agriculturists of Brittany have cheaper land, a more abundant supply of hay, and manual labour on more advantageous terms.

Does not common sense tell us that we must equalize the conditions by a protective octroi tariff? I demand that the duty on milk and butter should be raised by 1000 per cent., and still higher if necessary. The workman's breakfast will cost a little more, but see to what extent his wages will be raised! We shall see rising around us cow-houses, dairies, and barrel chums, and the foundations laid of new sources of industry. Not that I have any interest in this proposition. I am not a cowfeeder, nor have I any wish to be so. The sole motive which actuates me is a wish to be useful to the working classes. (Applause.)

Peter: I am delighted to see in this assembly statesmen so pure, so enlightened, and so devoted to the best interests of the people. (Cheers) I admire their disinterestedness, and I cannot do better than imitate the noble example which has been set me. I give their motions my support, and I shall only add another, for prohibiting the entry into Paris of the pigs of Poitou. I have no desire, I assure you, to become a pig-driver or a pork-butcher. In that case I should have made it a matter of conscience to be silent. But is it not shameful, gentlemen, that we should be the tributaries of the peasants of Poitou, who have the audacity to come into our own market and take possession of a branch of industry which we ourselves have no means of carrying on? and who, after having inundated us with their hams and sausages, take perhaps nothing from us in return? At all events, who will tell us that the balance of trade is not in their favour, and that we are not obliged to pay them a tribute in hard cash? Is it not evident that if the industry of Poitou were transplanted to Paris, it would open up a steady demand for Parisian labour? And then, gentlemen, is it not very possible, as M. Lestiboudois has so well remarked, that we may be buying the salt pork of Poitou, not with our incomes, but with our capital? Where will that land us? Let us not suffer, then, that rivals who are at once avaricious, greedy, and perfidious, should come here to undersell us, and put it out of our power to provide ourselves with the same commodities. Gentlemen, Paris has reposed in you her confidence; it is for you to justify that confidence. The people are without employment; it is for you to create employment for them; and if salt pork shall cost them a somewhat higher price, we have, at least, the consciousness of having sacrificed our own interests to those of the masses, as every good magistrate ought to do. (Loud and long-continued cheers.)

A Voice: I have heard much talk of the poor; but under pretext of affording them employment, you begin by depriving them of what is more valuable than employment itself, namely, butter, firewood, and meat.

Peter, Paul, and John: Vote, vote! Down with Utopian dreamers, theorists, generalizers! Vote, vote! (*The three motions are carried.*)

Scene III.—Twenty years afterwards.

Son: Father, make up your mind; we must leave Paris. Nobody can any longer live there—no work, and everything dear.

Father: You don't know, my son, how much it costs one to leave the place where he was born.

Son: The worst thing of all is to perish from want.

Father: Go you, then, and search for a more hospitable country. For myself, I will not leave the place where are the graves of your mother, and of your brothers and sisters. I long to obtain with them that repose which has been denied me in this city of desolation.

Son: Courage, father; we shall find employment somewhere else—in Poitou, or Normandy, or Brittany. It is said that all the manufactures of Paris are being removed by degrees to these distant provinces.

Father: And naturally so. Not being able to sell firewood and provisions, the people of these provinces have ceased to produce them beyond what their own wants call for. The time and capital at their disposal are devoted to making for themselves those articles with which we were in use to furnish them.

Son: Just as at Paris they have given up the manufacture of elegant dress and furniture, and betaken themselves to the planting of trees, and the rearing of pigs and cows. Although still young, I have lived to see vast warehouses, sumptuous quarters of the city, and quays once teeming with life and animation on the banks of the Seine, turned into meadows and copses.

Father: While towns are spread over the provinces, Paris is turned into green fields. What a deplorable revolution! And this terrible calamity has been brought upon us by three magistrates, backed by public ignorance.

Son: Pray relate to me the history of this change.

Father: It is short and simple. Under pretext of planting in Paris three new branches of industry, and by this means giving employment to the working classes, these men got the commune to prohibit the entry into Paris of firewood, butter, and meat. They claimed for themselves the right of providing for their fellow-citizens. These commodities rose at first to exorbitant prices. No one earned enough to procure them, and the limited number of those who could procure them spent all their income on them, and had no longer the means of buying anything else. A check was thus given to all other branches of industry and production, and all the more quickly that the provinces no longer afforded a market. Poverty, death, and emigration then began to depopulate Paris.

Son: And when is this to stop?

Father: When Paris has become a forest and a prairie.

Son: The three magistrates must have made a large fortune?

Father: At first they realized enormous profits, but at length they fell into the common poverty.

Son: How did that happen?

Father: Look at that ruin. That was a magnificent man-sion-house surrounded with a beautiful park. If Paris had continued to progress, Master Peter would have realized more interest than his entire capital now amounts to.

Son: How can that be, seeing he has got rid of competition?

Father: Competition in selling has disappeared, but competition in buying has disappeared also, and will continue every day to disappear more and more until Paris becomes a bare field, and until the copses of Master Peter have no more value than the copses of an equal extent of land in the Forest of Bondy. It is thus that monopoly, like every other system of injustice, carries in itself its own punishment.

Son: That appears to me not very clear, but the decadence of Paris is an incontestable fact. Is there no means, then, of counteracting this singular measure that Peter and his colleagues got adopted twenty years ago?

Father: I am going to tell you a secret. I remain in Paris on purpose. I shall call in the people to my assistance. It rests with them to replace the octroi on its ancient basis, and get quit of that fatal principle which was engrafted on it, and which still vegetates there like a parasitical fungus.

Son: You must succeed in this at once.

Father: On the contrary, the work will be difficult and laborious. Peter, Paul, and John understand one another marvellously. They will do anything rather than allow firewood, butter, and butchers' meat to enter Paris. They have on their side the people, who see clearly the employment which these three protected branches of industry afford. They know well to what extent the cowfeeders and wood-merchants give employment to labour; but they have by no means the same exact idea of the labour which would be developed in the open air of liberty.

Son: If that is all, you will soon enlighten them.

Father: At your age, my son, no doubts arise. If I write, the people will not read; for, to support their miserable existence, they have not much time at their disposal. If I speak, the magistrates will shut my mouth. The people, therefore, will long remain under their fatal mistake. Political parties, whose hopes are founded on popular passions, will set themselves, not to dissipate their prejudices, but to make merchandise of them. I shall have to combat at one and the same time the great men of the day, the people, and their leaders. In truth, I see a frightful storm ready to burst over the head of the bold man who shall venture to protest against an iniquity so deeply rooted in this country.

Son: You will have truth and justice on your side.

Father: And they will have force and calumny on theirs. Were I but young again! but age and suffering have exhausted my strength.

Son: Very well, father; what strength remains to you, devote to the service of the country. Begin this work of enfranchisement, and leave to me the care of finishing it.

Scene IV.—The Agitation.

Jacques Bonhomme: Parisians, let us insist upon a reform of the octroi duties; let us demand that they be instantly brought down to the former rate. Let every citizen be free to buy his firewood, butter, and butchers' meat where he sees fit.

The People: Vive, vive la Liberte!

Peter: Parisians, don't allow yourselves to be seduced by that word, liberty. What good can result from liberty to purchase if you want the means—in other words, if you are out of employment? Can Paris produce firewood as cheaply as the Forest of Bondy? meat as cheaply as Poitou? butter as cheaply as Normandy? If you open your gates freely to these rival products, what will become of the cowfeeders, woodcutters, and pork-butchers? They cannot dispense with protection.

The People: Vive, vive la Protection!

Jacques Bonhomme: Protection! but who protects you workmen? Do you not compete with one another? Let the wood-merchants, then, be subject to competition in their turn. They ought not to have right by law to raise the price of firewood, unless the rate of wages is also raised by law. Are you no longer in love with equality?

The People: Vive, vive l'Egalite!

Peter: Don't listen to these agitators. We have, it is true, raised the price of firewood, butchers' meat, and butter; but we have done so for the express purpose of being enabled to give good wages to the workmen. We are actuated by motives of charity.

The People: Vive, vive la Charite!

Jacques Bonhomme. Cause the rate of wages to be raised by the octroi, if you can, or cease by the same means to raise the prices of commodities. We Parisians ask for no charity—we demand justice.

The People: Vive, vive la Justice!

Peter: It is precisely the high price of commodities which will lead, *par ricochet,* to a rise of wages.

The People: Vive, vive la Cherte!

Jacques Bonhomme: If butter is dear, it is not because you pay high wages to the workmen, it is not even because you make exorbitant profits; it is solely because Paris is ill-adapted for that branch of industry; it is because you wish to make in the town what should be made in the country, and in the country what should be made in the town. The people have not more employment—only they have employment of a different kind. They have no higher wages; while they can no longer buy commodities as cheaply as formerly.

The People: Vive, vive le Bon Marche!

Peter: This man seduces you with fine words. Let us place the question before you in all its simplicity. Is it, or is it not, true, that if we admit firewood, meat, and butter freely or at a lower duty, our markets will be inundated? Believe me there is no other means of preserving ourselves from this new species of invasion but to keep the door shut, and so maintain the prices of commodities by rendering them artificially rare.

Some Voices in the Crowd: Vive, vive la Rarete!

Jacques Bonhomme: Let us bring the question to the simple test of truth. You cannot divide among the people of Paris commodities which are not in Paris. If there be less meat, less firewood, less butter, the share falling to each will be smaller. Now there must be less if we prohibit what should be allowed to enter the city. Parisians, abundance for each of you can be secured only by general abundance.

The People: Vive, vive l'Abondance!

Peter: It is in vain that this man tries to persuade you that it is your interest to be subjected to unbridled competition.

The People: A bas, à bas la Concurrence!

Jacques Bonhomme: It is in vain that this man tries to make you fall in love with restriction.

The People: A bas, à bas la Restriction!

Peter: I declare, for my own part, if you deprive the poor cowfeeders and pig-drivers of their daily bread, I can no longer be answerable for public order. Workmen, distrust that man. He is the agent of perfidious Normandy, and derives his inspiration from the provinces. He is a traitor; down with him! (The people preserve silence.)

Jacques Bonhomme: Parisians, what I have told you to-day,

I told you twenty years ago, when Peter set himself to work the octroi for his own profit and to your detriment. I am not, then, the agent of Normandy. Hang me up, if you will, but that will not make oppression anything else than oppression. Friends, it is not Jacques or Peter that you must put an end to, but liberty if you fear it, or restriction if it does you harm.

The People: Hang nobody, and set everybody free.

XIV. SOMETHING ELSE.

What is restriction?"

"It is partial prohibition."

"What is prohibition?"

"Absolute restriction."

"So that what holds true of the one, holds true of the other?"

"Yes; the difference is only one of degree. There is between them the same relation as there is between a circle and the arc of a circle."

"Then, if prohibition is bad, restriction cannot be good?"
"No more than the arc can be correct if the circle is irregular."
"What is the name which is common to restriction and prohibition?"
"Protection."
"What is the definitive effect of protection?"
"To exact from men *a greater amount of labour for the same result.*"
"Why are men attached to the system of protection?"
"Because as liberty enables us to obtain the same result with less labour, this apparent diminution of employment frightens them."
"Why do you say apparent?"
"Because *all labour saved can be applied to something else.*"
"To what?"
"That I cannot specify, nor is there any need to specify it."
"Why?"
"Because if the sum of satisfactions which the country at present enjoys could be obtained with one-tenth less labour, no one can enumerate the new enjoyments which men would desire to obtain from the labour left disposable. One man would desire to be better clothed, another better fed, another better educated, another better amused."
"Explain to me the mechanism and the effects of protection."
"That is not an easy matter. Before entering on consideration of the more complicated cases, we must study it in a very simple one."
"Take as simple a case as you choose."
"You remember how Robinson Crusoe managed to make a plank when he had no saw."
"Yes; he felled a tree, and then, cutting the trunk right and left with his hatchet, he reduced it to the thickness of a board."
"And that cost him much labour?"
"Fifteen whole days' work."
"And what did he live on during that time?"
"He had provisions."
"What happened to the hatchet?"
"It was blunted by the work."
"Yes; but you perhaps do not know this: that at the moment when Robinson was beginning the work he perceived a plank thrown by the tide upon the seashore."
"Happy accident! he of course ran to appropriate it?"
"That was his first impulse; but he stopped short, and began to reason thus with himself:—
"'If I appropriate this plank, it will cost me only the trouble of carrying it, and the time needed to descend and remount the cliff.
"'But if I form a plank with my hatchet, first of all, it will procure me fifteen days' employment; then my hatchet will get blunt, which will furnish me with the additional employment of sharpening it; then I shall consume my stock of provisions, which will be a third source of employment in replacing them. Now, *labour is wealth.* It is clear that I should ruin myself by appropriating the shipwrecked plank. I must protect my *personal labour*; and, now that I think of it, I can even increase that labour by throwing back the other plank into the sea.'"

"But this reasoning was absurd."

"No doubt. It is nevertheless the reasoning of every nation which protects itself by prohibition. It throws back the plank which is offered it in exchange for a small amount of labour in order to exert a greater amount of labour. It is not in the labour of the Customhouse officials that it discovers a gain. That gain is represented by the pains which Robinson takes to render back to the waves the gift which they had offered him. Consider the nation as a collective being, and you will not find between its reasoning and that of Robinson an atom of difference."

"Did Robinson not see that he could devote the time saved to *something else?*"

"What else?"

"As long as a man has wants to satisfy and time at his disposal, there is always something to be done. I am not bound to specify the kind of labour he would in such a case undertake."

"I see clearly what labour he could have escaped."

"And I maintain that Robinson, with incredible blindness, confounded the labour with its result, the end with the means, and I am going to prove to you..."

"There is no need. Here we have the system of restriction or prohibition in its simplest form. If it appear to you absurd when so put, it is because the two capacities of producer and consumer are in this case mixed up in the same individual."

"Let us pass on, therefore, to a more complicated example."

"With all my heart. Some time afterwards, Robinson having met with Friday, they united their labour in a common work. In the morning they hunted for six hours, and brought home four baskets of game. In the evening they worked in the garden for six hours, and obtained four baskets of vegetables.

"One day a canoe touched at the island. A good-looking foreigner landed, and was admitted to the table of our two recluses. He tasted and commended very much the produce of the garden, and before taking leave of his entertainers, spoke as follows:—

"'Generous islanders, I inhabit a country where game is much more plentiful than here, but where horticulture is quite unknown. It would be an easy matter to bring you every evening four baskets of game, if you would give me in exchange two baskets of vegetables.'

"At these words Robinson and Friday retired to consult, and the argument that passed is too interesting not to be reported *in extenso.*

"Friday: What do you think of it?

"Robinson: If we close with the proposal, we are ruined.

"F.: Are you sure of that? Let us consider.

"R.: The case is clear. Crushed by competition, our hunting as a branch of industry is annihilated.

"F.: What matters it, if we have the game?

"R.: Theory! it will no longer be the product of our labour.

"F.: I beg your pardon, sir; for in order to have game we must part with vegetables.

"R.: Then, what shall we gain?

"F.:. The four baskets of game cost us six hours' work. The foreigner gives us them in exchange for two baskets of vegetables, which cost us only three hours' work. This places three hours at our disposal.

"R.: Say, rather, which are substracted from our exertions. In this will consist our loss. *Labour is wealth*, and if we lose a fourth part of our time, we shall be less rich by a fourth.

"F.: You are greatly mistaken, my good friend. We shall have as much game, and the same quantity of vegetables, and three hours at our disposal into the bargain. This is progress, or there is no such thing in-the world.

"R.: You lose yourself in generalities! What should we make of these three hours?

"F.: We would do *something else*.

"R.: Ah! I understand you. You cannot come to particulars. Something else, something else—this is easily said.

"F.: We can fish, we can ornament our cottage, we can read the Bible.

"R.: Utopia! Is there any certainty that we should do either the one or the other?

"F.: Very well, if we have no wants to satisfy we can rest. Is repose nothing?

"R.: But while we repose we may die of hunger.

"F.: My dear friend, you have got into a vicious circle. I speak of a repose which will subtract nothing from our supply of game and vegetables. You always forget that by means of our *foreign trade* nine hours' labour will give us the same quantity of provisions that we obtain at present with twelve.

"R: It is very evident, Friday, that you have not been educated in Europe, and that you have never read the *Moniteur Industriel*. If you had, it would have taught you this: that all time saved is sheer loss. The important thing is not to eat or consume, but to work. All that we consume, if it is not the direct produce of our labour, goes for nothing. Do you want to know whether you are rich? Never consider the satisfactions you enjoy, but the labour you undergo. This is what the *Moniteur Industriel* would teach you. For myself, who have no pretensions to be a theorist, the only thing I look at is the loss of our hunting.

"F.: What a strange conglomeration of ideas! but...

"R.: I will have no buts. Moreover, there are political reasons for rejecting the interested offers of the perfidious foreigner.

"F.: Political reasons!

"R.: Yes, he only makes us these offers because they are advantageous to him.

"F.: So much the better, since they are for our advantage likewise.

"R.: Then by this traffic we should place ourselves in a situation of dependence upon him.

"F.: And he would place himself in dependence on us. We should have need of his game, and he of our vegetables, and we should live on terms of friendship.

"R.: System! Do you want me to shut your mouth?

"F.: We shall see about that. I have as yet heard no good reason.

"R.: Suppose the foreigner learns to cultivate a garden, and that his island should prove more fertile than ours. Do you see the consequence?

"F.: Yes; our relations with the foreigner would cease. He would send us no more vegetables, since he could have them at home with less labour. He would take no more game from us, since we should have nothing to give him in exchange, and we should then be in precisely the situation that you wish us in now.

"R.: Improvident savage! You don't see that after having annihilated our hunting by inundating us with game, he would annihilate our gardening by inundating us with vegetables.

"F.: But this would only last till we were in a situation to give him *something else*; that is to say, until we found something else which we could produce with economy of labour for ourselves.

"R. Something else, something else! You always come back to that. You are at sea, my good friend Friday; there is nothing practical in your views."

"The debate was long prolonged, and, as often happens, each remained wedded to his own opinion. But Robinson possessing a great ascendant over Friday, his opinion prevailed, and when the foreigner arrived to demand a reply, Robinson said to him—

"' Stranger, in order to induce us to accept your proposal, we must be assured of two things:

"' The first is, that your island is no better stocked with game than ours, for we want to fight only with *equal weapons*.

"' The second is, that you will lose by the bargain. For, as in every exchange there is necessarily a gaining and a losing party, we should be dupes, if you were not the loser. What have you got to say?'

"' Nothing,' replied the foreigner; and, bursting out a-laugh-ing, he regained his canoe."

"The story would not be amiss, if Robinson were not made to argue so very absurdly."

"He does not argue more absurdly than the committee of the Rue Hauteville."

"Oh! the case is very different. Sometimes you suppose one man, and sometimes (which comes to the same thing) two men working in company. That does not tally with the actual state of things. The division of labour and the intervention of merchants and money change the state of the question very much."

"That may complicate transactions, but does not change their nature."

"What! you want to compare modern commerce with a system of barter."

"Trade is nothing but a multiplicity of barters. Barter is in its own nature identical with commerce, just as labour on a small scale is identical with labour on a great scale, or as the law of gravitation which moves an atom is identical with that same law of gravitation which moves a world."

"So, according to you, these arguments, which are so untenable in the mouth of Robinson, are equally untenable when urged by our protectionists."

"Yes; only the error is better concealed under a complication of circumstances."

"Then, pray, let us have an example taken from the present order of things."

"With pleasure. In France, owing to the exigencies of climate and habits, cloth is a useful thing. Is the essential thing to *make it*, or to *get it?*"

"A very sensible question, truly! In order to have it, you must make it."

"Not necessarily. To have it, some one must make it, that is certain; but it is not at all necessary that the same person or the same country which consumes it should also produce it. You have not made that stuff which clothes you so well. France does not produce the coffee on which our citizens breakfast."

"But I buy my cloth, and France her coffee."

"Exactly so; and with what?"

"With money."

"But neither you nor France produce the material of money."

"We buy it."

"With what?"

"With our products, which are sent to Peru."

"It is then, in fact, your labour which you exchange for cloth, and French labour which is exchanged for coffee."

"Undoubtedly."

"It is not absolutely necessary, therefore, to manufacture what you consume."

"No; if we manufacture something else which we give in exchange."

"In other words, France has two means of procuring a given quantity of cloth. The first is to make it; the second is to make something else, and to exchange this something else with the foreigner for cloth. Of these two means, which is the best?"

"I don't very well know."

"Is it not that which, *for a determinate amount of labour, obtains the greater quantity of cloth?*"

"It seems so."

"And which is best for a nation, to have the choice between these two means, or that the law should prohibit one of them, on the chance of stumbling on the better of the two?"

"It appears to me that it is better for the nation to have the choice, inasmuch as in such matters it invariably chooses right."

"The law, which prohibits the importation of foreign cloth, decides, then, that if France wishes to have cloth, she must make it in kind, and that she is prohibited from making the something else with which she could purchase foreign cloth."

"True."

"And as the law obliges us to make the cloth, and forbids our making the something else, precisely because that something else would exact less labour (but for which reason the law would not interfere with it) the law virtually decrees that for a determinate amount of labour, France shall only have one yard of cloth, when for the same amount of labour she might have two yards, by applying that labour to something else!" "But the question recurs, 'What else?"

"And my question recurs, 'What does it signify?' Having the choice, she will only make the something else to such an extent as there may be a demand for it."

"That is possible; but I cannot divest myself of the idea that the foreigner will send us his cloth, and not take from us the something else, in which case we would be entrapped. At all events, this is the objection even from your own point of view. You allow that France could make this something else to exchange for cloth, with a less expenditure of labour than if she had made the cloth itself?"

"Undoubtedly."

"There would, then, be a certain amount of her labour rendered inert?"

"Yes; but without her being less well provided with clothes, a little circumstance which makes all the difference. Robinson lost sight of this, and our protectionists either do not see it, or pretend not to see it. The shipwrecked plank rendered fifteen days of Robinson's labour inert, in as far as that labour was applied to making a plank, but it did not deprive him of it. Discriminate, then, between these two kinds of diminished labour—the diminution which has for effect privation, and that which has for its cause satisfaction. These two things are very different, and if you mix them up, you reason as Robinson did. In the most complicated, as in the most simple cases, the sophism consists in this: *Judging of the utility of labour by its duration and intensity, and* *not by its results*; which gives rise to this economic policy: *To reduce the results of labour for the purpose of augmenting its duration and intensity.*" *

* *See ch. ii. and iii. of Sophimes, first series; and Harmonies Économiques, ch. vi.*

XV. THE LITTLE ARSENAL OF THE FREE-TRADER.

If any one tells you that there are no absolute principles, no inflexible rules; that prohibition may be bad and yet that restriction may be good,

Reply: "Restriction prohibits all that it hinders from being imported.":

If any one says that agriculture is the nursing-mother of the country,

Reply: "What nourishes the country is not exactly agriculture, but corn."

If any one tells you that the basis of the food of the people is agriculture,

Reply: "The basis of the people's food is corn. This is the reason why a law which gives us, by agricultural labour, two quarters of corn, when we could have obtained four quarters without such labour, and by means of labour applied to manufactures, is a law not for feeding, but for starving the people." If any one remarks that restriction upon the importation of foreign corn gives rise to a more extensive culture, and consequently to increased home production,

Reply: "It induces men to sow grain on comparatively barren and ungrateful soils. To milk a cow and go on milking her, puts a little more into the pail, for it is difficult to say when you will come to the last drop. But that drop costs dear."

If any one tells you that when bread is dear, the agriculturist, having become rich, enriches the manufacturer,

Reply: "Bread is dear when it is scarce, and then men are poor, or, if you like it better, they become rich *starvelings*."

If you are further told that when bread gets dearer, wages rise, Reply by pointing out that, in April 1847, five-sixths of our workmen were receiving charity,

If you are told that the wages of labour should rise with the increased price of provisions,

Reply: "This is as much as to say that in a ship without provisions, everybody will have as much biscuit as if the vessel were fully victualled."

If you are told that it is necessary to secure a good price to the man who sells corn,

Reply: "That in that case it is also necessary to secure good wages to the man who buys it."

If it is said that the proprietors, who make the laws, have raised the price of bread, without taking thought about wages, because they know that when bread rises, wages naturally rise, Reply: "Upon the same principle, when the workmen come to make the laws, don't blame them if they fix a high rate of wages without busying themselves about protecting corn, because they know that when wages rise, provisions naturally rise also."

If you are asked what, then, is to be done?

Reply: "Be just to everybody."

If you are told that it is essential that every great country should produce iron,

Reply: "What is essential is, that every great country should have iron."

If you are told that it is indispensable that every great country should produce cloth,

Reply: "The indispensable thing is, that the citizens of every great country should have cloth."

If it be said that labour is wealth,

Reply: "This is not true."

And, by way of improvement, add: "Phlebotomy is not health, and the proof of it is that bleeding is resorted to for the purpose of restoring health."

If it is said: "To force men to cultivate rocks, and extract an ounce of iron from a hundredweight of ore, is to increase their labour and consequently their wealth,"

Reply: "To force men to dig wells by prohibiting them from taking water from the brook, is to increase their *useless labour*, but not their wealth."

If you are told that the sun gives you his heat and light without remuneration,

Reply: "So much the better for me, for it costs me nothing to see clearly."

And if you are answered that industry in general loses what would have been paid for artificial light,

Rejoin; "No; for having paid nothing to the sun, what he saves me enables me to buy clothes, furniture, and candles."

In the same way, if you are told that these rascally English possess capital which is dormant,

Reply: "So much the better for us; they will not make us pay interest for it."

If it is said: "These perfidious English find coal and iron in the same pit,"

Reply: "So much the better for us; they will charge us nothing for bringing them together."

If you are told that the Swiss have rich pasturages, which cost little:

Reply: "The advantage is ours, for they will demand a smaller amount of our labour in return for giving an impetus to our agriculture, and supplying us with provisions."

If they tell you that the lands of the Crimea have no value, and pay no taxes,

Reply: "The profit is ours, who buy corn free from such charges."

If they tell you that the serfs of Poland work without wages,

Reply: "The misfortune is theirs and the profit is ours, since their labour does not enter into the price of the corn which their masters sell us."

Finally, if they tell you that other nations have many advantages over us,

Reply: "By means of exchange, they are forced to allow us to participate in these advantages."

If they tell you that under free-trade we are about to be inundated with bread, *bouf à la mode*, coal, and winter clothing, Reply: "In that case we shall be neither hungry nor thirsty."

If they ask how we are to pay for these things?

Reply: "Don't let that disquiet you. If we are inundated, it is a sign we have the means of paying for the inundation; and if we have not the means of paying, we shall not be inundated."

If any one says: I should approve of free-trade, if the foreigner, in sending us his products, would take our products in exchange; but he carries off our money,

Reply: "Neither money nor coffee grows in the fields of Beauce, nor are they turned out by the workshops of Elbeuf. So far as we are concerned, to pay the foreigner with money is the same thing as paying him with coffee."

If they bid you eat butcher's meat,

Reply: "Allow it to be imported."

If they say to you, in the words of the *Presse*, "When one has not the means to buy bread, he is forced to buy beef," Reply: "This is advice quite as judicious as that given by M. Vautour to his tenant:

"'Quand on n'a pas de quoi payer son terme,
Il faut avoir une maison à soi.'"

If, again, they say to you, in the words of *La Presse*, "The government should teach the people how and why they must eat beef,"

Reply: "The government has only to allow the beef to be imported, and the most civilized people in the world will know how to use it without being taught by a master."

If they tell you that the government should know everything, and foresee everything, in order to direct the people, and that the people have simply to allow themselves to be led, Reply by asking: "Is there a state apart from the people? is there a human foresight apart from humanity? Archimedes might repeat every day of his life, 'With a fulcrum and lever I can move the world;' but he never did move it, for want of a fulcrum and lever. The lever of the state is the nation; and nothing can be more foolish than to found so many hopes upon the state, which is simply to take for granted the existence of collective science and foresight, after having set out with the assumption of individual imbecility and improvidence."

If any one says, "I ask no favour, but only such a duty on bread and meat as shall compensate the heavy taxes to which I am subjected; only a small duty equal to what the taxes add to the cost price of my corn,"

Reply: "A thousand pardons; but I also pay taxes. If, then, the protection which you vote in your own favour has the effect of burdening me as a purchaser of corn with exactly your share of the taxes, your modest demand amounts to nothing less than establishing this arrangement as formulated by you:

Seeing that the public charges are heavy, I, as a seller of corn, am to pay nothing, and you my neighbour, as a buyer of corn, are to pay double, viz., your own share and mine into the bargain.' Mr Corn-merchant, my good friend, you may have force at your command, but assuredly you have not reason on your side."

If any one says to you, "It is, however, exceedingly hard upon me, who pay taxes, to have to compete in my own market with the foreigner, who pays none,

Reply:

"1st, In the first place, it is not your market, but our market. I who live upon corn and pay for it, should surely be taken into account.

"2d, Few foreigners at the present day are exempt from taxes.

"3d, If the taxes you vote yield you in roads, canals, security, etc., more than they cost you, you are not justified in repelling, at my expense, the competition of foreigners, who, if they do not pay taxes, have not the advantages you enjoy in roads, canals, and security. You might as well say, 'I demand a compensating duty because I have finer clothes, stronger horses, and better ploughs than the hard-working peasant of Russia.'

"4th, If the tax does not repay you for what it costs, don't vote it.

"5th, In short, after having voted the tax, do you wish to get free from it? Try to frame a law which will throw it on the foreigner. But your tariff makes your share of it fall upon me, who have already my own burden to bear."

If any one says, "For the Russians free-trade is necessary to enable them to exchange their products with advantage," (Opinion de M. Thiers dans les Bureaux, April 1847),

Reply: "Liberty is necessary everywhere, and for the same reason."

If you are told, "Each country has its wants, and we must be guided by that in what we do." (M. Thiers),

Reply: "Each country acts thus of its own accord, if you don't throw obstacles in the way."

If they tell you, "We have no sheet-iron, and we must allow it to be imported," (M. Thiers),

Reply: "Many thanks."

If you are told, "We have no freights for our merchant shipping. The want of return cargoes prevents our shipping from competing with foreigners," (M. Thiers),

Reply: "When a country wishes to have everything produced at home, there can be no freights either for exports or imports. It is just as absurd to desire to have a mercantile marine under a system of prohibition, as it would be to have carts when there is nothing to carry."

If you are told that assuming protection to be unjust, everything has been arranged on that footing; capital has been embarked; rights have been acquired; and the system cannot be changed without suffering to individuals and classes,

Reply: "All injustice is profitable to somebody (except, perhaps, restriction, which in the long run benefits no one). To argue from the derangement which the cessation of injustice may occasion to the man who profits by it, is as much as to say that a system of injustice, for no other reason than that it has had a temporary existence, ought to exist for ever."

XVI. THE RIGHT HAND AND THE LEFT.

Report Addressed to the King.

Sire,

When we observe these free-trade advocates boldly-disseminating their doctrines, and maintaining that the right of buying and selling is implied in the right of property (as has been urged by M. Billault in the true style of a special pleader), we may be permitted to feel serious alarm as to the fate of our national labour; for what would Frenchmen make of their heads and their hands were they left to their own resources?

The administration which you have honoured with your confidence has turned its attention to this grave state of things, and has sought in its wisdom to discover a species of *protection* which may be substituted for that which appears to be getting out of repute. They propose a *law to prohibit your faithful SUBJECTS FROM USING THEIR RIGHT HANDS.*

Sire, we beseech you not to do us the injustice of supposing that we have adopted lightly and without due deliberation a measure which at first sight may appear somewhat whimsical. A profound study of the system of protection has taught us this syllogism, upon which the whole doctrine reposes:

The more men work, the richer they become;

The more difficulties there are to be overcome, the more work;

Ergo, the more difficulties there are to be overcome, the richer they become.

In fact, what is protection, if it is not an ingenious application of this reasoning—reasoning so close and conclusive as to balk the subtlety of M. Billault himself?

Let us personify the country, and regard it as a collective being with thirty millions of mouths, and, as a natural consequence, with sixty millions of hands. Here is a man who makes a French clock, which he can exchange in Belgium for ten hundredweights of iron. But we tell him to make the iron himself. He replies, "I cannot, it would occupy too much of my time; I should produce only five hundredweights of iron during the time I am occupied in making a clock." Utopian dreamer, we reply, that is the very reason why we forbid you to make the clock, and order you to make the iron. Don't you see we are providing employment for you?

Sire, it cannot have escaped your sagacity that this is exactly the same thing in effect as if we were to say to the country, "Work with your left hand, and not with the right."

To create obstacles in order to furnish labour with an opportunity of developing itself, was the principle of the old system of restriction, and it is the principle likewise of the new system which is now being inaugurated. Sire, to regulate industry in this way is not to innovate, but to persevere.

As regards the efficiency of the measure, it is incontestable. It is difficult, much more difficult than one would suppose, to do with the left hand what we have been accustomed to do with the right. You will be convinced of this, Sire, if you will condescend to make trial of our system in a process which must be familiar to you; as, for example, in shuffling a pack of cards. For this reason, we flatter ourselves that we are opening to labour an unlimited career.

When workmen in all departments of industry are thus confined to the use of the left hand, we may figure to ourselves, Sire, the immense number of people that will be wanted to supply the present consumption, assuming it to continue invariable, as we always do when we compare two different systems of production with one another. So prodigious a demand for manual labour cannot fail to induce a great rise of wages, and pauperism will disappear as if by enchantment.

Sire, your paternal heart will rejoice to think that this new law of ours will extend its benefits to that interesting part of the community whose destinies engage all your solicitude. What is the present destiny of women in France? The bolder and more hardy sex drives them insensibly out of every department of industry.

Formerly, they had the resource of the lottery offices. These offices have been shut up by a pitiless philanthropy, and on what pretext? "To save the money of the poor." Alas! the poor man never obtained for a piece of money enjoyments as sweet and innocent as those afforded by the mysterious urn of fortune. Deprived of all the enjoyments of life, when he, fortnight after fortnight, put a day's wages on the *quaterne*, how many delicious hours did he afford his family! Hope was always present at his fireside. The garret was peopled with illusions. The wife hoped to rival her neighbours in her style of living; the son saw himself the drum-major of a regiment; and the daughter fancied herself led to the altar by her betrothed.

"C'est quelque chose encor que de faire un beau rêve!"

The lottery was the poetry of the poor, and we have lost it.

The lottery gone, what means have we of providing for our *protegees?* Tobacco-shops and the post-office.

Tobacco, all right; its use progresses, thanks to the *distinguees* habits, which august examples have skilfully introduced among our fashionable youth.

The post-office!... We shall say nothing of it, as we mean to make it the subject of a special report.

Except, then, the sale of tobacco, what employment remains for your female subjects? Embroidery, network, and sewing,—melancholy resources, which the barbarous science of mechanics goes on limiting more and more.

But the moment your new law comes into operation, the moment right hands are amputated or tied up, the face of everything will be changed. Twenty times, thirty times, a greater number of embroiderers, polishers, laundresses, seamstresses, milliners, shirtmakers, will not be sufficient to supply the wants of the kingdom, always assuming, as before, the consumption to be the same.

This assumption may very likely be disputed by some cold theorists, for dress and everything else will then be dearer. The same thing may be said of the iron which we extract from our own mines, compared with the iron we could obtain in exchange for our wines. This argument, therefore, does not tell more against gaucherie than against protection, for this very dearness is the effect and the sign of an excess of work and exertion, which is precisely the basis upon which, in both cases, we contend that the prosperity of the working classes is founded.

Yes, we shall be favoured soon with a touching picture of the prosperity of the millinery business. What movement! What activity! What life! Every dress will occupy a hundred fingers, instead of ten. No young woman will be idle, and we have no need, Sire, to indicate to your perspicacity the moral consequences of this great revolution. Not only will there be more young women employed, but each of them will earn more, for they will be unable to supply the demand; and if competition shall again show itself, it will not be among the seamstresses who make the dresses, but among the fine ladies who wear them.

You must see then, Sire, that our proposal is not only in strict conformity with the economic traditions of the government, but is in itself essentially moral and popular.

To appreciate its effects, let us suppose the law passed and in operation,—let us transport ourselves in imagination into the future,—and assume the new system to have been in operation for twenty years. Idleness is banished from the country; ease and concord, contentment and morality, have, with employment, been introduced into every family—no more poverty, no more vice. The left hand being very visible in all work, employment will be abundant, and the remuneration adequate. Everything is arranged on this footing, and the workshops in consequence are full. If, in such circumstances, Sire, Utopian dreamers were all at once to agitate for the right hand being again set free, would they not throw the whole country into alarm? Would such a pretended reform not overturn the whole existing state of things? Then our system must be good, since it could not be put an end to without universal suffering.

And yet we confess we have the melancholy presentiment (so great is human perversity) that some day there will be formed an association for right-hand freedom.

We think that already we hear the free Dexterities, assembled in the Salle Montesquieu, holding this language:—

"Good people, you think yourselves richer because the use of one of your hands has been denied you; you take account only of the additional employment which that brings you. But consider also the high prices which result from it, and the forced diminution of consumption. That measure has not made capital more abundant, and capital is the fund from which wages are paid. The streams which flow from that great reservoir are directed towards other channels; but their volume is not enlarged; and the ultimate effect, as far as the nation at large is concerned, is the loss of all that wealth which millions of right hands could produce, compared with what is now produced by an equal number of left hands. At the risk of some inevitable derangements, then, let us form an association, and enforce our right to work with both hands."

Fortunately, Sire, an association has been formed in defence of left-hand labour, and the Sinistristes will have no difficulty in demolishing all these generalities, suppositions, abstractions, reveries, and utopias. They have only to exhume the Moniteur Industriel for 1846, and they will find ready-made arguments against freedom Of trade, which refute so admirably all that has been urged in favour of right-hand liberty that it is only necessary to substitute the one word for the other.

"The Parisian free-trade league has no doubt of securing the concurrence of the workmen. But the workmen are no longer men who can be led by the nose. They have their eyes open, and they know political economy better than our professors. Free trade, they say, will deprive us of employment, and labour is our wealth. With employment, with abundant employment, the price of commodities never places them beyond our reach. Without employment, were bread at a halfpenny a pound, the workman would die of hunger. Now your doctrines, instead of increasing the present amount of employment, would diminish it, that is to say, would reduce us to poverty.

"When there are too many commodities in the market, their price falls, no doubt. But as wages always fall when commodities are cheap, the result is that, instead of being in a situation to purchase more, we are no longer able to buy anything. It is when commodities are cheap that the workman is worst off."

It will not be amiss for the Sinistristes to intermingle some menaces with their theories. Here is a model for them:—"What! you desire to substitute right-hand for left-hand labour, and thus force down, or perhaps annihilate wages, the sole resource of the great bulk of the nation!

"And, at a time when a deficient harvest is imposing painful privations on the workman, you wish to disquiet him as to his future, and render him more accessible to bad advice, and more ready to abandon that wise line of conduct which has hitherto distinguished him."

After such conclusive reasoning as this, we entertain a confident hope, Sire, that if the battle is once begun, the left hand will come off victorious.

Perhaps an association may be formed for the purpose of inquiring whether the right hand and the left are not both wrong, and whether a third hand cannot be found to conciliate everybody.

After having depicted the Dexteristes as seduced by the apparent liberality of a principle, the soundness of which experience has not yet verified and the Sinistristes as maintaining the position they have gained, they go on to say:—

"We deny that there is any third position which it is possible to take up in the midst of the battle! Is it not evident that the workmen have to defend themselves at one and the same time against those who desire to change nothing in the present situation, because they find their account in it, and against those who dream of an economic revolution of which they have calculated neither the direction nor the extent?"

We cannot, however, conceal from your Majesty that our project has a vulnerable side; for it may be said that twenty years hence left hands will be as skilful as right hands are at present, and that then you could no longer trust to gaucherie for an increase of national employment.

To that we reply, that according to the most learned physicians the left side of the body has a natural feebleness, which is quite reassuring as regards the labour of the future.

Should your Majesty consent to pass the measure now proposed, a great principle will be established: All wealth proceeds from the intensity of labour. It will be easy for us to extend and vary the applications of this principle. We may decree, for example, that it shall no longer be permissible to work but with the foot; for this is no more impossible (as we have seen) than to extract iron from the mud of the Seine. You see then, Sire, that the means of increasing national labour can never fail. And after all has been tried, we have still the practically ex-haustless resource of amputation.

To conclude, Sire, if this report were not intended for publicity, we should take the liberty of soliciting your attention to the great influence which measures of this kind are calculated to confer on men in power. But that is a matter which we must reserve for a private audience.

XVII. DOMINATION BY LABOUR.

In the same way that in time of war we attain the mastery by superiority in arms, do we not, in time of peace, arrive at domination by superiority in labour?"

This is a question of the highest interest at a time when no doubt seems to be entertained that in the field of industry, as in the field of battle, the stronger crushes the weaker.

To arrive at this conclusion, we must have discovered between the labour which is applied to commodities and the violence exercised upon men, a melancholy and discouraging analogy; for why should these two kinds of operations be thought identical in their effects, if they are essentially different in their own nature?

And if it be true that in industry, as in war, predominance is the necessary result of superiority, what have we to do with progress or with social economy, seeing that we inhabit a world where everything has been so arranged by Providence that one and the same effect—namely, oppression—proceeds necessarily from two opposite principles?

With reference to England's new policy of commercial freedom, many persons make this objection, which has, I am convinced, taken possession of the most candid minds among us: "Is England doing anything else than pursuing the same end by different means. Does she not always aspire at universal supremacy? Assured of her superiority in capital and labour, does she not invite free competition in order to stifle Continental industry, and so put herself in a situation to reign as a sovereign, having conquered the privilege of feeding and clothing the population she has ruined?"

It would not be difficult to demonstrate that these alarms are chimerical; that our alleged inferiority is much exaggerated; that our great branches of industry not only maintain their ground, but are actually developed under the action of external competition, and that the infallible effect of such competition is to bring about an increase of general consumption, capable of absorbing both home and foreign products.

At present, I desire to make a direct answer to the objection, leaving it all the advantage of the ground chosen by the objectors. Keeping out of view for the present the special case of England and France, I shall inquire in a general way whether, when, by its superiority in one branch of industry, a nation comes to outrival and put down a similar branch of industry existing among another people, the former has advanced one step towards domination, or the latter towards dependence; in' other words, whether both nations do not gain by the operation, and whether it is not the nation which is outrivalled that gains the most.

If we saw in a product nothing more than an opportunity of bestowing labour, the alarms of the protectionists would undoubtedly be well-founded. Were we to consider iron, for example, only in its relations with ironmasters, we might be led to fear that the competition of a country where it is the gratuitous gift of nature would extinguish the furnaces of another country where both ore and fuel are scarce.

But is this a complete view of the subject? Has iron relations only with those who make it? Has it no relations with those who use it? Is its sole and ultimate destination to be produced? And if it is useful, not on account of the labour to which it gives employment, but on account of the qualities it possesses, of the numerous purposes to which its durability and malleability adapt it, does it not follow that the foreigner cannot reduce its price, even so far as to render its production at home unprofitable, without doing us more good in this last respect, than harm in the other?

Pray consider how many things there are which foreigners, by reason of the natural advantages by which they are surrounded, prevent our producing directly, and with reference to which we are placed in reality in the hypothetical position we have been examining with reference to iron. We produce at home neither tea, coffee, gold, nor silver. Is our industry *en masse* diminished in consequence? No; only in order to create the counter-value of these imported commodities, in order to acquire them by means of exchange, we detach from our national labour a portion less great than would be required to produce these things ourselves. More labour thus remains to be devoted to the procuring of other enjoyments. We are so much the richer and so much the stronger. All that external competition can do, even in cases where it puts an end absolutely to a determinate branch of industry, is to economize labour, and increase our productive power. Is this, in the case of the foreigner, the road to domination!

If we should find in France a gold mine, it does not follow that it would be for our interest to work it. Nay, it is certain that the enterprise would be neglected if each ounce of gold absorbed more of our labour than an ounce of gold purchased abroad with cloth. In this case we should do better to find our mines in our workshops. And what is true of gold is true of iron.

The illusion proceeds from our failure to see one thing, which is, that foreign superiority never puts a stop to national industry, except under a determinate form, and under that form only renders it superfluous by placing at our disposal the result of the very labour thus superseded. If men lived in diving-bells under water, and had to provide themselves with air by means of a pump, this would be a great source of employment.

To throw obstacles in the way of such employment, as long as men were left in this condition would be to inflict upon them a frightful injury. But if the labour ceases because the necessity for its exertion no longer exists, because men are placed in a medium where air is introduced into their lungs without effort, then the loss of that labour is not to be regretted, except in the eyes of men who obstinately persist in seeing in labour nothing but labour in the abstract.

It is exactly this kind of labour which machinery, commercial freedom, progress of every kind, gradually supersedes; not useful labour, but labour become superfluous, without object, and without result. On the contrary, protection sets that sort of useless labour to work; it places us again under water, to bring the air-pump into play; it forces us to apply for gold to the inaccessible national mine, rather than to the national workshops. All the effect is expressed by the words, depredation of forces.

It will be understood that I am speaking here of general effects, not of the temporary inconvenience which is always caused by the transition from a bad system to a good one. A momentary derangement accompanies necessarily all progress. This may be a reason for making the transition gently and gradually. It is no reason for putting a stop systematically to all progress, still less for misunderstanding it.

Industry is often represented as a struggle. That is not a true representation of it, or only true when we confine ourselves to the consideration of each branch of industry in its effects upon similar branches, regarding them both in thought apart from the interests of the rest of mankind. But there is always something else to be considered, namely, the effects upon consumption, and upon general prosperity.

It is an error to apply to trade, as is but too often done, phrases which are applicable to war.

In war the stronger overcomes the weaker.

In industry the stronger imparts force to the weaker. This entirely does away with the analogy.

Let the English be as powerful and skilful as they are represented, let them be possessed of as large an amount of capital, and have as great a command of the two great agents of production, iron and fuel, as they are supposed to have; all this simply means cheapness. And who gains by the cheapness of products? The man who buys them.

It is not in their power to annihilate any part whatever of our national labour. All they can do is to render it superfluous in the production of what is acquired by exchange, to furnish us with air without the aid of the pump, to enlarge in this way our disposable forces, and so render their alleged domination as much more impossible as their superiority becomes more incontestable.

Thus, by a rigorous and consoling demonstration, we arrive at this conclusion, that labour and violence, which are so opposite in their nature, are not less so in their effects.

All we are called upon to do is to distinguish between labour annihilated, and labour economized.

To have less iron because we work less, and to have less iron although we work less, are things not only different, but opposed to each other. The protectionists confound them; we do not. That is all.

We may be very certain of one thing, that if the English employ a large amount of activity, labour, capital, intelligence, and natural forces, it is not done for show. It is done in order to procure a multitude of enjoyments in exchange for their products. They most certainly expect to receive at least as much as they give. *What they produce at home is destined to pay for what they purchase abroad.* If they inundate us with their products, it is because they expect to be inundated with ours in return. That being so, the best means of having much for ourselves is to be free to choose between these two modes of acquisition, immediate production, and mediate production. British Machiavelism cannot force us to make a wrong choice.

Let us give up, then, the puerility of applying to industrial competition phrases applicable to war,—a way of speaking which is only specious when applied to competition between two rival trades. The moment we come to take into account the effect produced on the general prosperity, the analogy disappears.

In a battle, every one who is killed diminishes by so much the strength of the army. In industry, a workshop is shut up only when what it produced is obtained by the public from another source and in greater abundance. Figure a state of things where for one man killed on the spot two should rise up full of life and vigour. Were such a state of things possible, war would no longer merit its name.

This, however, is the distinctive character of what is so absurdly called industrial war.

Let the Belgians and the English lower the price of their iron ever so much; let them, if they will, send it to us for nothing; this might extinguish some of our blast-furnaces; but immediately, and as a necessary consequence of this very cheapness, there would rise up a thousand other branches of industry more profitable than the one which had been superseded.

We arrive, then, at the conclusion that domination by labour is impossible, and a contradiction in terms, seeing that all superiority which manifests itself among a people means cheapness, and tends only to impart force to all other nations. Let us banish, then, from political economy all terms borrowed from the military vocabulary: to fight with equal weapons, to conquer, to crush, to stifle, to be beaten, invasion, tribute, etc. What do such phrases mean? Squeeze them, and you obtain nothing... Yes, you do obtain something; for from such words proceed absurd errors, and fatal and pestilent prejudices. Such phrases tend to arrest the fusion of nations, are inimical to their peaceful, universal, and indissoluble alliance, and retard the progress of the human race.

www.ingramcontent.com/pod-product-compliance
Lightning Source LLC
LaVergne TN
LVHW080158090726
842905LV00036B/679

* 9 7 8 3 9 8 8 6 8 7 0 6 7 *